Military Families

Chicken Soup for the Soul: Military Families
*101 Stories about the Force Behind the Forces*ˢᴹ
Amy Newmark. Foreword by Miranda Hope.

Published by Chicken Soup for the Soul Publishing, LLC www.chickensoup.com
Copyright ©2017 by Chicken Soup for the Soul Publishing, LLC. All Rights Reserved.

Photo of Amy Newmark courtesy of Susan Morrow at SwickPix
Photo of Miranda Hope courtesy of Ronda Ann Gregorio
All other photos courtesy of USO, Inc. ©2017 All Rights Reserved
USO will receive royalties of $.60 per copy of the book sold.

Cover and Interior by Daniel Zaccari

Distributed to the booktrade by Simon & Schuster. SAN: 200-2442

Publisher's Cataloging-In-Publication Data
(Prepared by The Donohue Group, Inc.)

Names: Newmark, Amy, compiler. | Hope, Miranda, writer of supplementary
    textual content.
Title: Chicken soup for the soul : military families : 101 stories about
    the force behind the forces / [compiled by] Amy Newmark ; foreword by
    Miranda Hope.
Other Titles: Military families : 101 stories about the force behind the
    forces
Description: [Cos Cob, Connecticut] : Chicken Soup for the Soul, LLC
    [2017]
Identifiers: LCCN 2017936101 | ISBN 978-1-61159-967-1 (print) | ISBN
    978-1-61159-266-5 (ebook)
Subjects: LCSH: Families of military personnel--United States--Literary
    collections. | Families of military personnel--United States--
    Anecdotes. | United States--Armed Forces--Military life--Literary
    collections. | United States--Armed Forces--Military life--Anecdotes. |
    United Service Organizations (U.S.)--Literary collections. | United
    Service Organizations (U.S.)--Anecdotes. | LCGFT: Anecdotes.
Classification: LCC U766 .C45 2017 (print) | LCC U766 (ebook) | DDC
    355.10973--dc23

PRINTED IN THE UNITED STATES OF AMERICA
on acid∞free paper

25 24 23 22 21 20 19 18 17   01 02 03 04 05 06 07 08 09 10 11

101 Stories about the Force Behind the Forces℠

Amy Newmark
Foreword by Miranda Hope

Chicken Soup for the Soul, LLC
Cos Cob, CT

Changing the world one story at a time®
www.chickensoup.com

Table of Contents

❸
~On the Move, Again!~

❹
~Staying Strong at Home~

❺
~Patriotism in Action~

❻

~The Faces of the Forces~

❼

~Ready to Serve~

❽
~Coming Home~

❾
~The Lighter Moments~

❿
~Saying Goodbye~

⑪
~Through the Generations~

Foreword

Throughout his celebrated life, Bob Hope, my grandfather, embodied the American Dream. Through hard work and great talent, he rose from humble means to become, at one time, the most famous man on earth. He was a talented singer-dancer-actor-comedian. He was an innovator in every medium he touched: stage, radio, TV, film and stand-up comedy. But it was through his United Service Organizations (USO) tours to entertain service members abroad that he encountered his favorite audience and created his most enduring legacy.

During the week of Christmas, 1987, I accompanied my grandfather on one of his last tours with the USO. We flew around the globe that week — flying west from Los Angeles to arrive eight days later in Los Angeles. Bob Hope performed seven shows along the way, in various remote corners of the globe, in the heat of an air base in the Philippines, in the vast waters of the Persian Gulf, on a snow covered Army base in Northern Italy. The schedule was unrelenting: set up, break down, sleep on the plane.

I was seventeen, helping with cue cards and costumes, and I had never known such exhaustion. I came home and slept for two days. My grandfather spent that week reviewing hundreds of pages of possible material, writing, fine-tuning and performing seven shows flawlessly, meeting with service men and women and statesmen, and even attending a midnight Christmas mass in the weight room in the bottom of the USS Midway aircraft carrier in the middle of the Persian Gulf. At the time, he was eighty-four years old.

That's when I really saw that he was cut from a different and extraordinary cloth. I saw a tireless work ethic, a roll-up-your-sleeves and do-what-needs-to-be-done attitude, a serve-those-who-serve humility, a commitment to choosing to comfort others over one's own comfort, a total lack of narcissism or vanity, and an absolute inability for it to even occur to him to complain. He knew that he wasn't just bringing jokes and Super Bowl Cheerleaders, but that he was also bringing humanity and courage and home. He took his talents to the center of a crisis and used them to heal. He had a wonderful time doing it.

And the audience had a wonderful time receiving it. If you look on YouTube and watch a clip from Bob "Somewhere in the Pacific" Hope 1943 and then watch a clip of Bob "Persian Gulf" Hope 1987, you'll hear the same roar from the audience of service men and women. It is a thrilling, deafening, adoring sound. It is the sound of thousands of human souls, far from home, in a frightening, uncertain terrain welcoming this man, as their brothers, mothers, uncles, sisters, fathers, and grandfathers welcomed this same man to their own battlefields. This man, who in his forties, in his eighties and in every decade between, flew away from ease and comfort to strengthen their lonely, dedicated hearts at Christmas, to lift not just the morale of his audience, but the morale of his nation and to do it with tireless grace, wit and charm.

"Only in America," he told me on that trip, as we made our way through monarchies and flew over dictatorships. "Only in America could a stonemason's son from Cleveland who left school after the third grade to support his family, have this life that I have now." He loved this country. He loved how it rewarded his hard work and talent. He never took for granted his freedom and he loved the men and women who defended it.

It was that trip and his commitment that sparked in me a desire to serve. We know that many veterans returning from war are not thriving in civilian life. There are plenty of reasons why and many ways in which they need support, but the fact remains — they *need* and *deserve* it. Through the Bob & Dolores Hope Foundation, I am honored to partner with charities that feed, clothe and shelter veterans and help them to thrive through meaningful work.

I hope that you enjoy the stories relayed here in the pages of *Chicken Soup for the Soul: Military Families*. I am pleased to know that a portion of the book sales will go to support the USO and their commitment to "strengthen America's military service members by keeping them connected to family, home and country." Such a noble cause! And, an accurate description of Bob Hope's greatest legacy. May these stories not just move and entertain you, but *strengthen* you as well, wherever you may be, currently deployed, returned from deployment, or holding down the fort at home as a spouse, child, parent or friend of a service man or woman. You are, as the USO says, "the force behind the forces."

~Miranda Hope
Vice President, Bob & Dolores Hope Foundation

Military Families

It Takes a Village

The Common Denominator

Family is not an important thing; it's everything.
~Michael J. Fox

In December 1999, with orders in hand, my twenty-five-year-old son Ty boarded a plane in Kosovo and headed for Germany. For the first time, he would spend Christmas outside the United States and apart from relatives.

Because I didn't understand how the military operated, I envisioned the worst. *Would my son spend an icy Christmas Eve outdoors on guard duty? Would he eat a cold turkey sandwich alone in his apartment?*

I shouldn't have fretted.

The day before Christmas, Ty called home. "Mom, a chief warrant officer and his wife invited me to dinner tomorrow. They also invited another single lieutenant and two married lieutenants and their wives. I knew you'd be worried I'd spend Christmas alone, so I want you to know I have plans."

The chief and his family gave Ty the gift of hospitality. They also gave me a present because, for the first time, I beheld the strength of military family life.

I've caught other glimpses during Ty's years of service. Some revealed simple acts of kindness. When Ty deployed, his friends stateside checked each week to make sure his car still ran and his townhouse pipes hadn't frozen. He did the same for them when he came back and they deployed.

Ty phoned the day he returned to the United States from an overseas deployment. As a thirty-two-year-old captain, he'd taken and brought back 163 soldiers under his command. Most were between the ages of eighteen and twenty-two.

"How are they doing?" I asked.

"Mostly okay. They have to contact me if they get into trouble. Saturday at 0200, one of my soldiers called. The first thing he said was, 'Sir, I wrecked my car.'"

I marveled. "If you ever have kids, you'll already know how to deal with them when they're that age."

"Yeah, well…"

After we hung up, I realized Ty considered his soldiers part of his family. His military family. Brothers and sisters in arms who protect one another.

Other categories of family, primarily kin related by blood and marriage, can strengthen the military clan. In a phone conversation Ty told me he places great importance on family. "Mom, today the doctor asked me how I consistently maintain a positive attitude." In 2005, a roadside blast injured him. Since then, he's dealt with chronic pain and ongoing medical procedures.

He continued, "I told the doc the first thing that came to mind: 'My family supports me.'"

We do. When he deploys, we send cards, letters, and e-mails of encouragement. We ship care packages, which usually include home-made cookies for Ty and his soldiers.

On his latest assignment, in Washington State, he lives near grandparents, aunts, uncles, and cousins. My sister Jannet invites him to holiday dinners and family functions. She drives him to medical procedures. When he flies to trainings, she takes him to the airport and brings him home when he returns.

He goes with family members to the symphony, pizza parlors, and movies. They drop by to visit and make sure Ty has food in his house when he's recuperating.

Ty's cousins are like brothers and sisters. They provide him with friendship, comic relief, and opportunities to participate in the give-and-take of relationships.

When Ty deployed to the Middle East, I joined Blue Star Mothers, an organization of moms with sons and daughters in the military. We moms worked well together. Our chapter shipped thousands of care packages each year.

Later, while visiting with Ty, I said, "Supporting our troops and veterans gives us moms something positive to do."

"That's great." He furrowed his brow. "You'll never know the emotional burdens adult family members put on some of my soldiers. They're already giving everything they have during training or completing their missions while also watching each other's backs and staying alive. They don't have any energy left over to take care of their moms and wives who are falling apart from fear. I understand they're afraid. But it makes the soldiers' jobs that much harder when family members dump their fears and guilt on those who need absolute focus to keep themselves and the soldiers to the left and right of them alive."

As a woman, I understood some of the anxieties of the moms and wives. I also silently thanked my friends in Blue Star Mothers because we'd encouraged and shored up one another to be brave and strong for our adult children serving in the military.

During another deployment to the Middle East, Ty couldn't always keep in contact with us, so I obsessively watched news reports for information. I held my breath as I searched for a glimpse of him in televised news programs that depicted fierce fighting and bombings.

While on a business trip during that time, my friend Betty noticed I wasn't as talkative as usual with our group of co-workers. As we walked to our rooms after dinner, she asked, "What's wrong?"

"I haven't heard from Ty in two months." The lump in my throat kept me from saying more.

Betty had prayed for Ty for years, including his latest deployment. We stopped in the empty hallway, and she prayed with me. The next day, I received a brief e-mail from Ty. "Hi, Mom. Everyone's okay." After he returned stateside, I learned he'd led missions into forward areas without U.S. mail delivery, e-mail access, or phone service.

The answer to prayer, Ty's short message, lifted my spirits and kept my hope alive until the next time he contacted me.

Diverse types of families strengthen the military. These people reflect American demographics with respect to race, religion, age, gender, socioeconomic status, and education. Yet, regardless of the composition of the different kinships and their contributions to the military's family, they all share a common denominator: love.

Love for the men and women who serve our country.

~Linda Jewell

Thank You for Your Service

One of the deep secrets of life is that all that is really worth the doing is what we do for others.
~Lewis Carroll

"Thank you for your service." After more than twenty years of active duty in the military, I still blush at this comment. It's always nice to hear, but it makes me feel awkward. I don't think my enlistment is some amazing thing worth special attention.

In high school, I worked on comics instead of homework. My above-average grades could have netted the scholarship I needed, but classmates with better scores beat me out. With little money and few options, the recruiter's pitch and the thought of a stable paycheck sounded pretty good.

Even so, I deeply appreciate the occasional free cup of coffee, surprise discount on dinner, or simple expression of gratitude.

I never expect it or demand it. I chose this life with a decent understanding of what it entailed. And my wife, who also served, chose to marry into the military with first-hand knowledge of what that meant. We walked into it with eyes wide open.

My kids, on the other hand, were drafted into this life at birth. They've spent the majority of their lives in a foreign country that is more home to them than the United States whose uniform their dad puts on each day. My brother-in-law calls them his Japanese niece and nephews, despite their blond hair and pale skin.

They endure the transitions and challenges of military family life with patience and resilience, but it takes a toll. They've lost touch with friends in our moves across the world. Even when we stay in one place for a few years, other families get orders and friends move away.

Although modern technology makes communication instantaneous and easy, our time overseas still separates us from family on both sides. My kids have grandparents, aunts, uncles, and cousins they see every few years at best. Such is the price they pay for a decision they never made.

But sometimes we find, or create, "family" in unexpected places.

A few years ago, we moved to Nebraska and settled into the Omaha community. My children made some friends in the neighborhood with practiced ease and speed born of years of temporary but meaningful connections. My wife and I also sought out places to connect.

Shortly before the move, I committed to "this whole writing thing" I'd toyed around with over the years. I realized that being in the States meant access to writing groups and seminars. With a quick Google search and an e-mail I found the monthly critique group I'd attend for the next two and a half years.

My wife and I met with published authors and amateur writers who welcomed us and helped us learn the craft. A kind widow nicknamed "the lion-hearted" Kat hosted the group and provided the relentless yet constructive criticism the rest of us seemed too timid or kind to give. Her warm and inviting home became a peaceful refuge we looked forward to each month. We encouraged one another, developed friendships and watched each other's skills improve.

With Christmas approaching, the group made plans for a casual gathering that included our families. I showed up at our host's house with my wife and four kids, and found out that, for various reasons, no one else could attend that night. So the planned party became Kat and the Williamsons instead.

With a two-year-old, a seven-year-old, a middle-school boy and a teenage girl, Kat had her hands full. But we played silly games, the old-fashioned sort that involved talking face-to-face, telling jokes and stories, and interacting with people instead of electronic devices. Then Kat brought out thoughtful Christmas gifts for the kids to enjoy, along with a fruit-filled Jell-O dish for dessert.

That night, we left with stomachs and hearts filled with cheer.

Later that week, I got an e-mail from Kat, thanking me for coming and especially for bringing the children.

"I didn't think about your four kids when you and Jami came to critique group each month. Seeing them in the house made me realize they are far away from family just like you are. And I thought about how long it's been since the laughter of little children echoed in this house. I know I can't replace family, and I wouldn't want to try, but I thought, 'Well, maybe I can be a surrogate grandma to those kids.' So I'd like to have you all back for your son's birthday next month, and then have you visit every month after that."

Kat saw it as supporting the troops in general while ministering to a specific family's needs. And she made good on her invitation. For the next year and a half, we regularly visited and shared our celebrations, birthdays, holidays, and everyday lives with this wonderful woman who saw my kids and said, "I could do something special for them."

Kat's hospitality and love blessed not just me but my entire family, especially those "drafted" in. So, while I'm sure she doesn't need to hear it, I'll say it anyway: To Kat, and to the many people across America (and with our troops overseas) who reach out in similar ways to touch the lives of military members and families, thank you for your service. It matters more than words can say.

~David M. Williamson

Why Every Moment Counts

When we realize the shortness of life, we begin to see
the importance of making every moment count.
~Dillon Burroughs

While the USO offers many programs to America's troops and their families, Operation Birthday Cake is one that has always been very near and dear to my heart. It can take hours or weeks to coordinate the logistics, but the program has a big impact. Not only does the service member know that someone back home is thinking of him or her, but a loved one who is far away gets to feel connected on a special day.

A Marine mom contacted me in April 2015 to schedule a surprise for her son's birthday on May 6th. We had surprised him with a last-minute-request cake the previous year since she had just found out about the program. This year, she contacted us with ample time to make sure we would be able to surprise him once more as he celebrated another birthday away from home. Then, the unforeseeable happened. She contacted me on Friday, May 1st, with the news that he would be deploying that weekend for a humanitarian relief effort in Nepal after a large earthquake. Immediately, I responded that I did not have time to order a cake from the bakery, but I would do my best to coordinate with his unit to surprise him before he left, or possibly send a belated cake upon his return.

On Monday morning, May 4th, I contacted his unit and was happy to find out he had not left yet, but was scheduled to leave in the next day or so. I went to the commissary bakery to get a cake to deliver that afternoon. I arrived at his workplace and was escorted in secretly. Holding the cake, I started singing "Happy Birthday." His whole unit was already gathered around as they were prepping for their departure, but they knew the surprise was coming. Without missing a beat, they all joined in to wish their brother-in-arms a happy day. It was incredibly heartwarming to see a tightknit unit joining to celebrate as more than workmates… they were a family.

That service member left the next day with his unit. Unfortunately, he did not return. There was a helicopter crash, and he and a fellow Marine, who sang him "Happy Birthday" with the entire group just days before, were killed.

Sometimes, it may not seem like a big deal if an Operation Birthday Cake request is a day late. Sometimes, it is frustrating to get a request for a birthday that is only a day or so away as the requestor just found out about the program. Sometimes, it is frustrating to make last minute changes or rearrange dates and times to accommodate unforeseen changes in their schedules. While we suggest a two-week window for cake requests to ensure ample time for planning, there are always exceptions. Thus, I always tried to make a cake happen, and so did the rest of the USO Okinawa team. The USO's slogan is "Every Moment Counts." This was one of those true defining moments.

Cases like this show how something as small as a birthday cake can mean so much. When he died, I contacted his mom to offer my condolences and to see how she wanted us to move forward with his group photo on our Facebook page. She replied:

Thank you, Andrea. You can leave the pictures up. I am so thankful we were able to get that cake to him. Everything was up in the air surrounding his departure, but you all helped wish him a happy birthday, and I'm so thankful you did. His friends have said he was very happy to receive that cake. Thank you for all that you do.

~Andrea Holt

Yellow Ribbons

Ye cannot live for yourselves; a thousand fibres
connect you with your fellow-men.
~Henry Melvill

The following are excerpts from letters #50, #51 and #52 that we received from our son Darren while he was deployed in Saudi Arabia with the 82nd Airborne Division during the Gulf War from August 2, 1990 to February 28, 1991. Today is the first time in the twenty-five years since the war ended that I've taken them out of the faded cardboard box and reread them, and I wonder how I ever managed to get through those seven terrifying months.

Mom, it is not looking good over here. It sounds like bombing will start long before you get this letter. I don't know what the outcome of this deployment will be, but all the guys are willing to do whatever it takes. I just want you all to remember I love you and miss you tons. I can't wait to see you again. (I will see you again.)

Mom, I just want you to know I'm still safe. But we should be fighting by the time you get this letter. Don't worry, Mom, I'm going to come home. Nobody is going to keep me from watching Timmy and Elijah grow up.

Dear Mom and Dad. This will be the last of my letter writing for a long time. I will be moving out for combat. Just remember I love you with all my heart. Maybe I'm not the best son you ever had, and I probably never told you enough, but I love you and Dad very, very much. Now we have to pray that we see one another soon.

Writing to Darren daily and baking cookies to send in care packages for him and his buddies kept me busy and made me feel like I was contributing what I could to support our troops. I prayed constantly, and I leaned on the shoulders of my family and friends. Darren's best Army buddy's mother contacted me by letter, and LaDonna and I became fast pen pals, trying our best to keep each other's spirits high. We wrote each other nearly every single day.

But what unequivocally filled my heart with pride and strengthened my soul were the countless thoughtful people throughout the United States who showed their patriotic support for our troops.

Among the letters in the box, I found one written to Darren from a complete stranger who got his mailing address from a newspaper listing of all the soldiers serving in the Gulf.

This gentleman, Nick, wrote:

The patriotic fever of us folks back here continues to manifest itself as strongly as ever… almost like each succeeding day must surpass the previous one. No let-up around the country. For instance, would you believe our national anthem made the top 40 charts this week? Whitney Houston sang it at the start of the Super Bowl, and 78,000 fans went "ape." It's the high mark of excellence; they show it over and over again.

Of all the numerous ways Americans showed their support for our troops, my favorite will always be the yellow ribbons — beautiful yellow ribbons from sea to shining sea!

Darren had asked his sister Jacqui and her girlfriend Julie if they'd tie a yellow ribbon on the arm of the statue in the Veterans Memorial

Square in our small town of Sandy, Oregon. The *Sandy Post* published a photo of the girls honoring his request.

Soon after, the VFW tied yellow ribbons to branches of the tall arborvitae trees that formed a border for the square — each ribbon bore the name of a soon-to-be veteran serving in the Gulf War. The plan was for each soldier, upon his homecoming, to take down the ribbon bearing his name. I held my breath and prayed for that day to come.

Every house in town eventually displayed yellow ribbons on their trees, in their windows, or on their fences. Car windows had yellow ribbons. People wore T-shirts imprinted with yellow-ribbon designs or ribbon pins on their lapels. Women even wore yellow ribbons in their hair. Yellow ribbons were everywhere.

My friend LaDonna wrote me that her house was covered with yellow ribbons, and their little town of Osage, Iowa, was adorned much like Sandy, Oregon.

From news reports, we could see that towns throughout the entire country were showing similar support for our troops with united displays of yellow ribbons.

Jacqui even decorated her Christmas tree that year with nothing but yellow ribbons tied in beautiful bows. She didn't have the heart to celebrate Christmas without honoring our troops in a significant way. It was stunning and perfectly patriotic, and the next best thing to having Darren home for the holidays.

Darren celebrated his twenty-second birthday in the Saudi Arabian desert, preparing with his unit to spearhead the attack into Iraq.

It was a long and exhausting seven months for both the troops and their families. But the united support of so many caring persons on the home front lightened the burden tremendously.

On February 28th, we were ecstatic when President George Bush declared victory in his address to the nation. He said Iraq's army was defeated, and our military objectives had been met. The war was over!

Completely relieved of worry, but too overwhelmed to relax, all I wanted to do was call LaDonna. Although we had never in our seven months of friendship talked on the phone, I dialed her number almost instinctively. When I heard her voice for the first time, it was as though the weight of the world was lifted off my shoulders. Like our sons, we had survived this war together.

We laughed, cried, and praised God for over an hour on that phone call, and we knew our families would be friends forever. We also knew there were families whose sons or daughters would not return, and our hearts hurt terribly for them.

Darren's company returned to Fort Bragg, North Carolina, in the middle of March. On March 23rd, he arrived at Portland International Airport to be greeted by a crowd of friends and family all wearing yellow-ribbon T-shirts.

On his way home, Darren stopped in Sandy and proudly removed the yellow ribbon bearing his name from the emerald green branch of the arborvitae tree. That ribbon lies among the letters in the humble cardboard box.

~Connie Kaseweter Pullen

A Magical Gift

We believe distributing copies of God's Word plants
powerful seeds God can use according to
His own timing…
~The Gideons International website

Magic lived in every hotel room of all the vacations of my childhood. In the top drawer of each nightstand was a Bible stamped "Placed by the Gideons."

I asked my mother who the Gideons were and she told me, "They are good folk who bring hope and wisdom and comfort to those who need it." I pestered my mother to describe a Gideon to me, but alas, she had never seen one.

I thought that a Gideon must be magical indeed. I envisioned elves with turned-up slippers, bells on their toes, stocking hats, and pointed ears. Did a Gideon look like Snap, Crackle, or Pop? A teddy bear? A fairy-like Tinkerbell? Peter Pan? Mr. Smee?

On the endless car trips my family took in our Pontiac station wagon, well before the interstate highway system was built, my imagination ran to the Gideons. From West Virginia to Florida to California and all places in between, the Gideons had placed a Bible in every room. They had been there before me. They must have known I was coming. That idea, like a warm hug, brought me such peace.

I grew up, married into the Army, and moved all over the United States. Although the Gideons receded into my childhood fantasies, I would occasionally open a hotel room drawer, and sure enough, a

Gideon had been there before me. Even as an adult, seeing that familiar Bible gave me a sense of peace and comfort.

In August 1990, safety and comfort for all of us seemed in jeopardy. Iraq had invaded Kuwait, and for all we knew, World War III was at hand. My husband had deployed with his unit, the 2nd Battalion, 327th Infantry of the 101st Airborne Division out of Fort Campbell, Kentucky. The waiting spouses of the unit quickly formed support groups and "chains of concern"—telephone trees wherein each spouse called up and down the chain to check on other spouses. We had all sorts of group functions and get-togethers. Since this was before cell phones, Skype, and social media had become common, we relied on each other, the U.S. mail, and an occasional phone call from our husbands.

Although my husband was away for ten months, I received only two phone calls. But I considered myself lucky. In previous wars, who had even that?

It was the letters that sustained the families, and the activities that kept up our spirits. Every week, I would have "pajama parties" at our house wherein any spouse or family member was welcome to spend the night. We watched movies, played board games, made crafts, and ate endless potluck meals. I was never without a full house.

On February 24, 1991, the ground war of Desert Storm began. This set off the longest one hundred hours of most of our lives. The shock and awe were terrifying to us all. My home was nearly bursting with frightened people on that February night. Every time the bell rang, I would answer the door and more people would flood in. I have never known exactly how many people were in our house that night.

One time that night I opened the door, not to a military spouse, but to a civilian man. He said to me, "We think you all could use some hope and comfort tonight. Where would you like these?"

There on my porch were stacks and stacks of wonderful Bibles. Gasping, I opened the door wide, and he and his friends brought them in.

He said to me, "God bless you. We are praying for you," and he left before I could regain the power of speech.

And there it was: "Placed by the Gideons."

So now I know. There are real live Gideons out there. I know. I have seen them. They look like regular men. They walk among us, often overlooked, but always there.

The Gideons brought hope and comfort and wisdom to the families of the 2nd Battalion, 327th Infantry when we needed it most.

~Anne Oliver

We Can Do That!

All the kindness which a man puts out into the world
works on the heart and thoughts of mankind.
~Albert Schweitzer

Before coming to work seven years ago as a volunteer for the USO at our center in Times Square in Manhattan, I would describe my experience with the military as two-fold: (1) navigating life with my late father, an infantryman who was drafted and served on the German front during World War II and was discharged many years before I was born; and (2) growing up with my brother, ten years older than me, a draftee who served stateside as an Army doctor during the Vietnam years.

My father returned from battle with psychological wounds so severe that they impacted every aspect of his post-Army life and so deep that they were invisible to all but those closest to him. Although ultimately blessed with long years and many successes in his life, my dad remained haunted to the end by his traumatic wartime experiences. Sadly, he was born in a time when there was too little knowledge of these issues, let alone services that might ameliorate them. The understanding and the access to modalities that could have helped him achieve a more self-accepting, integrated and peaceful life would come much later. To my dad, comfort was simply not attainable, even when offered in the form of a child's love, a wife's unwavering and steady adoration, or an acknowledgement of gratitude for his being part of "the greatest generation," an epithet that seemed deserved even then when I was too young to know what those words actually meant.

Alas, the mere mention of "Army" was prohibited in our house, as though the word itself could conjure danger. As children we were forbidden to look at the few pictures we found of my father in uniform; we later learned they had somehow survived his earlier purge. Nor were we allowed to watch *M*A*S*H* on television while Dad was in the house. There was never an explanation for his erratic behavior, his bouts of depression, his mercurial outbursts, or his crippling fears and anxieties, leaving four children struggling to make sense of their dad, and hoping and praying that someone would "fix" him. It was a high order that eluded the best minds of the time, none of whom seemed to know exactly what needed fixing or how.

My brother had it easier. After all, he entered as an officer doctor, was kept stateside, and had access to the most current science and every service available at that time to help him cope. What my brother did *not* have was the understanding, let alone the gratitude, of any of his non-military peers. His unseen trauma, shared almost unilaterally by all who served during the Vietnam years, was living with the shame he was made to feel for having served, willingly or not, in a military that was vilified by most everyone in his generation. He left the Army with his own set of internal scars that, like our father before him, were painfully visible to those of us closest to him.

Of course, I had it easiest of all. I was born at exactly the right time to have access to emerging and cutting-edge science and literature that allowed me to contextualize and put my experiences in perspective and to formulate a dedicated response. That plan did not include my joining the military; it did, however, lead me to make a fervent personal commitment that those who serve "under my watch" would never experience the loneliness of my father and brother. I am not a physician, therapist, historian or genius. I am simply a daughter and sister who chooses to devote myself, in my own small way, to ensuring that no service members will ever feel that their wounds are invisible, their service unappreciated, or that they and their families are alone on their journeys.

Of the countless opportunities I am given every day to fulfill this personal mission to which I'm dedicated, a particular instance stands out. A family of five entered the USO center one morning when I was staffing the front desk. The young mom presented her military ID showing a status of Retired on Disability. Upon signing her husband and three young children into our system, she began to unravel in ways that looked all too familiar to me. Her husband glanced at me and whispered that they were "dealing with some PTSD issues" and asked if there was any place in our center to give his wife her meds and allow her the space to relax. I motioned to him to bring his wife to our café, get some water from the cooler, and position her at the computer farthest from the door in the least visible spot.

In the meantime, I offered the kids a foosball table, some Xbox games, and some snacks. With the kids settled and Mom seemingly regaining composure, I brought Dad back to the front desk and asked if he thought it would be possible to have the entire family attend a Broadway show, courtesy of the USO. As fate would have it, we had in our possession some wonderful tickets donated by Disney to one of their top-rated, family-friendly productions. It was a small gesture on our part that yielded a reaction one might expect when offering someone a winning mega millions lottery ticket. And then, reality. Yes, he and the children would cherish an opportunity to do something fun and "normal" with Mom — and he was relatively certain her medication could get her through the show — but if she needed to leave abruptly, which happened often, they would require an aisle seat. And that is when he got a dose of USO reality. Yes, we will do whatever we can to ensure you get the seats you need, he was told.

Sometimes, our guests call, e-mail, or write to us, articulating the profound impact of the small acts of kindness they receive at the USO. I never heard back from this family, nor did I expect to. They expressed everything I needed to know as they walked out our doors, giggling together, and turning those tickets over and over in their hands. When they thought they were out of eyeshot of our center, we saw them gleefully jumping up and down.

~Raya Levi

My Father's Voice

*Teaching is one of the noblest of professions. It requires
an adequate preparation and training, patience,
devotion, and a deep sense of responsibility.*
~Calvin Coolidge

I never heard my father's voice. There were photographs of him, and I know his handwriting from the letters he wrote to my mother. But I always wondered how he sounded. Did his voice reflect the French Canadian dialect of his parents' speech? Or did it have a masculine North Jersey sound to it? Was he soft spoken or a deep baritone? I will never know because he died in World War II when I was just an infant.

Louis La Pointe, my father, enlisted twice before he was finally accepted into the U.S. Army. The war was raging, and like most of his friends, he felt duty-bound to defend his country. He shipped out filled with hopeful idealism, but he never returned home. I became what the government called a "war orphan." As tragic as it was for my mother and me, this is not a sad story. Most people who hear it call it "inspiring." It's about friendship, loyalty, and keeping promises.

After the war ended, my father's friends returned home to the neighborhood and learned that their childhood friend was killed in action. His "old gang" from Jersey City's DeKalb Avenue decided that they wanted to do something special to remember him. Someone asked the question, "What would Louie want?" I don't know how long they tossed the idea around, but as a group they finally agreed on an answer:

He would want his daughter, Lois, to have the same opportunities he would have given her. And to them that meant a college education. But how could a bunch of regular Joes make such a thing happen? They resolved to form an organization and raise the tuition money by sponsoring special fundraising events. It would be called The Louis La Pointe Association.

It was in this spirit of friendship that The Louis La Pointe Association was conceived. I was only two years old, but my future was being decided by a group of men I didn't even know. I came to refer to them by the name my mother used. She called them "The Club." Every Christmas, Easter, and birthday, I would get dressed up in my best outfit because members of The Club were paying us a visit.

The only member whom I clearly recall was Stanley Moore. He owned the local pub where they held their meetings. He was the Club's treasurer for life. It was assumed that because he was a businessman, he could manage money. I guess the others took turns coming to see us, but Mr. Moore was a constant. Like caring uncles, they indulged me with special gifts. Once I received a gold locket with a real diamond chip in the center. I wore it for years until I lost it on a class trip. One Easter they presented me with a three-foot-tall chocolate bunny. Right out of the store window. I was about to tell them that I didn't like sweets, but my mother squeezed my hand as a signal, and I kept quiet.

Every year, The Louis La Pointe Association held a dinner dance as a fundraiser. I dreaded attending this adult event. As a child, I felt self-conscious and awkward walking into the hall with my mother and hearing whispers of "There's little Lois." But, of course, I had to be there. I didn't understand that these events provided the means to build my college fund. They were honoring my father's memory by raising money for *my* future.

In addition to forming the Club, the men petitioned the Jersey City Council to construct a playground in the neighborhood. They labored tirelessly to see this dream become a reality. When I was seven years old, my mother and I sat on the grandstand in the pouring rain and watched the parade of association members walk to the spot where the Louis La Pointe Park was dedicated. From the weeds of a vacant lot rose a beautiful playground for the local children to enjoy. It proudly displayed a white stone monument and a plaque that bore my father's name.

This was a tremendous accomplishment for a small group of buddies who believed in the American dream and their ability to make a difference. Many years later, my son Jason was present at the park's re-dedication ceremony. He wore his Marine Corps dress uniform and delivered an eloquent speech in which he thanked the La Pointe Association for its efforts on my behalf. How proud my father would have been to know that his grandson was also serving his country. The park still stands in the place where my dad grew up, a testimony to the goodwill of his friends, who believed in keeping their promises.

Thanks to the efforts of the La Pointe Association, I did attend college. When I received my degree in English, I made a big decision. I asked myself how I could possibly repay the Club for all they had done for me. The answer was so obvious, and yet it had eluded me. I decided that I would try to inspire children to succeed even if it seemed that the odds were against them. I was proof that was possible. I would become a teacher.

Fortunately, there was a teacher shortage in New Jersey at the time, and I had three job offers. I applied for an Emergency Teaching Certificate, and I walked into a sixth grade classroom the September following my graduation. At the end of my first day, I realized that this was the place where I belonged. It meant returning to college at night to earn a permanent teaching certificate that was followed by a master's degree. This time, I was paying the tuition, and thanks to The Louis La Pointe Association, I was able to do it.

The highlight of my career was in 1987 when I became the New Jersey Teacher of the Year. At a large gathering that honored the outstanding teachers in each county, I stood at the microphone and told the story of a young man going off to war, only to be killed on the battlefields of Italy. I held back his name, but I described the efforts of his friends to help his infant daughter achieve her potential. They wanted to provide her with tuition money for a college education. After many years of fundraising, they accomplished their goal. I explained how, as a college graduate, she wanted to pay back the gift of an education that they had given her. And so she chose a profession that would help children become all they could be. She became a teacher.

I paused and closed my speech with the words, "That young man's name was Private Louis La Pointe, and I'm Louie La Pointe's daughter." Spontaneously, 1,400 teachers stood and applauded. The standing ovation lasted for several minutes. And amid their cheers, I could finally imagine my father's voice. He was saying, "Good job, daughter. I am very proud of you and of my friends in the Club. Their friendship and loyalty have made all this possible."

~Lois La Pointe Kiely

Military Is Family

The family is one of nature's masterpieces.
~George Santayana

After my parents and only sister died, I had no one to love and no one to love me. Fortunately, I served twenty-two years and ten months in the United States Air Force. I still have friends whom I have known and loved for over thirty years. They are the men and women I served with while on active duty. Even after we retired, we kept in touch by becoming members of military groups.

I also volunteer for the USO. When guests come into our Welcome Center, I am saying hello to my brethren. We joke as families do about the different branches of the Armed Forces we served in. We have a kinship no one can ever understand unless they wore the uniform of our great country.

I am no longer lonely. I love so many who come through the USO center, and I know they love me. Imagine meeting a Medal of Honor recipient and, after I saluted him (something all military does in the presence of a Medal of Honor recipient), he hugged me. This old man with the glorious past hugged *me*. I loved him instantly.

This happens so often. We all know what our history is. We see the scars, the limping, the prosthetics, the families striving to smile when Mom or Dad is leaving for an extended deployment. We cry with them. We hug, and it is as if we are indeed brothers, sisters, grandparents, sons, and daughters of the many who serve.

When it comes to those who serve in our Armed Forces and their families, we care about each other. We laugh when a toddler decides to say hello to all the guests in our USO center. That toddler is our baby. We cry when the remains of one of our brothers or sisters who died in combat comes home with the American flag covering their coffin. We hug the moms, dads, sisters, and brothers and all the family members of the hero who gave all for America. And we cry, too, because the one who died is our brother or sister.

I firmly believe there is nothing that comes close to being part of a military family. We all love our country, we stand and salute our flag, we kneel when we ask God to keep our family safe, and we enjoy the company of each other by sharing stories of our experiences when we wore the uniform of America's Armed Forces.

We attend church services together, active-duty and retired members of the military, praising God and praying for America and our friends and family deployed to dangerous zones. We congregate at the chapel on our military installations. We seek counsel from our chaplains, who themselves are military.

Yes, we *are* family. We are not alone. We have people whom we love and who love us back. Our bond cannot be broken. No more loneliness — only a true feeling of being part of a very special family.

~Dolores Incremona

Getting on Base

*I like to see a man proud of the place in which he
lives. I like to see a man live so that his
place will be proud of him.*
~Abraham Lincoln

My husband and I entered military life a little backwards. We lived in the civilian world first, and then decided to sell my husband's private practice and join the United States Air Force in 2014.

In the fall of 2014, we received our first assignment to Joint Base Elmendorf-Richardson, Alaska. My husband left a month before us to secure a house on base for our family. We moved from our home in Arizona, leaving our family, friends, jobs, and the kids' schools to make the trek north.

We were entering a whole new world. There was terminology I didn't understand. There were times I was in a conversation with others, and they used acronyms that sounded like a different language. I did not know that PCS meant Permanent Change of Station or COLA meant cost of living allowance. I didn't know a hangar was where planes were stored. I did not even know what the "flight line" was.

Nonetheless, it was very exciting to live on base. There were the BX (Base Exchange), commissary, gas stations, library, gym, parks for kids, indoor swimming, ski hill, and anything you could ever want inside a little community. There was just one thing missing—family and friends! We moved right before Thanksgiving. To our surprise, we were invited to Thanksgiving dinner by a neighbor who had just met us!

At the dinner, I was telling the military wives how I had to sell our house and one of our cars "by myself." I had to make sure the movers did everything right "by myself" and a whole long list of other things "by myself." The women just laughed and said, "Welcome to the military!" It made me realize these women do this every few years, and this is just a part of their lives!

I learned quickly that if I didn't get out there and meet people, I was never going to make friends in my new military world.

When the kids and I arrived, my husband purchased a new vehicle for us. I had no idea where anything was or how to get anywhere. The second day, when my husband went to work, I had an interview at the children's new school. I went to the garage to start the car to warm it up. Coming from Arizona, we weren't used to colder temperatures. As I walked away from the car, I heard a beep. Uh-oh. Somehow, I had locked the car door while the engine was running, and my only set of keys and cell phone were inside the car.

I knocked on the neighbor's door to ask to use their phone. I knew my husband's cell phone didn't work inside the hospital building where he worked, and I didn't know his office phone number! Fortunately, my neighbor worked at the hospital and knew the number and I reached him and got the location of the other set of keys.

Locking the keys in my car was one good way to meet new friends! This neighbor taught me everything I needed to know about the neighborhood and the base. After meeting her, I learned about the local women's Bible study, the monthly neighborhood Bunco, where the gym was, and more. I don't know what I would have done without her. She and I became quick friends!

One day when driving home around 5:00 p.m. on base, I saw a bunch of vehicles pulled over to the side of the road. This usually meant there was some type of wildlife to be seen, like a moose or bear. But this day was different. I saw men standing outside their cars with their hats off at attention. I saw children standing with their hands over their hearts. Then I heard the national anthem playing over the loudspeaker throughout the base. I soon learned that every day at 5:00 p.m., the national anthem plays, and no matter if you're walking or driving, you stop to pay respect to our country.

Many mornings, while driving to work I see soldiers running or marching in the streets. Many times, I hear the men yelling "Hooah!" in the distance. At times, I even hear the cannons exploding for training sessions. At first, this scared me, but now I am used to it.

The one sound we can never miss on the base is the sound of the F-22 Raptor jets soaring high above our house. Sometimes, we can even feel the house shake when they fly overhead. I also discovered that I can never leave my house without my military ID or I will not be able to get back on to base! I have learned this the hard way a few times when I had to make a phone call to my husband and ask, "Can you please bring me my ID?"

One thing that is hard to get used to is the moving trucks. It seems as quickly as I meet people, they are gone. The goodbyes get hard. The neighbors and friends I meet become a part of my military family. Without them, life would be hard away from everyone we left.

The longer I live on base, the more I'm involved in the community, the more I realize how blessed I am. I love how military families come together to make a meal for the family whose husband is deployed. We step in to cut the grass, watch children, or fulfill some small need while the spouse is away keeping our country safe.

Every day, I get to live next to the men and women who serve and protect our nation. I get to see firsthand their sacrifice and hard work.

When paratroopers practicing for a rescue mission are jumping from their planes, parachuting from the sky, I see freedom. When I hear the sound of the trumpet playing the national anthem and children standing still on the playgrounds with hands over their hearts, I hear and see freedom. When a neighbor comes home after serving four months in Iraq, completing a mission to keep us safe and protected from things we should never see — and hands me an American flag that flew on his plane — I am touching freedom. I am proud to be called a military wife, standing beside my husband in the United States Air Force.

~Heather Gillis

Why I Became a USO Volunteer

*Sometimes, the best way to help someone
is just to be near them.*
~Veronica Roth

This was my second child, but the first I would deliver in a foreign country. It was 2002. My husband and I were stationed in Darmstadt, Germany, but we lived on post in military housing in Langen. My son was three years old, and we were preparing to welcome his sister into the family. I was very nervous about having my baby in a hospital that was forty-eight miles away in Heidelberg. That's quite a risky distance when in labor.

This second pregnancy was unlike my first. My son was induced, so I went in on a scheduled day to give birth. Like my first, though, my mother would be there. Thankfully, her plane was expected to arrive from Oklahoma on the afternoon of January 28th. I had no idea what natural labor felt like, yet that's what I experienced just after midnight on January 28th. The dull ache in my lower back and small contractions didn't seem like the Braxton Hicks contractions I was accustomed to. I called the nurses' station at the Army hospital in Heidelberg to ask for advice. The nurse told me to time my contractions, and when they were closer together, come in to get checked out.

As the night wore on, I called my dad to see if my mom had made her flight and told him I might be having the baby that day. He informed me that my grandmother had had several mini strokes and had to be taken to the hospital. My mom almost didn't make her flight, taking care of my grandmother's needs. My aunt told her to go and be with me. After speaking with my father, I called the nurse again and told her that I was on my way. The pain was unbearable.

My next call was to a nearby friend. She was also a military wife, raising two small children of her own. She agreed to watch my son for however long we needed her. My husband dropped him off as I gathered my things and made my way down two flights of stairs. With every step, my belly hardened with contractions. I noticed the lights of our car coming down the street, made my way into the front seat, and ordered my husband to drive.

My husband drove as fast as he could on the Autobahn. I prayed to God to let us make it to the hospital. No one wants to give birth on the side of the road. Once we made it, I prayed again for them to let us through the checkpoints in time. After September 11th, every military installation in Europe was on high alert. This was a time when people had to exit the vehicle, open all doors, the hood, and the trunk. I was in no condition for any of that. The guard must have taken one look at me and decided it was okay to wave us through. Two prayers answered, and I was extremely thankful.

As I was taken into Labor and Delivery, the nurses set me up on the monitors and machines. One nurse laid me flat on my back. Something was wrong, and I asked her to sit me up. She said I needed to lie back, but I told her I couldn't breathe. A compromise was made. I was propped up midway. The doctor barely made it before my daughter decided to pop into this world.

Once my daughter was cleaned, I saw her for only a moment. My husband had to go to Frankfurt to pick up my mother, but first he had to stop by his unit to sign out on leave. He wasn't aware that soon after he left, the doctor told me the reason I couldn't breathe. My heart was failing. I needed to be medically evacuated to Landstuhl Regional Medical Center. My daughter would travel by ambulance and be kept in the nursery while I would be in ICU.

I didn't want to leave without my family. I asked if we could wait until my husband returned, but the answer was no. I had no choice but to leave on a Black Hawk helicopter immediately. They said I could call my mother to tell her where to meet me. I explained that we had no cell phones, and she was on a plane. I asked them to notify the Frankfurt Airport USO and have them meet my mother to fill her in on what was happening, and to call my husband's unit to tell him when he arrived to sign out on leave.

As I was being loaded onto the helicopter, my mind raced with questions about whether the calls were made, where my baby was, and if my son was being picked up. I said another prayer to God, asking Him to watch over my children, guide my mother, and protect my husband as he drove across Germany to pick up our family.

My prayers were answered yet again. I recall waking up at the hospital to my husband telling me that he rushed to pick up my mom at the airport. She was waiting with USO volunteers who had paged her after her flight landed. They asked her to wait in their lounge until my husband got there. They picked up my son and drove to Landstuhl to be with our daughter who made it safely to the nursery. I will never forget how grateful I was to have the support of a strong military community. At each step of the way, I was cared for, prayed over, and comforted. After a week in ICU, a long recovery was ahead of me. I spent another week in the hospital after another episode of heart failure.

Eventually, we left Germany and headed to Fort Hood, Texas, but I never forgot about how the USO volunteers sat with my mom and prayed for us after she got off the plane. Their kindness for a stranger prompted me to become a volunteer at the Fort Hood USO. Later, when we were stationed at Fort Lee, Virginia, I heard they were opening a new USO. I inquired about volunteering and was told they were looking for staff members to manage the USO. This is where I say, "The rest is history!" I've been the USO center director ever since.

~Kasinda Thomas

Chapter 2

Military Families

★ Growing Up Military ★

11

Like a Dandelion

Dandelions, like all things in nature, are beautiful
when you take the time to pay attention to them.
~June Stoyer

I make my way through the horse pasture, the warm summer wind blowing my hair in swirls around my face. Spring rains have given way to sunshine, fields of green and warm temperatures. I wade through the long grasses, happy to be rid of my raincoat and umbrella, and lift my face to the sun. The green meadow around me is dotted with purples, whites, and yellows from delicate looking Queen Anne's lace to the spiky thistles of Greater Knapweed. I push my doll carriage along with me, the perfect receptacle for all of the beautiful wildflowers I'll pick today.

As far as the eye can see, dandelions are in various stages of bloom and perfect for making a crown to rest atop my head. Impatient, I choose dandelion crowns over daisy chains, as their thick milky stems make it easier to create notches and loop them together. As I wander through the wildflowers and grasses, I pluck all the colors I see, excited about the wild bouquet I'll be bringing home. Here and there, I come across dandelions gone to seed and use them like bubble wands.

I pluck a white, fuzzy dandelion, fill my lungs with air and exhale in short bursts. The tiny seedlings take flight, some landing just feet away, others lifting high on gusts of wind and traveling as far as the eye can see. There is purpose to these tiny seeds, each traveling and landing in an unknown spot and planting its roots before again going to seed and traveling far across the fields. The dandelion is me and every other military brat who has spent a childhood repeatedly flying, planting roots, and flying away again.

"Where are you from?" It is a simple question complicated by my father's Air Force service. By the time I was twelve, I had lived in four states and three countries. "Home" was wherever my family resided at the time.

I wouldn't trade my childhood as a military dependent for any other existence. Military life taught me discipline and resilience, exposed me to different cultures, and provided my family a lifetime of memories.

Like the dandelion, military children grow up everywhere, quickly planting roots before being swept away to try new places. We thrive wherever our "seeds" land and make friends with ease, deeply rooted in the shared experience of military life. We blossom and thrive in new environments before being swept away in the wind of our military parents' move to new stations.

I was one of the many military children dispersed across Europe and Asia during the end of the Cold War in the 1980s, with a parent whose overseas station served to protect our homeland. One of my favorite pictures from childhood is a picture of myself as a toddler, sitting in a lush, green field in Germany, a dandelion crown atop my head and ruins in the background. It was a telling juxtaposition of new and old, hope and destruction.

The resilience we military children display is not only needed for our frequent moves, it's also part of our bravery when a military parent is away serving. My father worked swing shifts and long days as an air traffic controller, often broken by weeks away training. Scary as it was to find that my father had been called away in the middle of the night, his "emergency duffle" missing from our coat closet, I knew that he was doing something important. Well after one of those disappearances, I learned that my father had been called away to prepare and carry out the 1986 air strike on Libya. I'm proud that my father was in the control tower for such a pivotal military maneuver.

My mother was the glue that held our family together. She often had no idea of my father's classified whereabouts, but she reassured us despite the unease she surely felt inside. She kept us calm, maintained a sense of normalcy in our household, and cared for a baby and a preschooler on her own while my father worked night shifts in the control tower.

I grew up on air bases protected by fences. I'd ride my bike around the streets, venturing out for hours with my friends, and exploring dark corners and buildings on our old World War II Royal Air Force base. That freedom was only interrupted twice when our base went on lockdown, the gates closed against the threat of attack. Relegated to backyard play, I was irritated by such restrictions, but deep down I was afraid of what those closed gates represented.

Three elementary schools, three middle schools, and one high school stretching across two continents — that was my childhood. I've yet to plant deep roots with my own little family, having found a spouse who shares my love of travel and new experiences. The dandelions of my youth, which represent my childhood as a military dependent, have new meaning now that I have a son. He blows the seeds into the spring and autumn winds, and we watch their fuzzy parachutes fly away toward possibility. I'm reminded of how grateful I am for my own childhood.

~Lauren B. Stevens

12

Missing My Father

Love is missing someone whenever you're
apart, but somehow feeling warm inside
because you're close in heart.
~Kay Knudsen

I t was the early 1990s, and my dad had just received orders for Germany, where we would spend the next three years. I was thirteen, fumbling through my transition to a young adult. So much personal growth would follow in this period of my life, shaping who I would become as an adult. But as I look back on those memories, one thing is consistently missing — my father.

He usually flew to our next duty station to get housing in order, and we would join him a short time later along with our lives packed neatly in boxes. With this particular move, I don't recall him being around much longer beyond our welcoming to the new city, country, and home. There were rumors about a deployment before we even arrived, and on December 1, 1994, he left for Macedonia.

He had been gone many times before for training field exercises, but this was his first deployment. He would be gone for six months, patrolling the borders between Macedonia and Serbia.

After Macedonia, he was home through the summer, just long enough for us to reconnect. Integrating back into home life was made easier through my mother. She wrote to him often while he was away to keep him informed of everything that was happening with my brother, sister, and me. She helped him maintain that connection with us, which helped him ease back into normalcy without feeling like he had skipped a beat.

Unfortunately, just a few months after his return, he was sent off to training exercises, with another rumored deployment. He left for Bosnia on December 24, 1995.

I'll never forget that snowy Christmas Eve. We dropped him off at a train station and said goodbye in what felt like a second. I hated that they made him leave on Christmas Eve. It was the first time I had ever seen my mother cry.

Saying goodbye wasn't new, and the distance wasn't new, but the situation was. Bosnia was more worrisome. He would be one of the first troops in, paving the way for others to arrive after clearing the area of landmines and setting up camp. It was a fresh war, and it was difficult as a teenager to understand what was happening there and what it meant for him to be a part of it.

When we gathered around our Christmas tree the next morning, we tried our best to make it feel normal. Mom made coffee and put on music as she did every Christmas morning. My brother took my dad's place passing out the presents.

Shortly after we started opening gifts, we heard a knock at the door. We were stunned. Who could possibly be at the door this early on Christmas morning? My mom answered, and it didn't take long for us to realize that it was Dad! It had snowed so much that the trains couldn't leave, so they let the soldiers go home for a few hours to spend Christmas with their families. The presents no longer mattered, but we finished opening them anyway, this time with genuine happiness because we had Dad back to share it all with.

He left again a few short hours later.

The following months felt like years. He wasn't able to write often, as they were constantly on the move. He described their arrival by convoy like driving into a black-and-white movie, destruction surrounding them. They set up camp in a blown-out schoolyard. They spent weeks there without bathrooms, sleeping upright in their vehicles in freezing temperatures until tents eventually arrived.

We were unaware of the hardship he was enduring and had settled back into our normal routines at home. But I missed him. He wasn't there when I wanted to sit by him on the couch or at the dinner table to tell him about my day at school. I acknowledged the gap when we celebrated my sister's birthday without him... and then his, and Mom's, and every holiday in between.

We were gathered around the table for dinner one night when the news caught our attention — reports of the first solider killed in Bosnia. We dropped whatever we were doing and gathered around the TV to listen for every detail, every clue, to figure out if it was him or not. I hated that feeling of not knowing. My mom was the voice of reassurance, which at the time I thought meant she somehow knew he was safe, so it eased my concern. Looking back as an adult, I realize she was just trying to keep us calm and leave the worrying to her. At this time, in 1995, we didn't have cell phones or the Internet, and he certainly had limited communication in a front-line war zone. It was impossible to know what was going on and if he was safe. We just had to wait for the next letter or a surprise phone call, and hope we didn't get an unwanted knock on the door.

When we finally got letters from Dad, it was like Christmas! I'm not sure about my brother and sister, but I read my letters over and over until the next one arrived. Dad always made me laugh at his lame attempts to relate to me with the latest slang words. But they gave me comfort, and it felt like he was with me whenever I read them.

He described getting our letters the same way — like it was Christmas. Getting a package full of civilian food gave him the comfort of home and a little bit of normalcy. My sister and I would write about our issues with Mom, which he interpreted to mean that everything was just fine. In the greater scheme of things, it was just a normal day back at home. Our letters would snap him right back into who he was, a reminder of his identity as a father and a husband. They also reassured him that we were okay, and he could remain focused on his mission — which meant everything to his safety and the safety of his troops.

After many more months of letters, he eventually made it home safely. We were stationed back in the States, where he immediately left for another three months.

The constant coming and going put us on an emotional roller coaster, but we somehow made it through Dad's twenty-year Army career with an even closer bond. The distance made us more appreciative of our time together and certainly taught me that family mattered most in life. Many soldiers don't make it home. I don't take for granted that mine did, even years after his retirement.

~Erica Kyle

13

When Dad Is the Boss

*Culture, the acquainting ourselves with the best that
has been known and said in the world, and thus
with the history of the human spirit.*
~Matthew Arnold

The weekly diversity dinner at my Navy Lieutenant Commander's house began like normal: *"Sprechen sie Deutsch?"* [Do you speak German?] *"Nein, ich mag nicht sprechen Deutsch."* [No, I don't like speaking German.]

Unfortunately, that was not the answer my father wanted to hear. Since he had been trained in the diplomatic corps, my father spoke several languages, as did my mother. They were determined that their children, who had been born long after my father's overseas deployment, would have the same benefits as the rest of the children in our military officers' neighborhood.

So, at least once a week, we were not allowed to speak anything but the designated language at the dinner table. If you said, "Pass the potatoes, please," you would be ignored. But *"Passez les pommes de terre, s'il vous plait"* got the desired result on French night. We lived with little dictionaries to help us. Even today, I still have several. In addition to speaking multiple languages and reading stories about different cultures, we also ate foods from other countries since my mother cooked exotic dishes to match the evening's conversation and study.

I came to love French and Spanish, but German and Hebrew… not so much. We all found Japanese impossibly difficult to speak, but fascinating. In fact, I ended up marrying a man from Japan and working for a number of years for a large Japanese company. So those little lessons lingered long after the dinner-table conversation was over.

Neither I nor my sister got to live overseas, as many of my fellow Navy "brats" did, but we did travel extensively in the United States. My father oversaw a number of U.S. bases. About every eighteen months, the family was packed up and shipped from one end of the country to the other. My mother became an expert at never unpacking too much — only keeping out those things absolutely necessary to our comfort.

When not living on base, military officers from all branches tended to congregate together into communities where they would understand each other's trials, and the kids could relate to living a life so different from the rest of the world. Before my father retired, I never attended the same school for a full two-year period. Military communities sprang up in new areas, so everything was the latest and greatest — but not so great for the kids hungry for long-lasting friendships.

My father was gone for months during the Cuban Missile Crisis. The only time I saw him during that period was when I crept downstairs to find him with his head in his hands, poring over some computer printouts. I sneaked a look at what was on them and didn't understand the figures. Years later I did, when I remembered seeing numbers in the millions, and words like "loss of life and destruction of homes." Military commanders, and consequently their families, learned to live with the constant reality that war could destroy countless lives if the worst-case scenario happened.

Discipline in a military family was very similar to what was expected between soldiers or sailors and their officers. I can't remember when I didn't call my mother "ma'am" or my father "sir" — or any other parents, for that matter. While we were allowed to run around to our heart's content during the day, being in before the streetlights came on was mandatory. If we failed in that task, every mother on the street would make sure we got home immediately and wouldn't hesitate to apply necessary discipline to a rebellious kid.

Because of the fluid nature of families being shipped in and out of the United States, we learned how to get along with many new people and held on loosely to any attachments. Years later, I still kept in touch with kids who were stationed around the world: Germany, Hawaii, Japan, and elsewhere. Doing so made us keenly aware that the United States was wonderful, but there were many other places with different beliefs and lifestyles. Ours weren't necessarily the "right" ones. People didn't survive long being arrogant in another country that was hosting them.

To create a feeling of community, our parents put together local carnivals and stage plays. Nothing professional, but it pulled together those left behind so they could get to know each other. The creativity that arose from a bit of paint and cardboard was amazing. And the variety of foods one could find! After all, wives brought back the cooking traditions of not only their own land, but from every other place they had lived.

The flip side was that we never really had a home in the traditional sense. My mother loved beautiful objects and a well-decorated place. Sadly, moving things cross-country over and over again tended to destroy them, but she taught us how to make things as nice as possible quickly and on a very limited budget. It was the only way to bring a sense of normalcy to life. After growing up and moving out on my own, the rhythms of moving constantly and seeking change stayed in my blood for many years.

All the kids I knew were proud of their parents' military service. We had friendly competitions between each other over which branch was the bravest and the best. But we all felt a strong sense that we were somehow uniquely bonded. Unlike the rest of the world, we lived through the sadness of departures and the joy of reunions.

I think the wives left behind were, and still are, as brave as any deployed soldier or sailor. They had to keep a calm home, raise the children, balance a ridiculously tight budget, and be upbeat and happy when their spouses returned — no matter for how short a time. Military commanders' wives had an even more difficult time, because just as their husbands led their troops, the wives were expected to pull the other spouses together to do whatever charitable activities needed to be done, and also support them during horrendous losses and wars.

Despite that, I wouldn't have traded all the interesting experiences and new places I saw up and down the coasts of America for anything. Being a Navy brat gave me the confidence to try new things and meet new people, and isn't that what life is really all about?

~Kamia Taylor

14

Far but Never Too Far

There is a good reason they call these ceremonies
"commencement exercises." Graduation is
not the end; it's the beginning.
~Orrin Hatch

Being a military dependent is hard, whether you're a spouse or a child, when the military sends your loved one away. I got used to it during my childhood. Some days hurt more than others. Birthdays and Christmas were particularly hard. Oddly enough, I think graduation from high school was the worst. After years of changing schools and moving often, reaching that threshold toward adulthood is an even bigger achievement than it is in civilian life.

In a Department of Defense school, graduation is a bit different. I remember looking at my classmates toward the end of senior year knowing that I wouldn't see them again after graduation. There would be no ten or twenty-five year reunions for us. Our base might not even exist then. Some of us were going back to the States for college. Many others were joining the military, and we knew, since we were already at war, exactly what that meant for them. I suppose that tamped down the typical excitement surrounding graduation. It was a mixed bag—a combination of elation and anticipation mixed with sadness, knowing these few who were with me through so many hard times would never be there again.

My small class was relatively lucky. The majority of our service member parents were not deployed for graduation. For two of my classmates, though, that was not the case. Approaching graduation was particularly hard on them. Grandparents were making an especially long venture to come to Germany and see them graduate. Their mothers were there, too, but their fathers would not be. They were in Iraq.

We supported them as much as we were able to with something that is not typically seen in teens—a unique awareness and the maturity to show compassion. We were teenagers in so many rebellious ways, and yet, through shared hardships unique to military life, we saw things with a perspective unusual to our youth.

I was class president at the time, which meant that graduation planning was my responsibility. I remember being particularly worried about it going well. I suppose knowing that it was the last time we would all be together weighed on me. I wanted to get it right. It wasn't a monumental task really, but at the time it felt insurmountable. More than anything, I wanted everyone to have a shared moment that was special.

We arranged for extra seating from the base. We had so many family members flying in from the States that our school didn't have enough chairs. Since I wanted it to be really special, we rejected the typical commissary flat cake, and my mom made a gorgeous five-tier, five-foot-long cake with a fountain dyed blue for our school colors. The tiers of the cake were connected by stairways, and graduation figures were placed on them. We'd been so disappointed with the figures we ordered—they only came in a generic white male or female. Most of my classmates were minorities, so we repainted them to resemble each of the graduates. I remember poring over the class photos, matching hair colors and facial hair. We even included details like ankle tattoos. I remember how crazy everyone went as they began arriving early for the ceremony and saw my mom assembling the cake. The reactions were priceless. Everyone wanted a picture with the cake. Apparently, it even wound up being shown on American Forces Network in the week after graduation.

As we were getting ready, there were the expected tears. This was goodbye, but I think most of us choked back our own tears to be strong for our two peers whose fathers would not be there as they walked in the procession and received their diplomas. It was heartbreaking to see them try and hide the hurt that we all knew they were feeling.

Friends and families filled the cafeteria — which was our auditorium, too — and we got ready to walk in. We had to enter the hall and then split off because there was a table blocking the way, and we couldn't continue down the center of the aisle. No one really liked the arrangement I had made, but it was very important. So we split off at the table, walked to the edges of the room, crossed in front of the stage and filed up to the chairs on the stage where we took our seats. I'm not sure we actually managed to pay much attention to the principal's remarks. I think we were all focusing on not tripping when it was time to get up. We had each written a short speech — a perk of having few graduates — and while they were read, we handed out roses to those teachers and family who had gotten us through the years leading up to that point. Despite being nervous and focused on ourselves in that moment, I don't think anyone failed to see the two reserved empty seats.

Midway through the ceremony, instead of progressing to the next student's speech, I was called up. I hadn't told my classmates about that part; there were too many variables that could have led to it being canceled at the last minute, and I didn't want to get their hopes up. But everything, thankfully, went well. I walked up to the podium and introduced two very special guests.

A bright light flashed from the table in the aisle, and a projector came on, broadcasting a movie-screen sized image onto the cafeteria wall. A pair of soldiers in desert camouflage and helmets stood side by side and waved at their kids. We were broadcasting the graduation ceremony live to their base in Iraq, and they were broadcasting a live feed back to us. The two sergeants watched from a war zone as their children, tears streaming down their cheeks, accepted their diplomas. I don't think there were any dry eyes in the entire gathering. They told their children they were proud of them, they loved them, and they would be home as soon as they could. It was an amazing moment.

Even now, and it has been years, I still tear up when I think about the astounding strength of military bonds, both familial and friend. We may never see each other again, but time and distance mean nothing to that love and support.

~C. Solomon

15

Forgotten Heroes

Courage is to feel the daily daggers of
relentless steel and keep on living.
~Douglas Malloch

O peration Desert Storm is when it first hit me. It's the children. They are the forgotten heroes. And since then, as I watch with the rest of the country while American soldiers leave their families as they are headed to war, my eyes are always on the children.

Having been a military dependent for the first eighteen years of my life, I was called a military brat. I didn't mind. I wore the name with pride. My stint as a dependent, though not ideal, was filled with extraordinary experiences and faraway places. Being the child of the military is a rewarding life. But there are sacrifices, too.

My tenure as a military brat spread me over four states, three European countries and eight schools by the time I was twelve. Friends were like tulips, here today and gone tomorrow. Home was wherever my father was stationed. And my military family was closer to me than my blood relatives.

I have a multitude of memories. My children, all grown now with kids of their own, grew up tolerating my nostalgia for military life. Most of the time, it would be while watching television. Scenes of London, England, always stirred up my storehouse of favorite memories.

"Hey, I've been there!" I'd chime in. "I rode past Buckingham

Palace on a red double-decker bus!"

My kids would just shrug their shoulders. "Yes... we know, Mom... you've been everywhere."

They were not at all impressed as I shared for the millionth time: "I once stood so close to Queen Elizabeth I could reach out and touch her."

But their indifference didn't matter to me. I knew how fortunate I had been. I belonged to a unique club—I was the child of an American serviceman.

After my dad retired, I married and moved into the house that had been my parents' home. I craved roots and had no desire to ever move again. But every now and then, I peek into my treasure chest of childhood memories of the military life. That life made me who I am.

One day, while sitting down with my morning cup of coffee, I tuned in to the *Today* show. Suddenly, the camera zoomed in on a flag-waving crowd, cheering a busload of soldiers deploying to war. I stopped my coffee cup short of reaching my mouth. My insides were shaking. My heart was pounding. In my mind, I yelled at the crowd: "Wait a minute! Stop all of that patriotic joy!"

My mental outburst surprised me. But the news report had triggered something deep inside of me. Tears rolled down my face as a scene from decades ago replayed in my mind—a painful memory.

I was twelve years old when my dad deployed to Vietnam. No time of year is a good time to send a loved one off to war, but the day after Christmas seemed particularly cruel. Shortly after dawn, next to a blinking Christmas tree, I hugged my dad goodbye. No waving flags. No patriotic fanfare. Just an uncomfortable silence as my mother, four brothers and I watched him walk out the door.

As soon as he drove out of sight, I ran upstairs to my room and collapsed onto my bed. Burying my face in my pillow, I cried and cried until my sheets were soaked and there was nothing left to spill. My broken heart was dry.

I couldn't handle the thought of my dad going to war. My imagination set in motion unthinkable scenarios. *He could die! How could I live without my daddy?*

I was so wounded that morning, I felt like a casualty of war. But I was the child of an American serviceman. And that's just the way it is.

Finally, as military children so often must do, I accepted what I could not control. I threw myself into school activities and new friends.

Watching the nightly news became a ritual. I was bombarded with the sights and sounds of war: ricocheting bullets, bomb blasts and flag-draped coffins. The disturbing pictures tortured me. I longed to hear that the war was over. I begged God: "Please, Lord, end this war now so my daddy can come home."

My prayers were not answered right away. The war did not end immediately. But one day the phone rang, and I heard on the other end: "Hi, hon."

It was him!

"Daddy, where are you?"

"I'm on my way home, honey."

But I knew he wasn't supposed to be home for another three months.

"Why?" I quizzed him as the conversation turned serious. "Are you hurt? Have you been wounded?"

"No, honey," he assured me. "I'll see you in a couple days."

A few days later, he was home, safe and sound, but the dad who came back to me was not the one who left. The war had left its mark. Physically, he was fine; mentally, he was wounded.

A part of him was missing in action for many years. As with many Vietnam vets, his readjustment was long and difficult. Finally, although it was long after I had children of my own, he found his way back.

In spite of the pain of separation while my dad was at war, in spite of never knowing where I would live from one year to the next, and in spite of bidding my friends goodbye far too often, I treasure my history as the child of a military man. I wear it like a badge of honor.

If it were up to me, I would pin medals on every child of every American soldier and thank them for their service to our country. I don't think most Americans realize what the children of our servicemen and servicewomen endure for our sake. Their bravery goes unnoticed. But I understand because I am one of them. And I will never forget. I am the child of an American soldier.

~Teresa Anne Hayden

Not from Nowhere

Where thou art, that is home.
~Emily Dickinson

"Ah, travelers checks. You must be on vacation. Where are you from?" It was the summer of 1995. I remember that because I had just graduated from high school. My parents were at the end of a three-year tour in Japan, and we were back in the U.S. visiting family before I headed down south to begin my adventures in college. My favorite aunt and I were doing what we loved — spending the day at a mall in good old St. Louis.

I had my own spending money saved up from babysitting, but it was in the form of travelers checks. Everywhere I spent money, it was obvious that I was not a local for this reason alone. Now, the friendly clerk in front of me was curious.

"Define 'from,'" I laughed.

You see, to a military brat, the question "Where are you from?" is relative. At a young age, we sometimes looked to our parents for help in answering that question. We became accustomed to being given "the look," which is given by people who can't understand why such a simple question would be met with such hesitance and uncertainty. With age, came the wisdom of being able to discern *why* the question was being asked, and an appropriate answer could usually be given accordingly.

In this case, I wasn't sure how to answer. The clerk looked confused and rephrased what she thought was the same question. "Where do you live?"

"Well, I'm in the middle of a move, so... if you want to know where I'm moving *from*, the answer is Japan. But I'm headed to Arkansas in a couple weeks for college."

"Oh! You're Japanese?" she asked.

"No, I'm American," I said, giving my aunt a sideways glance. Didn't my blond hair and green eyes rule that out? "My dad was just stationed in Japan."

By this time, the clerk was intrigued with my life story. How strange my life must seem to someone who quite possibly has spent her entire life living on the same street, and whose longest road trip may very well have kept her within the confines of her own state.

"And you're headed to Arkansas, you said? That's a long way off. You must have family down there?"

"No, not really. My family roots are an hour east of here, in Illinois."

"Really?" she replied. "So, you must have been born and raised in Illinois then, before your family moved to Japan?"

"Um... no. I was born in Wyoming, actually."

"Have you been back to visit?" she asked.

"No, I was just a baby when we left. I don't remember anything about it."

"Did you move to Japan from there?"

"Actually, we lived in Florida before Japan."

By this time, my aunt was laughing, and I was becoming mildly annoyed because there's really no simple answer to the question "Where are you from?" when you're a military brat.

The friendly clerk then asked me how many places I've lived, and as I rattled off the states, her eyes showed her disbelief.

To me, having moved so often and having lived in so many different places was no big deal. It was the norm. Military brats move to an exciting new place, get settled, make friends, and in two years' time, they're saying goodbye to their new friends, who are now more like family, and they're moving on. They pack up, move somewhere else new and exciting, get settled, make more new life-long friends, and in two years' time — yup! — they're gone again. Repeat this process until adulthood. Some folks might find such a lifestyle unsettling, but to me it was just the way life was.

In the first eighteen years of my life, I lived in fifteen different houses, eight different states, and two countries. I attended seven different schools. Each time we moved, our hearts were torn in two because, as military families know, friendships form so quickly, run so deeply, and the bonds become so strong in that setting.

But we knew two things — we'd always stay in touch, and there would be new friendships forged in our new home that would be just as strong. My wedding was a perfect example of the strength and longevity of military friendships. My ring bearer came up from Georgia to be a part of our special day. I had babysat for his family in Japan. The twins who passed out flowers to our guests traveled from Colorado to join us. I had also babysat for them in Japan. My maid of honor was my seventh-grade best friend from Florida. A friend from Arkansas sang at our wedding. The Japanese baby who was my namesake had an entire family in attendance. These people *are* our family.

To the clerk at the mall, my life must have seemed like one big adventure. I am sure she would have continued to question me had there not been a line of customers behind us. And the stories I could have told! My high school years alone were enough to fill a book. I lived in an apartment on an Air Force base with Mt. Fuji on the horizon. Our church was a blend of American and Japanese cultures, and we had so many wonderful memories there. My school's athletic department brought in competitors from all over the Far East. I had classmates from Korea, Germany, and the Philippines. My senior class trip was to Saipan, where we spent three days and two nights on the beach and in the shopping district. For Christmas break one year, my family flew to Korea for a shopping spree that lasted several days. How many kids can boast of a childhood like this?

I've heard it said before that military brats are from nowhere. Someone once said it's a bit like being a permanent exile, with no place to call home. But I don't *feel* "homeless." I feel, rather, that I've had many homes. I've embraced so many different places, and when

I look back at each one, I am overcome with such sweet nostalgia that I might as well have lived there my entire life. I still don't have a neat, tidy, packaged answer for the question "Where are you from?" but I can now answer with a smile on my face. In my heart, I know that home is everywhere. And *that*, friendly store clerk, should have been my answer.

~Mati Stark

A Different Kind of Hero

The simple act of caring is heroic.
~Edward Albert

Four hundred miles out in the Atlantic Ocean aboard the aircraft carrier USS America, my exhausted father had just finished his shift as aviation maintenance chief for his squadron. He wanted nothing more than to fall into his bunk. As he turned off the light, his thoughts turned automatically to his family. He wondered how I had done in the Georgia State Spelling Bee that we had gone to the day before.

Before he could doze off, however, the light snapped on again. The skipper and executive officer stepped in.

"Afraid I've got some bad news, Chief," the skipper said. A Red Cross telegram read: *"Wife and two children critically injured in car accident. Recommend transportation home by fastest means possible."*

"Where's my third child?" Dad asked, fearing the worst. "I have three kids. What's happened to the third one?" Neither man knew.

Suddenly, in the middle of an aircraft carrier staffed with enough personnel to populate a small city, my father felt completely helpless and alone.

It took two days for Dad to get home. In the meantime, he learned the details of our accident. My mother, my sister and brother, and I were on our way home from the spelling bee with my school sponsor when a speeding car broadsided my sponsor's car. My sister, like my sponsor, had escaped with only cuts and bruises. But my mother's legs and ribs were broken, my six-year-old brother's leg was broken so badly he was in a body cast, and my pelvis was so seriously fractured that a sling-style traction supported my hips.

Through a medicated fog and one good eye (my right eye was injured), I was glad to see Dad appear at my bedside. I heard his reassuring words, "Everything's going to be alright. Old Dad's here." I drifted back to sleep, knowing I could count on my father to help us through. I tried not to think about the fact that his squadron had been doing carrier qualifications for a nine-month deployment to the Mediterranean and that at some point he would have to return to the ship.

He came to the hospital daily, making sure we had the best of care. Whatever we needed or wanted, whether it was an adjustment to my brother's cast or pie from a nearby diner, Dad provided it while also caring for my sister and our dog at home. Eventually, we were all discharged, but the stress continued as we tried to recuperate in a mobile home crowded with wheelchairs and other hospital equipment. Dad handled all the responsibilities of the house and yard despite caring for three incapacitated people. Unfortunately, no close friends or relatives lived nearby to help him with his burden. While the rest of the world concentrated on the Watergate break-in, the North Vietnamese advance on Saigon, and the terrorist attacks at the summer Olympics in Munich, Dad focused on getting us through each day and helping us gain our independence again.

I learned things about my father that summer that I will always remember. Though he knew more about fixing jet engines than a fourteen-year-old girl's hair, he gently combed out my long tangled mess, still full of paint and glass, and braided it. He made shorts to fit over my brother's body cast and made pickles when our garden produced way too many cucumbers. When we went to physical therapy, he had to wheel or carry each of us out of our home, fit us into the car, unload us into the building one at a time, and then do that all in reverse after the appointment. It made for a long day, but he never complained.

When we were finally able to limp along without assistance, we told Dad goodbye with many tears and prayers because his ordeal was not yet over. The USS America had been reassigned to Vietnam, so he had to travel to Travis Air Force Base outside San Francisco to get a "space available" seat on a plane going to Clark Air Base in the Philippines where the ship was being serviced at U.S. Naval Base Subic Bay.

He slept on two chairs in Travis's passenger terminal for a week, trying to be ready when a seat was announced over the loudspeaker. Finally, he caught a C-5 going to Hawaii, thinking there would be flights from their air base to Clark, but none was available. Needing to make some kind of forward progress, Daddy hitched a ride on a C-141 headed to Wake Island in the middle of the Pacific, sleeping on the cargo plane's floor for the entire trip. The C-141 crew, after delivering their cargo, received their next assignment — Clark Air Base — and let him ride along again. Once he reached Clark, he still needed to reach the USS America before it left, but the bus from Clark to Subic Bay wasn't running. Overhearing that a C-141 crew was taking groceries there, Daddy told them his situation, and they said if he could squeeze in, he could go.

When they landed, he hurried to the operations office where he could call a taxi to get to the ship, only to hear that one wouldn't be coming for a while. Frustrated, he walked back outside — and saw a cab headed in his direction. Daddy stepped out in front of it, promising the driver a generous tip as he commandeered the cab. The driver protested but quickly delivered him to the USS America. After traveling for nearly 10,000 miles, living off vending machine snacks, and going without a shower or shave for twelve days, he reported to the commander and said, "I'm back aboard, Skipper."

Before he left, I slipped a note into Daddy's flight bag telling him how much I appreciated everything he had done for us, not knowing the trials he would have to endure before finally getting to read it. Later, I received a letter from him. The letter was full of encouragement and the assurance that the work had been "no trouble at all" and that he would "do it all over again if necessary but hope it never will be."

I still have that note, and I often think about how Dad gladly cared for us for weeks. My father may not have been the kind of war hero we see in movies, but he was a hero to me that summer and always will be.

~Lisa Hyman Johnson

Sergeant Lilly's Boots

A man does what he must — in spite of personal
consequences, in spite of obstacles and dangers
and pressures — and that is the basis
of all human morality.
~John F. Kennedy

The early 1960s were filled with a palpable sense of imminent danger and fear. The drama of the Cold War was unfolding, and the potential for nuclear attacks was on everyone's mind. Nikita Khrushchev had banged his shoe on a table at the United Nations while threatening America and the free world. Most Americans paid at least modest attention to civil defense.

On this particular Sunday afternoon in October 1962, we weren't thinking about civil defense. Instead, my family was topping off an inspiring worship service with fried chicken and mashed potatoes at the Non-commissioned Officers Club at Scott Air Force Base. I was looking forward to the apple pie à la mode.

Our meal was interrupted by an airman who spoke to my father privately. Dad came back to the table and said that we had to depart immediately. I couldn't imagine what was more important than dessert.

On the way home, Dad explained that he had received orders to go on a mission and had only a brief time to pack. He could not tell us where he was going or the nature of the mission. It was strangely quiet and somber in the Ford station wagon that day.

Once home, Dad pulled me aside and said, "Son, I'm not sure where I'm going or when I will be back. There's some trouble in the world, and I have to help fix it. I need you to be a man and take care of things around here and help your mother. Now, get my boots and polish them real shiny for me. Son, I'm counting on you."

Soon, we were back at the base, where Dad kissed Mom and hugged my sister and me. We watched in wonder as he walked through the gate toward the plane that would take him away from us to an unknown destination.

Upon his return, we discovered that his mission had involved preparation for a possible conflict with Cuba and Russia for which he later received a special commendation. Over time, we learned how close we had come to nuclear war.

To this day, when someone asks me if I remember the Cuban Missile Crisis, I respond with: "Yes, I shined Sergeant Lilly's boots!"

~Pastor Gary C. Lilly

Comfort Crew

*Our mission is to deliver proven strategies to prepare
every military child for the unique challenges they
face, so they positively impact themselves,
their families, and our country.*

*~Mission statement of The Comfort
Crew for Military Kids*

I am sitting here in my office at The Comfort Crew for Military Kids headquarters in Austin, Texas, drinking a cup of tea and reflecting on my last nine years of touring with the USO. The Comfort Crew created the "With You All the Way! Tour" to strengthen our military families. The Tour took us to sixteen different countries, delivering this program to more than 200,000 military children around the world. I have collected many stories during all the years of touring with the USO, and a few come to mind.

One story in particular occupies a very special place in my heart. I had just finished a presentation at a school on a base in North Carolina. After my presentation, a little boy approached me.

He told me that he had been moved by the performance and wanted to thank me for coming to his school. Then he took a deep breath and told me that his mother died in a car accident a few years earlier, and his dad was currently deployed. He was very worried that his dad might not come back.

We had a very touching conversation, and I shared some ideas about how to manage his stress and the fears he had about losing his dad. As I finished talking, he put up his finger and asked if I wouldn't mind waiting a minute because he needed to get something from his classroom.

He dashed off and returned a few minutes later. He held out a patch his father had given him before he left. The boy told me he carried that patch with him every day. He kept it in his desk at school and slept with it under his pillow.

He handed the patch to me. I marveled at it.

"What a wonderful gift your dad gave you."

"It's for you."

I told the boy that I couldn't take the patch because it was a special gift and so important to him. But he insisted, and I didn't want to hurt his feelings by rejecting his gesture. I put it in my wallet and said I'd take care of the patch for him and look after it in case he needed it back.

Then he said something that touched my heart.

"I want you to keep the patch forever. You support so many people. I want to support you."

We spend a lot of time traveling during our USO tours. To keep me occupied while logging thousands of miles on airplanes, I often doodle on stones. I call them "Hope ROCKS!"

During one of our USO World Tours, I was at a school on a base in Germany and met a little girl who was having a very difficult time. She was distraught and sobbing while trying to tell me how she was feeling.

I happened to have one of my hope stones in my pocket, and I gave it to her. I told her that whenever she felt sad or anxious or lonely, she should hold it in her hand and know there is someone with her all the way.

She smiled and hugged me and thanked me for the rock. She wouldn't let go. Her teacher had to pry her arms away. "Thanks for the stone," she said as the teacher led her back to her classroom. "I'll keep it forever."

Eight months later, we were at another school at a different base in Germany. After my performance, I saw a teacher standing nearby with her class. Suddenly, she put her hand to her mouth and pointed at me. She was sobbing.

Then I saw a blur out of the corner of my eye. Before I knew what was happening, I was almost knocked off my feet by a child who ran up and hugged me. She looked up, and I recognized her immediately. It was the same girl to whom I had given the stone eight months before. She had moved and was now at a different school on another base.

She was sobbing, but smiling at the same time.

"I'm so happy to see you," I said.

"Me, too," she said. "My daddy is deployed. But look."

She reached into her pocket and brought out a crumpled and frayed Kleenex. She unraveled it, and inside was the stone I had given her all those months before. The doodles were practically worn off the sides.

"You kept it?" I asked, smiling. "You made my day."

Her teacher, who was standing nearby and still in tears, said, "She carries that stone with her every single day."

"My dad is still deployed, and the stone gives me hope," she said.

I looked over at my business partner, Woody Englander, who was standing nearby. He started to cry, and so did I.

The little girl carefully re-wrapped the rock in the Kleenex and put it back into her pocket. Then she noticed me wiping my tears.

She stepped forward and gave me a giant hug.

"It's okay," she said, patting my back while hugging me. "It's okay."

It's amazing that while I was supporting her, she in turn was supporting me.

One of the things I do to help me manage all the feelings I carry from all the children we meet is to write about my experiences in a journal. At every performance, I encourage kids to do the same. The result is amazing. An e-mail I received after one visit sums it all up.

Dear Mr. Trevor Romain,
You spoke at my school when I got the With You All the Way movie box and that journal. My dad was gone 3 times and I felt like he did not know us. I sometimes got so sad it hurt inside and I was real depressed because it feels like he is not my same dad. But I promise your movie helped a lot. I wrote my ideas down in my

journal and my dad read it and you know what? He cried. And when he cried I knew that he cared and I felt so much better to know that he got his feelings back and I got my dad back. Thank you for the USO and your helping.
Delissa

~Trevor Romain

Chapter 3

Military Families

★ ★ On the Move, Again! ★ ★

20

What Is a Military Wife?

A thing is mighty big when time and
distance cannot shrink it.
~Zora Neale Hurston

She's moving… Moving far from home… Moving two cars, three kids and one dog… All riding with *her*, of course. Moving sofas to basements because they won't go in *this* house. Moving curtains that won't fit. Moving jobs and certifications and professional development hours. Moving away from friends. Moving toward new friends, moving her most important luggage: her trunk full of memories.

She's waiting… Waiting for housing. Waiting for orders. Waiting for deployments. Waiting for phone calls. Waiting for reunions. Waiting for the new curtains to arrive. Waiting for him to come home for dinner…

They call her "Military Dependent," but she knows better: She is fiercely *In*-dependent. She can balance a checkbook, handle the yard work, fix a noisy toilet, and bury the family pet. She is intimately familiar with drywall anchors and toggle bolts. She can file the taxes, sell a house, buy a car, or set up a move… all with *one* Power of Attorney.

She welcomes neighbors who don't welcome her. She reinvents her career with every Permanent Change of Station (PCS) order. She locates a house in the desert, the Arctic, or the Deep South, and learns to call them all "home." She *makes* them all home.

Military Wives move fast. They leap into decorating, leadership, volunteering, career alternatives, churches, and friendships. They don't have fifteen years to get to know people. Their roots are short but flexible. They plant annuals for themselves and perennials for those who come after them.

Military Wives quickly learn to value each other: they connect over coffee, rely on the spouse network, accept offers of friendship and favors, and record addresses in pencil. They have a common bond. The Military Wife has a husband unlike other husbands; his commitment is unique. He doesn't have a "job"; he has a "mission" that he can't just decide to quit… He's on-call for his country 24/7.

But for her, the wife, he's the most unreliable guy in town! His language is foreign — TDY PCS OPR SOS ACC BDU ACU BAR CIB TAD EPR — and so a Military Wife is a translator for her family and his. She is the long-distance link to keep them informed, the glue that holds them together.

A Military Wife has her moments: She wants to wring his neck, dye his uniform pink, refuse to move to Siberia, but she pulls herself together. Give her a few days, a travel brochure, a long hot bath, a pledge to the flag, a wedding picture, and she goes. She packs. She moves. She follows.

Why? What for? You may think it is because she has lost her mind, but actually it is because she has lost her heart. It was stolen from her by a man who puts duty first, who longs to deploy, who salutes the flag, and whose boots in the doorway remind her that as long as he is her military husband, she will remain his Military Wife. She would have it no other way.

~Amy H. Fraher

21

Sharing Happiness

Since there is nothing so well worth having as
friends, never lose a chance to make them.
~Francesco Guicciardini

My phone rang this week, and for once it wasn't my kids or my husband or my mother or my carpool partner or my in-laws or one of those pre-recorded doctor's appointment confirmation messages. "Hey, Lisa, what have you been up to?" the other military spouse asked.

I was dumbfounded. It had been months since I had received a purely social call — it was as if I had forgotten what to do. My mind raced as I tried to remember how to engage in idle chitchat.

Why on earth is she calling me? I wondered. *I mean, we only know each other because our Navy husbands work together on base. And besides, I'm new, but she's lived here for years. She has plenty of other friends to call... there must be some problem.*

"Oh, you know, the usual... busy, busy, busy!" I lied, waiting for her to ask to borrow money, or give her a ride to the airport, or buy overpriced candles for her son's baseball team fundraiser.

"Well, listen, I really need some exercise... would you like to go on a power walk or something?"

You'd have thought I was a double winner on *The Price Is Right's* Showcase Showdown by the way I reacted.

"Really? Yes! I would love to! What time? Where do you want me to meet you? I'll go anywhere! I already have workout clothes on, so I am ready to go whenever you are, so just say the word and…"

"Nine-fifteen at the Park and Ride lot on Wonderwood Drive."

"You got it!"

I arrived twenty minutes early and sat there looking for her minivan. When she arrived, I bolted from my car as if it had burst into flames.

"Hi!" I yelled across the parking lot, waving enthusiastically, and startled her out of her morning haze. Thankfully, she didn't throw her van in reverse and screech out of the parking lot. In fact, she didn't try to escape at all.

My new friend stepped out of her van and simply said, "Hello!"

Thank goodness, I thought, *she probably thinks I just had a little too much caffeine this morning.*

For the next hour, we did what housewives do so well—analyzed, pondered, proclaimed, opined, pontificated, empathized, chastised, gossiped and even listened a little bit, all under the guise of exercise. I thoroughly enjoyed myself.

Back in the parking lot, my new friend suggested that we make the outing our new Thursday routine. I eagerly agreed, and nearly skipped back to my car with a goofy grin.

On the drive home, I thought, *Finally, a real friend. I can't wait for next Thursday. Boy, I wish we could meet Tuesdays and Thursdays. But maybe that's too much. I don't want to scare her away. Hmmm. Come to think of it, maybe I did come on too strong. I don't remember listening all that much, actually. I think I did most of the talking. Why do I always do that? She was probably wondering whether I'd ever shut up. I'll bet she will call and cancel next week because she thinks I'm an annoying blabbermouth….*

I pulled into my driveway, put the car in park, and looked at myself in the rearview mirror. Not only did I realize that my bangs had fallen into that unflattering middle part that made my face look like a full moon, it also occurred to me that this had all happened before.

Suddenly overwhelmed with that bizarre déjà vu sensation, I tried to recollect the past. It didn't take long for me to recognize that the internal conversation I just had with myself was the same one I had in 2008, 1998, 1996, 1994 and 1993—basically, every time the military had ordered us to move.

After every move, I busy myself with setting up our new life — new house, new schools, new doctors, new dentists, new music teachers, new gym, new church, new pizza place, new routines — a daunting task that keeps me occupied for several months. But once the new routines are in place, there's nothing left to do except get on with living.

And whether the Navy sends us to Poughkeepsie or Prague, boredom eventually sets in. I find myself dawdling on the Internet, throwing dinner together at the last minute, ignoring housework, and eating too much. I put on workout clothes every day, but never make it to the gym. I call my husband at work even though I know he won't have time to talk. I write long e-mails to friends from the past who are too preoccupied to write back. Even my own mother tries to get off the phone when I call, and my last resort, the family dog, has no good gossip to share.

To put it simply, I become bored out of my mind.

As I fixed my bangs in the rearview mirror, I remembered that human beings are tribal animals with genetically determined primal instincts. Our cave dwelling ancestors lived in groups, hunting, gathering, and sharing in order to ensure the survival of the community.

It's true, I get a little pathetic every time we move, but I realize it's because I'm only human. And although I'm in no danger of starving anytime soon (quite the contrary, in fact), I know that everyone needs a good friend or two to nourish the soul.

~Lisa Smith Molinari

Overseas!

*If you reject the food, ignore the customs, fear
the religion and avoid the people, you
might better stay home.*
~James A. Michener

After my husband notified me we'd be moving to Germany in a few months, I immediately started trying to learn German. My Facebook account got wise to my game (courtesy of software cookies stored from my computer searches), and started auto-populating with ads for any and all things German. And that's precisely how my first words learned in German came from a "click bait" story.

The German language has a reputation for mile-long words, and it's not without reason. This particular story ran with this theme, featuring a person saying a word in multiple languages, to highlight how different it sounded in German. For example, in English you would say hospital; in French, *hôpital*, but in German (as the linguist shouted for extra emphasis) — *Krankenhaus*! I quickly learned *kranken* means to suffer, and *haus* is, well, a house. And all nouns are capitalized because nouns are important. So in German, the hospital translates into the "suffer-house." An ambulance became *Krankenwagen*, of course, the "suffer-wagon." But what had me howling was seeing an ad for *Kranken-gymnastics*. It was a promo for CrossFit — the elite, uber-high-intensity workout program. But isn't it a lot more fun to think of CrossFit as the "suffer-gymnastics?"

Germany, I thought, *was going to be one heck of an experience.*

After serving on active duty myself as a mil-to-mil married couple, and now as a military spouse, I've discovered each military Permanent Change of Station (PCS) is always a bit different. All moves require an extensive amount of planning and preparation, but an international PCS ratchets that up a notch. To pull one off successfully requires a carefully orchestrated sequence of events and recommendations. Right up there with trust but verify all information given to you, and e-mail yourself a copy of everything, would be to have patience and keep your sense of humor intact.

The first order of business (and lesson in patience) before we left the States was starting the rounds of health certifications, both for ourselves and our rescue cat. Getting medically cleared for travel and country relocation takes time. Multiple forms are required of each family member, as well as appointments with medical staff. The military simply wants to ensure adequate medical care will be available for your family overseas. To do this, they need an exhaustive list of forms, records, and affidavits for each family member.

Humans understand this. Animals do not.

Our poor rescue cat (already a needy, curmudgeonly soul) carefully eyed the veterinarian on our first visit before allowing himself to be seduced with cat treats. After he got his microchip, though, the honeymoon was over, and the vet moved to our cat's permanent "do-not-trust list" — right up there with his cat carrier, the means of transporting him to this torture.

Our second visit involved a spy movie–style snatch-and-grab where I pounced on him while he was napping and quickly placed him in his carrier. This visit devolved into the vet and her technician being forced to wrap him in a towel like a cat burrito in order to stop him from biting. Also not a trust building move.

By the time we made it to the vet for his final round of paperwork and certifications, the cat was a hot mess. Literally. He peed in his carrier as I drove around the Washington, D.C. beltway.

After a final paperwork scare at the airport (resolved by a record I'd saved in my e-mail), husband, cat, and wife successfully boarded a plane for Germany.

We'd been in-country less than twenty-four hours before my husband started his in-processing onto our assigned Air Force base. As he completed the rounds of checklists required by base agencies, I went to my own form of in-processing: the spouse's orientation. I found myself excited, but there were definitely a few shell-shocked looking ladies at the table with me.

Our instructor did his best to cover a mountain of information in six short hours. He lectured on cultural customs and courtesies, explained why there are four different types of trashcans in Germany (hint: recycling), chided the American who shows up late to an appointment (as Germans are extremely punctual), and finally finished with a brief on holidays.

"Today is *Hexennacht!*" he gleefully announced. Or "Witches' Night." He explained that on this day, April 30th, witches are reputed to hold a celebration high in the mountains to await the arrival of spring the following day — May 1st.

And he cautioned us to hide our trashcans, doormats, and anything else we didn't want whisked off into the dark night, as Hexennacht was also a popular prankster's holiday among mischievous teens.

I smirked and immediately thought, *My legs are long enough — go pull someone else's*, as I Googled "Witches' Night" on my phone under the table.

He was totally not kidding!

Fortunately, our trashcans made it safely through the night, and I realized this was just the first holiday of many which the U.S. does not have — or if it does, it is celebrated quite differently.

But it's these differences that have made this move the best military adventure to date. It's the raised eyebrows of surprise at constantly learning something new. The proud smile of recognition and respect from an elderly lady once you greet her in her native tongue and hold a conversation with her. The grin from your local butcher when you can finally say *Hähnchenbrustfilets* (chicken breasts) instead of pointing at the word and holding up your fingers to indicate how many you'd like. The grin on your face when he returns the effort and gives you a cookbook featuring full color pictures and German labeling for every cut of meat you can order in his store.

The real fun of an international move, though, has been learning to open my heart and my mind to new experiences, languages, and customs.

The German language tends to have a word for everything and, true to form, they have a wonderful word I would like to share with you: *Gemütlichkeit*. Pronounced guh-moot-lish-KYTE, it describes a feeling we've all experienced, but may not have had the name for. The rough English translation is coziness or good cheer, but *Gemütlichkeit* really goes a step further. It encapsulates that feeling of belonging, of social acceptance, of leaving your troubles at the door and being surrounded by a group of your dearest friends. It's hard to put that feeling into a precise English word. We've felt it, but the Germans labeled it.

That's the feeling I know I'll leave Germany with, that warmth and feeling of belonging, of being warmly welcomed into their social structure — once I put myself in the position to receive it.

Once I truly began living like a local.

~Kristi Adams

23

Wings or Roots

There are only two lasting bequests we can hope to give
our children. One of these is roots; the other, wings.
~W. Hodding Carter II

A year and a half ago, I had my doubts. I remember packing the ski jackets and ice scrapers in the car while sweating in the sunshine of our San Diego driveway. It only got worse when we picked up the kids from Kindercare and watched them say goodbye to the teachers who had held them from the time they were babies! I was a crying mess, and I wondered at the time what kind of parents could take their kids away from so much love, stability, and happiness.

Fortunately, I was quickly comforted by the life we found when we arrived in Portsmouth, Rhode Island. We were welcomed from the moment we set foot in the snow, and we learned about life in a way we had never considered before. Justin still played football, and Annalise was already dancing the first Saturday morning we were there, but more importantly, we quickly learned so many new East Coast things. Justin learned how to collect a full meal off the beach with nothing but a pail, and Annalise has conquered the game of Popcorn on the trampoline. We know how and when to use the word "wicked," and I figured out how to decorate our house a new way.

John got another master's degree, and we have visited Boston, New

York, Washington, D.C., Baltimore, Philadelphia, Michigan, Virginia, Florida, Bermuda, the Bahamas, Newport yachts in the summer, the South Boston St. Patrick's Day Parade, Cape Cod, and Martha's Vineyard. We had a great time living on the East Coast.

Now, I find that I am again faced with the same challenge that I felt a year and a half ago: How do I successfully take these kids away from such a wonderful place?

The answer came to me last night as I was "sleeping" in my bed, surrounded by boxes, and shielding myself from the knees and elbows of the lovely children sleeping peacefully on either side of me: Our Navy family has wings.

As people go through life, they can choose to have wings or roots, but they cannot have both. With roots, they get to grow up in one place where they know everyone and everything. It is a wonderful and comfortable way to live. It's how I grew up.

With wings, my children grow up with experiences from all over the place and learn about the different cultures in the world they are living in. It's an adventurous and, from time to time, a somewhat scary way to live. It's a way of life that comes with "goodbye," but is always tempered with a warm "hello" when they arrive at the next place.

The truck arrives today, and our boxes will be loaded up. They'll head to California, and they will (hopefully) be waiting for us when we arrive. I'll try to hold it together as we drive out of Portsmouth, but I know I'll cry. I also know that when I see the first green road sign saying that we are in San Diego (still sixty miles from our house), I'll probably be flying with excitement. I'll have a hard time respecting the speed-limit signs asking me to drive my family safely the rest of the way to Chula Vista.

This is what I want to tell my kids: Wings are good! Wings show you the world and help you better understand the choices you will someday make when we do not make them for you. I never would have known life as I do today had I not decided to choose "wings" and drive my car to San Diego to give it a try. It was there that I met your dad, got married, bought a house, and was blessed with two beautiful children! We now continue that adventure together, in the Navy, as we explore our world together.

~Lisa Dolby

24

Military Families Can Thrive, Not Just Survive

Memories of our lives, of our works and
our deeds will continue in others.
~Rosa Parks

My lovely and indomitable wife and I spent more than twenty-nine years in the military. During these glorious years, we moved seventeen times. Sure, there were surprises and tears, apprehension and misgivings, but the years flew by, and the memories are joyful and sweet. It was hard when our children were young, but little did we know that those were the easy years! We had our three kids over a span of four years, so they were close in age, and they all had essentially the same needs — cribs, strollers, car seats, etc. — when they were young. Our family cars, typically vans and minivans early on, were always filled to the roof when we moved from one assignment to another.

The kids never fussed about moving. They were with Mom and Dad, and that was all that mattered… along with getting fed regularly and stopping early to go swimming! I recall leaving Arkansas in 1988 for the Pentagon. Our kids were five, four, and two, and we just drove and sang songs. We never let them see any of our worries about the new place. Instead, we created excitement about going someplace new.

As they grew older, the moves were less challenging physically but far more difficult emotionally. Once our children were in school and made friends, we were doomed! No more packing up the house, loading the cars and off we go. Now it was dealing with the anguish of leaving friends and schools, moving from our beloved house, and "going to someplace we've never heard of where we don't know anyone!"

I must say that we rarely ended up at a base that we hoped to go to. I never once made it even close to the state where I grew up: California. However, we *always* ended up loving our assignments and having fantastic adventures in new parts of the world. I remember one trip we took from RAF Mildenhall in England north to Scotland for about ten days in our U.S. full-sized van! We had a ball, saw amazing sights, and drove on some of the tiniest roads we'd ever seen. And I don't think many of the Scots had ever seen a vehicle that big on their roads in the middle of the Highlands. But we saw Loch Ness (no Nessie), William Wallace's giant sword in Stirling Castle, and ate some amazing food along the way.

Even though our wonderful children got to be pros at packing and moving, they sure didn't like it. Without exception, they hated leaving and didn't want to go to the "new place," yet when we departed two or three years later, they hated to leave that place just as much! They dreaded the disruption, but loved the adventure and meeting new friends, and they've kept in touch with many of them.

Nearly all military children are on the high end of resiliency. We always told our kids that they are part of *our* family, that Mom and Dad started our family, and then we had them next. Even though Dad was in the military — a career he has dedicated his life to — we reminded them that we were all in this together. We also encouraged them to study and work hard so they could get into a college of their choice and finally have four years of stability!

As a family, we always tried to take some fun trips between jobs when we moved. We seldom drove directly to the new assignment, or if we did, we then headed out on a break. This also helped me in my work because it cleared my brain of all the old worries and prepared it for new challenges.

I recall one trip we took to Disney World in Orlando. We'd visited the resort a lot, but this was the only time we stayed on the property and paid for their family meal plan. We weren't sure how that was going to work out, so we were careful the first few days. As a result, we ended up on our last day with a *lot* of food money left over, so we took the family to one of the premier restaurants there and had a feast to remember. The kids ordered anything they wanted and then some, and we were there for a long time enjoying our family and the superb food. It is a family memory we still treasure, and the moral of the story is to find ways to make special occasions, even during a military move.

My adult life was focused on serving our country, and our family grew up and closer together during this time. Our experiences and memories are incredible and can't ever be taken away. We had a few "lows," but our "highs" were amazing, and we not only survived these life experiences, we thrived. Today, our children are all grown and successful in very different professions. I feel we gave them some extra tools and experiences to enjoy life, take risks, work through challenges, and endure when they find themselves out of their comfort zones. They also gained a strong sense of service before self, and now they each find ways to give back to others in need.

Deployment challenges today are different and in many ways more difficult for our service members, but I know they are coping and solving their problems in the same way — with love, compassion, discipline, and a sense of humor!

~B.E. Burda

25

Let's Date and Be Friends

Good friends help you to find important things
when you have lost them... your smile,
your hope, and your courage.
~Doe Zantamata

For the most part, I've always been a resilient person, adapting to change easily. Moving from Australia to America shortly after my husband and I got married was no big deal, but it helped me adapt to the constant moving of the military lifestyle.

I had left all my friends and family back in Sydney and decided to start a new life with my husband. One thing I wasn't prepared for was being a *new* military spouse, in a different country, and, boy, I was in for a lesson.

It was tough moving to a new country and leaving friends I had known since I was a little girl. They were my lifeline girlfriends; my shoulder to cry on, and the thought of having to put myself "out there" and make new friends scared the daylights out of me.

We had just moved to Biloxi, Mississippi, and I had a four-year-old and a six-month-old baby. Surrounded by nothing but piles of boxes, with no friends to help unpack and no Wi-Fi, my kids craved attention from someone other than my husband and me. Truth is, I could have taken the kids to the park, but I didn't want to go alone!

I had the best support system at our last base, and finding new friends and rebuilding my support network was important to me so I wouldn't drive my kids or husband crazy. But I hated the "dating scene," and that's exactly what it felt like I had to do. I had to learn how to "date" other military spouses and hopefully be good enough and interesting enough for them. That way, they'd give me a second chance so I could show them how much fun I could be. I told myself I actually had to make an effort because new friends wouldn't find me in this house surrounded by cardboard boxes, drowning in packaging paper and tripping on random toys and Legos. Something needed to change, and I needed to make that change.

I don't know how many times I kept telling myself, *I've been brave enough to move to a new country. I can do this! I can make new friends. It's not that hard, is it?* But for some reason, a part of me didn't believe those words. I needed to get my act together because a possible new friend could walk by while I was stuck inside the house.

So I had a plan. After a long weekend, I got up on Monday morning and put on my new denim jeans, straightened my hair, dressed my kids, and hopped in the car to go to the local park. As we were pulling into the parking lot, I started to feel my insides turn sour. I sat in the car for about ten minutes still convincing myself. *I can do this. I can do this.*

After listening to my son yell at me for the tenth time about wanting to play on the swings, I decided to get out of the car, grab the kids and put on my game face. It was time to go shopping for a new friend. I walked through the playground gates and looked around. All of a sudden, I was craving a familiar face. Just one. I scanned the entire playground. Nothing. For some reason, I felt like I was setting myself up for failure before I had even started. I kept thinking about all the friends I had left behind in Sydney and how much I missed them.

But watching my son run to the swings, and seeing how excited he was to be around other kids, I knew I had to do this — not just for me, but for *him*. So after running around after my son for fifteen minutes, I took him to the swings and, sure enough, I met my first candidate: Ashley. She had a son two years older than mine and a welcoming voice that said, "Hi, how are you?" It was time for me to make my move.

After talking with her for forty minutes, we exchanged phone numbers and decided to meet up again the following week. Super excited, I told myself, *You did it! You made a friend!* It was an amazing feeling driving home from the playground that afternoon. I felt like I had struck gold!

But later that night, my inner pessimist decided to show up and convinced me that I wasn't good enough. My husband was lower rank than her husband, and I wondered how that would affect our relationship. Most military spouses don't carry their spouse's rank with them, but who knew how she would feel? *Was she looking for a new friend, too? Or did she have lots of friends and didn't have time for one more? Did I come across as too desperate?*

After two days of not hearing from Ashley, I decided to make the first move. Hoping not to sound too eager, I called and asked if she wanted to get the kids together. Sure enough, she was glad I called and invited us to come over to her house the very next day. And just before we said our goodbye, she asked, "Do you like Australian wine?" Instantly, I knew Ashley was a keeper — that one friend I had been looking for!

What a sigh of relief. I sealed the deal and didn't get rejected. I made a *new* friend! And she liked *Australian wine!*

After a few play dates, we decided to go out to lunch and catch up as adults, talking about books we loved, bases we had been to and wine we liked to drink. Even though I craved my Aussie friends, it felt great to finally find one friend I could bond with.

Because of Ashley's friendship, I didn't feel so lonely anymore. Through my new friendship with Ashley, I was able to meet other military spouses and make more friends. And even though we have both moved to different bases, and don't share glasses of wine as often as we used to (unless it's on FaceTime), I will never forget how much life I gained by finding the courage within to put myself out there for the sake of friendship. I felt blessed to have Ashley as my new American friend and learn how to make new friends.

Friendship truly is a precious and meaningful investment, and I couldn't have survived our duty station without my military spouse friends — who have now become my lifelong friends. And I'm hoping that one day, if we are lucky enough, we might get stationed together again.

~Ranishley Larsen

26

The Horror in My Rearview Mirror

In life, a person will come and go from many homes.
We may leave a house, a town, a room, but that
does not mean those places leave us.
~Ari Berk

"**O**h! Oh, no! No, no, no. Please don't tell me," I quietly pleaded. The words rushed forth, like an ambulance racing to an emergency. However, it was too late for help of any kind.

White-knuckling the steering wheel, I watched in horror as the scene played out in the rearview mirror. Like a perfectly choreographed ballet, my glance couldn't have been timed more perfectly. Unlike that same ballet, there was no rehearsal and the show was bombing.

Earlier that morning, an army of volunteers flowed from the church steps straight to our front door. It was moving day. A crowd of the finest, kindest North Carolina country folks arrived. It was the moving version of a barn-raising, a country congregation serving a military family. My mouth hung open at the sight.

My husband had left for an eight-month deployment just three weeks earlier, so I was trying to execute our move on my own — with three children under the age of seven. Our new house was only five miles down the road, but a move is a move. The same number of boxes and tape is needed to transport items five miles or five thousand miles.

Ample amounts of sweat, strength, and risk are required as well.

The community rose to the challenge, and a line of seventeen vehicles snaked along the quiet, country road, each carrying a load of boxes and other household goods. Everything was going great, until I looked in the rearview mirror and saw our walnut-brown upright piano — my friend and musical confidant for over twenty years — teetering on a trailer attached to the truck behind me.

I prepared myself for the crash — the sound of splintering wood and piano keys hitting piano wires was going to be awful. The explosion of black, white, and brown confetti would litter the country roadside and adjoining grassy ditch.

But that's not what happened.

The upright piano was anything but upright at the end of her fall, but she wasn't in a million pieces. She was in one — mostly. The well-used musical instrument was perched flat on her back, white and black keys still intact, reaching for the sky.

Busting all the way through her back, as if punching a hole in drywall, the trailer hitch had caught her. My beloved piano was positioned precariously across the hitch and angled supports of the trailer, mostly in one piece. The explosion of keys, however, didn't happen. There weren't a million pieces of black and white confetti strewn along the roadside like I envisioned.

For a concert pianist, this would have been a travesty. For me, a military spouse with memories and hands that continued to plink for fun as time allowed, it was an opportunity to be thankful. The piano was still alive and mostly well, regardless of the hole.

Several men had loaded the piano and secured her onto a flatbed trailer earlier that morning. They were there willingly, ready to assist a military family in any way they could. I couldn't cast blame in their direction, only gratitude. They were simply helping and had a small hiccup in the process. I'll be forever thankful for their willingness to offer their time, trucks, muscles, and sweat.

Later, a piano tuner investigated repair options. There weren't many. We concluded it best to simply leave the hole and memories alone, backing the piano against a wall to hide its newfound hole.

There was a small sound change with a note or two, but the difference was barely noticeable to an untrained ear.

The piano made many moves after its hitch encounter. Rolling across the United States in a container from the Atlantic shore to the Pacific, it traveled safely. It securely traversed the high seas, sailing halfway across the Pacific Ocean to the Hawaiian Islands and back.

Somehow, despite the hole and relocation weight allowances allotted by the military, the piano faithfully followed my family with each move. New locations brought new memories, new fingers tickling the ivories and plinking new tunes as well. That piano, hole and all, will always be a part of our family. The folks who helped our military family move that crazy October day, likewise, will always have a special spot in our hearts, fallen piano and all.

~Kristi Woods

27

Over the River and Off the Beltway

Grandmothers always have time to
talk and make you feel special.
~Catherine Pulsifer

"**G**rams, could we make brownies?" my daughter asks, already knowing the answer.

"Is the Pope Catholic?" replies my husband's mother, smiling up at Anna, who has at least half a foot on her.

Short but feisty. Born of Irish heritage. Humbly brought up in Ho-Ho-Kus, New Jersey. Married fifty-three years to a quintessential Italian. Raised five children. Hates housework and cooking. Loves her nine grandchildren.

Digging through her cupboards, Grams is surprised by what she has stockpiled. "Jesus, Mary and good Saint Joseph, here's some coconut. Ever made Girdle Stretchers, Anna? Oh, and I've got a bunch of cake mixes, and here's raisins, and a helluva lot of chocolate chips...."

Anna removes a baking pan, inadvertently causing a small but noisy avalanche, sending Grams' Westies, Patty and Murphy, scrambling into the dining room. Grams laughs, assuring her granddaughter that there's nothing she'll ever do to make her angry.

Anna and her sister transform the cozy blue kitchen into a science lab, eventually producing a batch of triple chocolate, peanut butter chip cupcakes, in which Grams happily indulges despite her diabetes.

A few days later, we are back in Grams' kitchen saying goodbye.

The Capital Beltway and Maryland I-270 take us out of the urban sprawl and into pastoral hills and forested mountains. Three hours into our drive, signs of civilization dwindle to tiny towns, coal trucks, and soft serve ice cream joints, as our minivan rolls deeper into rural Western Pennsylvania.

While the kids snooze, I make a mental "to-do list" of the things I need to do when we arrive at our final destination. Thankfully, our ninth military move from Mayport, Florida to Newport, Rhode Island has made our summer visits with the grandmothers a bit easier, since they both live on the way.

"Kids, wake up! We're almost at Grammy's house!" I say, peering into the rearview mirror at open mouths, drooping heads, and sprawled legs.

Once in the driveway, the girls run giggling from the minivan, sneaking up to Grammy's kitchen window to scare her. Mercifully, their plan is foiled by Oscar, the stereotypically Napoleonic Dachshund, whose sharp bark is as good as any home security system.

Grammy appears at the side door, miniature Cujo at her feet, forcing the girls to settle for a lame "Boo!" from the shrubs.

"Wait! Go back!" Grammy pleads. "You have to come through the Secret Garden!"

My mother was a first grade teacher for thirty years. Despite retirement, it's still in her blood. Sticking to the schedule, Grammy leads us back to the driveway so that we walk through the trees that she had carefully pruned and adorned with lanterns and birdhouses.

With Step 1 of her plan complete, we finally hug and kiss hello.

Much like at Grams's house, we congregate in the kitchen. With us seated at the booth she painted with red apples so many years ago, Grammy seizes the opportunity to have our undivided attention. She reaches into a kitchen drawer, retrieving four typed handouts, each colorfully highlighted and decorated with sparkly smiley face stickers.

"Kids, during your stay here at 'Grammy Camp,' there are some rules that must be followed," she says only half seriously.

"Seriously?" Anna replies, only half seriously.

The girls look at each other and smile. They know how Grammy is — a mix of *Romper Room's* corny but nurturing Miss Patti, *Hodgepodge Lodge's* nature-loving Miss Jean, and *The Magic School Bus's* scatterbrained Ms. Frizzle.

She goes over her "Camper's Guide to Health & Happiness," explaining the finicky plumbing that still uses well water, and upcoming "mandatory" participation in creative activities like making gourd birdhouses.

In the days to follow, we follow her plan. Before we know it, we are back in Grammy's kitchen, saying goodbye.

As my minivan rolls northward again to our next home in Rhode Island, I wonder what it would be like if we weren't a Navy family — if we lived closer and could visit Grams and Grammy all the time. Sunday for family dinners. Tuesday afternoons for homework help. Wednesday nights to watch TV together. Saturdays to help rake leaves.

Between the exits, I realize that, like priceless gemstones, the rarity of our time with Grams and Grammy is part of what makes it so precious. As I emerge from the Allegheny Mountains, golden shafts from the setting sun pierce the windshield. I lower the visor to shade my eyes and head onward, toward the horizon and our new home.

~Lisa Smith Molinari

28

Will Santa Find Us?

They err who think Santa Claus enters through the
chimney. He enters through the heart.
~Charles W. Howard

"**I** see it! I see it! The star! We need to get off at the next exit," I yelled. I wanted to make sure my dad heard me from the back of our blue 1968 Volkswagen Squareback. I was five and my sister was three. We were sitting on our makeshift bed: a thin, twin mattress complete with sheets, pillows, and blankets that fit perfectly behind the front seats and over the back seat, which was down flat. Our shoes were tucked neatly under the end of the mattress at the back hatch. Dolls and stuffed animals lined the sides. It was 1972, and seatbelts were optional.

"We found the hotel!" my sister yelled excitedly, as we started to bounce around in the back of the car, which prompted Mom to tell us to settle down.

The most important job my sister and I had each time our family moved was to find the hotel. We had to locate the big yellow star of the Holiday Inn each night. It was a comforting beacon in unfamiliar territory.

We had been driving all day, with a stop for lunch and twenty-minute breaks every couple of hours to stretch our legs. The sun had set hours ago, and we were eager to get out of the car and eat some dinner.

But first we needed to get off the freeway. I learned to draw comfort from the feel of the brakes as they took hold and the sounds of our car's engine downshifting while other cars and large semi-trucks continued to fly by on the freeway behind us. I knew we would safely settle in for the night in a new hotel room and eat dinner and breakfast at a new restaurant.

"Can we take an elevator to our room, please?" I asked as my mom put my shoes on me. The elevator ride in the hotel was another special treat of moving.

"We need to wait and see where our room is," Mom replied as she bundled us up in our coats and gloves.

We had just arrived in Pocatello, Idaho, my dad's new duty station. My parents had already explained that we would live in the hotel until they found a house. It was December, and there was an abundance of snow and ice on the ground. Christmas was coming, and that meant Santa!

"There's a Christmas special on TV tonight, and we can watch it if you don't take too long with your baths," Mom said after we came back to our room from dinner.

We cooperated with bath time and were quickly in our nightgowns. In 1972, if we didn't catch it on television, then we missed out until the next year.

The small color television with "rabbit ears" was on a stand against the wall, and my sister and I sat on the bed as we watched *The Little Drummer Boy*. Suddenly, I realized we were going to be in that hotel room on Christmas Eve and Christmas morning, and that meant something awful!

"Santa isn't bringing us any presents this year!" I wailed. "We aren't at home! We don't have a home this Christmas!" Tears streamed down my cheeks.

My parents looked at each other, startled by my outburst. My dad tried to reason with me. "Of course Santa will bring you presents this year. Why wouldn't he?"

"There is no chimney here. We don't even have a Christmas tree, and it's NOT OUR HOME! Santa only brings presents to kids who are in their homes. You said kids have to be home, in their own beds, asleep for Santa to come!" I was sobbing and wailing, heartbroken when I realized Santa would overlook my sister and me. I knew my bed, *all* of our beds, were on a big moving truck somewhere on the way to Idaho.

"Come over here, please," Dad said as my mom moved from her chair to tuck my sister into bed. I dragged myself over to the chair where my dad was sitting. He pulled me onto his knee and continued to try to calm me as he hugged me tightly. "We might not be in a house, and this hotel room is temporary, but remember, wherever we are, as long as we are together, we are home. Home is where we are together at night." My dad tried to console me as he kissed my forehead and hugged me close to his chest.

My mom gathered me up and tucked me into bed as she wiped the tears off my face and used a tissue to clean my nose. She tried to comfort me. "Try to sleep well tonight. Everything will look better in the morning."

It was hard to fall asleep that night. I was not convinced that Santa would find us even though my parents promised we would get a tree, and that Santa would know how to find us. After all, Santa was magical and would just know. But I knew Santa had rules, and we weren't following those rules.

Within a couple days, we had a tiny tree, barely large enough for its small stand. There wasn't much space for a Christmas tree in the hotel room, and it was the most Charlie Brownish tree I can remember. We made popcorn chains using a needle and thread, and then we decorated it while we sang Christmas carols. My parents were working hard to show us that Christmas was still possible in a hotel room, but I was not convinced.

The next day, Christmas morning, I woke up, looked under the tree, and saw presents! Still in our nightgowns, my sister and I looked through the presents under that scrawny yet glorious tree. I can't even remember now what was inside the wrapped presents, labeled in recognizable, shaky handwriting. I only remember my joy that Santa found us! We weren't in our beds, but he found us in that hotel room we called home.

~Daphne M. Jasinski

Military Families

★ Staying Strong at Home ★

29

Paper Chains

You never know how strong you are until being
strong is the only choice you have.
~Bob Marley

When people think of things that are strong enough to support them, they think of metal or wood. Things that are industrial strength. Things that they can stand on, sit on, jump up and down on. Ropes, trampolines — that sort of thing. But when I think of something that has the strength to support my family and me, I think about paper. Just a chain of paper. Links of different colors, held together by nothing more than a staple, a piece of tape or a dab of glue.

My first paper-chain experience was when my husband deployed to Iraq the first time. That first month, I felt like I was carrying the weight of the world on my shoulders. I had three little people depending on me, not to mention the little one growing inside me, and I was scared. I was searching for a lifeline, something physical to hold on to and hold us all up. So the paper chain was born.

I had first read about it in some getting-through-deployment magazine, but didn't give it much thought. The instructions said to make a chain in advance, and then remove a link every day leading to homecoming. It's impossible to do that, though, when you don't know how long they will be gone. What if we got down to two or three links, and there was an extension? How would I explain that to the kids? So, I came up with a different version of the paper chain.

We started it one night at our dining room table. I gave the kids safety scissors, construction paper, and markers. We cut the paper into strips big enough to write on, and then we curled them into a circle and hooked the two ends together. I told them we would make one a day until Daddy came home, hooking each one together and then using the chain to decorate the house for his homecoming. They liked the idea and jumped right in.

We started it in the summer, and the kids used bright blues, reds and greens — like a beach ball. They wrote messages on them like, "I love you, Daddy," and "Come home soon." As time went by, the colors changed. There were many pink links around the time the baby was born, and the messages changed, too. "It's a girl" and "I'm a big sister" were scribbled on strips of paper before they were added to the chain. In the fall, the colors became more subdued. We used orange and black for Halloween and the kids wrote, "I was a princess this year," and "Trick or treat, Daddy." Thanksgiving brought shades of brown and yellow, with messages like "Happy Turkey Day" and "I like pie." Of course, Christmas meant red and green and "Noel" or "Santa is coming!" It also meant we were only a month or so away from my husband's much-anticipated homecoming.

During the last month, the colors on the chain were not as important as the messages on each new link. We went back to "I love you, Daddy," and then at the end the paper loops were all yellow and said, "Welcome home."

I remember finally getting the call that homecoming was definitely on schedule. We bought new clothes, got the kids' hair cut, cleaned the house, and made signs. Before we knew it, we were walking out the door on our way to his unit to wait with the other families. I had to stop at the door because I had the strangest feeling I was forgetting something. As I surveyed the kids' playroom, I saw that paper chain. It was the history of our past six months, and I wanted to give it the place of honor it deserved. I took it to the dining room and draped it around the wall of the room like garland on a mantle so that my husband would be sure to see it.

After making sure it wouldn't fall, I ran out the door and jumped in the car to get my husband. The homecoming was like nothing I could have imagined. I stood holding the baby, now four months old, along with the other mothers, fathers, spouses and kids waiting to see their Marines. I was nervous and nauseous at the same time.

I tried to keep the three older kids in check while looking out the door for any sign of the bus. Then I saw it. When the buses opened their doors, and the Marines started coming off, the families couldn't be held back any more than an ocean wave. I stood in one spot, not wanting to be caught up in the crowd. I knew he would find me if I didn't find him, and I was right.

Finally, I saw him standing alone by the end of the bus, and he saw me at the same time. I showed the kids who I had found, and they got those first moments with Dad. Then I put his baby girl into his arms and watched the smile cross his face.

At home, we unloaded the car, and my husband got a much-needed shower. Then we all sat in the living room and talked. He went on and on about the night sky and how clear and beautiful it was there, and I was amazed that he had found beauty even in a combat zone. Then he asked about things at home. The kids went wild, all talking at once. I managed to get them quiet and asked them if they had shown Daddy their paper chain.

The chain came down from the wall, and the kids took turns explaining each link and the message on it. I stood in the doorway watching them get reacquainted with their dad. And I was amazed at the strength of that paper chain — how it was now being used to bridge the gap in my family caused by this deployment.

Later that night, when everyone went to bed, I took the chain to the garage. Initially, I had intended to toss it in the garbage because it had served its purpose. But when I got there, I could not throw it out. I realized that the chain, more than anything I could ever write myself, was a story. It told the story of our little family in our little corner of a Marine Corps base in North Carolina, and how our first deployment had changed us all but kept us linked together.

In the end, I carefully folded the chain and placed it in a plastic container on a shelf. When we moved, years after it had been packed away, I found it and opened the lid. I didn't take it out, just peeked at it before I closed it up and stuck it on the moving truck. It is in my closet now, along with another one just like it from the second deployment, and another from the third. If I ever need a chain strong enough to hold me up, I know just where to find one.

~Jennifer Mears Weaver

30

Stronger Than You Know

*You are braver than you believe, stronger than
you seem, and smarter than you think.*
~Author Unknown

I served honorably for twenty-three years in the United States
Air Force, and while I couldn't have done it without the training and support of my peers and leaders, I also couldn't have
done it without my wife, Mari.

Early in our marriage, deployments were easier. No kids to worry
about; no house to worry about. We would write letters to one another
and send care packages. Profess our love long-distance and stay in
touch as best we could, counting down the days until I came home
and was recognized with time off and medals for exceptional service.

In 2001, two things happened. First, I was assigned to a Combat
Communications unit in Oklahoma, one of the most forward-deployed
units in the entire Air Force. Second, we found out we were having
our first child.

Those first years in Oklahoma had their ups and downs — some
local field duty, but no deployments. Then, on May 31, 2004 at 0800, I
was given orders to deploy to Qatar in support of the war in Iraq — leaving the next morning at 0600. You can only imagine the thoughts
going through my head about telling Mari. She was six months into
a high-risk pregnancy and had a rambunctious two-year-old boy to

look after. This would not be welcome news.

Because I had so many appointments to complete that day, I couldn't break the news in person, and I had to do it over the phone. As soon as I told her, I could hear the anxiety in her voice. She took a deep breath and stopped her tears. She asked what I needed her to do and what errands she could take care of for me. She knew this was what had to get done, and she wanted to help me to do it.

I didn't get home that night until 1900. She had completed everything I asked for. She had spent the whole day being strong, but now needed to fall apart. When I hugged her, she told me what she'd accomplished. She came up with a game plan to take care of our son, Spencer, take care of the house, and have our baby while her husband was deployed in support of the war on terror.

The best and worst part of the deployment came on August 19, 2004. Mari called me right after Lauren was born and said everything was okay, but she called back a few hours later. Our daughter was having complications because she had been born with fluid in her lungs. She was in the NICU until further notice. Mari was upset, and I was scared. It was the most helpless feeling in the world for both of us.

Mari had to step up and be the mother of all moms. I still had twenty-three days left in country before I could go home, so Mari, with the help of family, took care of the house and Spencer, and made multiple trips to the hospital every day to see Lauren, all while recovering from major surgery. She had to be strong enough for all of us, taking care of the kids and keeping me in the loop on what was happening with our daughter. After a week, Lauren was able to go home, and our family was one step closer to being whole again.

I met Lauren for the first time on September 11, 2004. It was an awesome experience I will cherish as long as I can remember, walking through that airport to find my wife, her mom and our two children waiting to greet me. We were together, and it felt amazing.

Once again, I received a medal after that deployment for exceptional service, but I had also been given the tools and training to do the best job I could. Mari wasn't given any training to do the job placed in front of her, but she did it. And when things changed unexpectedly, she didn't back down. Mari didn't get a medal, but she received my utmost respect, admiration and love for her exceptional service.

I deployed once again in January 2010 to Baghdad, Iraq, for a six-month tour. This was going to be the last deployment before retirement. Mari once again took control of the house and made sure Spencer and Lauren had everything they needed, making it easier for me to be away from my family and get my job done.

On May 16, Mari sent an e-mail asking me to call her immediately. My stomach sank, thinking there was something wrong with the kids or, even worse, her. When I called, she told me to check my e-mail again because she'd just sent me something. I looked at this strange photo and she let me guess a few times before breaking the news — it was our roof, from the inside, after hailstones the size of softballs had punched through it. It was like looking at a map of the stars. Our town had been in the path of a devastating hailstorm that caused $500 million in damage.

Once again, Mari stepped up and performed exceptionally. She worked with the roofer and contractors to get everything done. She made it look easy, taking care of two small kids and dealing with major damage to our home all while I was deployed.

About a week later, on Memorial Day, Mari woke up at 0300 to dripping on her head where the roof had leaked into the bedroom. (The edge of a shingle had been chipped, and they didn't notice it the first time.) Three coats of latex paint formed a bubble holding over a gallon of water from dumping on her. She jumped up, moved the bed (which is usually hard for both of us to move together), and placed towels and buckets for the leaks. She got the contractor to our house in the early morning hours of a holiday to get the roof patched again because she didn't have any other option. She had to do it, and she did. She called me when she had it under control.

It was a rough deployment in Iraq, and after an extra month in country and nine days of travel, I finally made it home. Once again, my exceptional service was recognized with medals. Mari earned no medals, but did earn more of my admiration, respect and love.

My wife always puts the needs of her two young children and

husband in front of her own. This isn't because she received the training to do it; this is her instinct as a mother, and the added duties that come with being a military wife.

I retired in 2011. Our life in the military is behind us, but always with us. One day, as we were watching a news story about the hardships endured by a deployed service member, Mari said to me, "I could never be that strong."

Funny, because I always knew she was even stronger.

~Anthony W. Farthing

Pay It Forward
with a Hug

And if you see me, smile and maybe give
me a hug. That's important to me too.
~Jim Valvano

In December 2007, my husband of just eighteen months was more than 6,000 miles away. I had a cozy life near the beach; he had a less-than-cushy life in Baghdad, Iraq. America was just a few years into Operation Iraqi Freedom, and my soldier was on what would become a fourteen-month deployment to a war torn area. I was twenty-three years old and 900 miles from home, away for the first time — a military wife who hadn't yet settled in to the deployment life.

Church was one of my favorite places. I sang the worship songs at the beginning of the service with all my heart, hoping God would hear my number one request: *Please bring him home. Please bring him home alive and well.* At the time, mortars, rocket propelled grenades (RPGs), and improvised explosive devices (IEDs) were everywhere, and my husband lived in the middle of the muck.

Our church prayed specifically for members of the military one weekend a month. That year, the weekend landed right before Christmas, and many families would be missing their service members. I was missing mine terribly. Christmas parties without him, decorating without him, going home without him... nothing felt right. During the pastor's prayer, I started crying — sobbing, really. I was so lonely and sad.

The woman behind me must have seen or sensed my tears during the all-heads-bowed part because she laid a hand on me. Afterward, she tapped me on the shoulder and asked if my husband was overseas. I nodded, and she hugged me tight, like a mama bear with her cub. She told me that my husband and I were both strong, and we would be prayed for. It meant the world to me, and even though I was still sad for Greg to be gone, I was encouraged by the stranger's hug.

Two weeks later, I was sitting in the airport. Christmas had come and gone, and I was heading back from vacation. I noticed a soldier with his parents enter the terminal. The mom was doting on her son all the way down the vestibule, wiping lint off his backpack, checking to see if she had more snacks she could give him, and clutching tissue in both her hands. Once they got to his gate, her tears flowed like mine had in church just a couple weeks prior. She barely let him go as her husband stood next to her, holding her hand. Her brand new soldier walked away, heading into a life of sacrifice and courage.

My heart went out to this mother. I know that when she gave birth to this child, there was no way she could have known what this world would face, and that her son would be one of the few to sign up to defend our freedoms. Her heart was aching for the memories she wouldn't make with him now that he was leaving home, just as my heart ached for the moments I was missing with my soldier.

I made a choice, one that would be best understood in the military community. I went up to this perfect stranger, who stood weeping as her soldier son walked away, and gave her a hug, passing on the strength, encouragement, and faith the stranger in church had offered me. I assured her that he'd be well taken care of, that if he was strong and brave enough to sign up, he was strong and brave enough to serve. I listened as she cried, and I offered a simple companionship of understanding.

I hope that mom paid it forward, as I did, when she saw a military mom or wife hurting. We are so proud to stand beside and behind our soldiers. No matter the torrent of tears when they walk away, we live this life proud to be linked with the men and women who defend the very ground we stand on. We love our service members and we stand together to make sure we care for each other as well as they care for us.

~Elisa Preston

32

A Knock on the Door

We light our lamp, we stir our fire; we get ready to
pass a quiet and peaceful evening at the corner of
our hearth; tic, tac, someone knocks at the door...
~Claude Tillier

Safe in my home
there's a knock on my door.
Who could it be
at a quarter to four?
On a Tuesday, of all days,
while changing the bed.
That knock fills me instantly,
deeply, with dread.
Just who is standing
out there in the sun?
My heart begins pounding,
my mind says to run.
Not looking my best
but too worried to care.
Shaking and frightened
at who's waiting there.
Steeling my nerves
as all us wives do.
I go to the window
and peek on out through.

Praying I don't see
two men standing tall.
Somber in Dress Blues,
delivering the call.
But what I do see
makes me take a deep breath.
For it's simply my neighbor
who waits on the step.
I open the door
with my hands still quaking.
"May I borrow some sugar
to finish my baking?"
She looks at me strangely,
sees tears in my eyes.
Wondering what could be
making me cry.
But a knock on the door
can be more than it seems,
When your husband fights for
the U.S. Marines.

~Nicole M. Hackler

33

Semper Fidelis: My Life as a Marine Corps Wife

The gem cannot be polished without friction,
nor man perfected without trials.
~Chinese Proverb

I met my husband when I was just a kid, and we stayed friends as we grew up. After graduating from high school, he decided to join the military. He went on two deployments to Iraq, and we kept in touch throughout. I was there to welcome him home from his second deployment, and a little over a year later, he asked me to marry him. I happily accepted, but his third deployment was looming.

This time, he would be going to Afghanistan, and we didn't have time to plan a wedding. Like so many other military couples, we made a trip to the local courthouse so that we could be married before he left. Amusingly, several other couples from his unit got married on the same day; we joked about how we were all anniversary buddies.

Matt and I went on a honeymoon shortly before his deployment to Hawaii; a few weeks later, we found out that I was pregnant. We were thrilled and couldn't wait to welcome our first child into the world.

In the back of our minds, though, we worried about whether he would be home in time for the birth. He was leaving on the advance team, which means this deployment would be longer for him than the rest of the Marines in his unit. Nevertheless, we were excited and happily planned for the birth of our baby. We found out that our little bundle of joy was going to be a boy, and we named him Benjamin.

Not long into the deployment, things got scary. I was woken up in the middle of the night by a phone call, and it was Matt, explaining that he had been in an IED blast. He was all right, but he suffered a grade II concussion and had to be sent to the hospital for a week. Six men from Matt's unit — five Marines and one Corpsman — would die over the course of that deployment. I was constantly worried that Matt would be one of them, and every time I heard a car door slam, I would wait in fear for that dreaded knock on the door.

Things weren't easy on the home front, either. I was diagnosed with preeclampsia, a serious pregnancy complication that is often diagnosed after a sudden rise in blood pressure. Left untreated, it will develop into eclampsia, which causes seizures... and possibly, death. The only treatment is delivery of the baby. I knew that Matt was going to be coming home soon, though, so I begged the doctors to wait. They agreed, as long as I agreed to go to the hospital each day so that my baby and I could be monitored.

It was a race against the clock to keep Benjamin in as long as I could. We finally got a date for Matt's return, and we set a date for the birth of our baby two days later. Everything seemed to be going smoothly, but that would soon change. My vision started being affected by the preeclampsia, and Matt called the day before he was supposed to come home and announced that his flight had been delayed. The doctors refused to push the birth back any further, and I worried that I would end up having to give birth alone.

Thankfully, everything worked out. Matt came home the day I was scheduled to be induced, so I was able to go to his homecoming before we headed to the hospital to have the baby. Everything didn't go smoothly, but one emergency C-section later, we made it through. We were happy, but we knew he would be returning to Afghanistan in less than a year. We were prepared, though, and ready to tackle another challenge. Little did we know how much harder it was about to get.

A few months before Matt was set to leave, we learned I was pregnant again. This time, we knew that I would be having the baby alone; there was no getting around it. So I mentally began preparing myself, and we began making arrangements. But we got bad news fairly early in the pregnancy: the nuchal translucency screening had come back positive, meaning that our baby was at high risk of having Down syndrome.

I was referred to a high risk OB/GYN and asked if I wanted to have an amniocentesis and have a definitive diagnosis, or wait until the baby was born. I couldn't stand the uncertainty, so I decided to have the procedure.

Two days after Matt deployed to Afghanistan, I had the amniocentesis. Another Marine wife came with me and held my hand while I steadfastly looked at the ceiling, not wanting to see the needle. Three days later, I got the phone call from my doctor: The baby was a male, and the test was positive for Trisomy 21, or Down syndrome. I thanked him, deflected any questions, made my next appointment, and hung up the phone. Then I burst into tears, feeling like my entire world had been destroyed. I cried for days, unable to think of the tiny baby in my belly without sobbing. Matt, however, took the news wonderfully. He didn't mind that our child had Down syndrome. He wasn't scared like I was.

Slowly, I came around. I came to accept the diagnosis and stop fearing it. I started to educate myself on Down syndrome, and I realized how many of my fears were based on misconceptions. With my husband watching on Skype, and another military wife holding my hand, I gave birth to Wyatt. Far from the miserable experience I had imagined, it was a day full of joy and love. Wyatt was beautiful and healthy. Three weeks later, Matt came home, and our little family was complete.

Now, three years later, we have added two daughters and traded a career in the military for a career in law enforcement. And while we faced some incredibly difficult times during our five years together in the Marine Corps, I wouldn't trade them for anything. They made us stronger and brought us closer. Some of our best memories were because of the military. And I couldn't be prouder to stand beside a man who took an oath to serve this country… to serve as one of the few and the proud, always faithful — to his country, his Corps, and to me.

~Cassy Fiano-Chesser

Songs from Far Away

*Music expresses that which cannot be put into words
and that which cannot remain silent.*
~Victor Hugo

When my father deployed, the music went with him. The ukulele that I had watched him play as I grew up was abandoned. It played no lullabies, Christmas songs, or Happy Birthdays. No silly songs to cheer us up or perky tunes to make us dance. It sat there lifeless, just wood and strings.

"Time will fly by; you'll see," our mother soothed. We were used to Father being gone, after all, but never for so long or so suddenly. It had come as a surprise because we had just moved into a new duty station a few weeks before.

This had been our fourth Permanent Change of Station (PCS) in only two years, but we didn't mind so much. New people, places, and experiences were the privileges of military life. It was easy to make new friends, but it was harder to keep them. Military life taught us how to appreciate the people we had with us, for however long that might be. And the one consistency was us: Dad, Mom, my brother and sister, and me. Us versus the world. We rarely saw our actual relatives, but that was okay because the Army was our family.

Still, music was the thing that tethered my father to Hawaii, a reminder of his home and heritage. We learned about our ancestors and culture mostly through his music and songs. Music was how he shared our family traditions and expressed his love.

But with this PCS, everything was different. We were finally "home" in Hawaii and expected to fit into a place that we had only heard about in my parents' stories. Father had spent more than twenty years of service trying to get stationed back to his place of birth and the extended family he left behind. We were just arriving, awkward and clumsy in a half-civilian existence, and he was already making preparations to leave again, this time without us.

Suddenly, we were surrounded by cousins and aunties who grew up knowing each other and participating in a cultural heritage of which we only had a surface knowledge. They wove *lauhala* and dug for crabs. We didn't. They had learned recipes and customs from our *Tutu* (grandmother). But we hadn't. We were foreigners in our own family.

We didn't fit in, and the one person who made us fit — our father — was gone. Not just for a week of field training, or a month of Temporary Duty (TDY) somewhere in the United States, but indefinitely — thousands of miles away on foreign soil.

Without the structure that living on base provided, or the surety of my father's steady guidance, we were a ship without captain or compass. And that was when my father's ukulele called out to me. As I plucked the strings in a tuneless, random tempo, I felt closer to him and our Hawaiian roots. So I picked up an old song book and a chord chart, and I taught myself to play.

I would play and sing, and it was like my father was there. After my father eventually returned, he bought another ukulele, and we had a mini concert. He was shocked and proud that I had learned so much, so quickly. But what I really learned was that music has the power to do extraordinary things — tying us to our culture and each other, our past and our present.

When I went off to college, his ukulele went with me. When I missed home or felt like things just didn't fit, I would play and sing. And my songs would fill up all those empty spaces inside, tucked tightly like the corners of my dorm bed sheets… and everything would be okay.

~Misty Sanico

35

Story Time with Daddy

Books are lighthouses erected in the great sea of time.
~E.P. Whipple

I had the honor of marrying my best friend nearly fifteen years ago and, in doing so, I became a Navy wife. My husband, Rex, has been in the Navy for fourteen years. We have four children ranging in age from four to eleven. We are a close family even with the trials of separation we have encountered as a Navy family. Over the course of Rex's Navy career, we've spent the equivalent of more than four years apart due to deployments. His most recent deployment was for ten months in 2014–2015.

We call our family a "team." When he is away, our family misses out on playing with their dad on the playground, roasting marshmallows in the back yard, our family's pizza and movie night, and so many parts of our everyday family routine. Our team's story time each night is also one member short.

Thanks to United Through Reading, a nonprofit program that the USO hosted at their San Diego location, we were able to continue our tradition of reading together while Rex was away. United Through Reading videotapes service members reading books aloud, and then the USO location that hosts the program sends the videos to their families. The families are able to watch the videos at home and continue their bedtime story routine.

Our family has always loved to read, and it means the world to us that we can still incorporate Daddy into our regular bedtime routine when he is away. The kids pile on the couch with the books and videos he sends, and we all read along. He makes silly sounds and voices to keep the kids engaged. They love it, and we can clearly see the difference that continued reading has made in their lives.

The stories help our family stay connected while we are apart. They also help us reinforce the importance of reading to our kids, something that is very important to us as parents. Our nine-year-old, Annaleigh, always loved story time, but was never one to read on her own. Since Rex started reading to her with United Through Reading when he was away, she has started to fly through books. Now she even asks Rex to read chapter books on the videos!

The video recordings are so interactive; it's truly a piece of their daddy. They constantly ask to watch them over and over again. And if they are feeling down or having a bad day, we put in the United Through Reading videos, and there is immediate joy when they hear Daddy's voice. Rex says when he reads the stories for them on video, he starts to feel like he is right there in person. Even though he is on a U.S. Navy ship at sea, the program brings him home for a short time.

When Rex is deployed, it feels like there is a very large hole in the family dynamic. Rex says that by not being here and being able to do the things he usually does with the kids, he feels that he isn't as connected to them. It's hard on him, and it's hard on the kids.

Because of their hardship, at first I thought that the stories were just to help the kids stay connected to their daddy. Soon, I realized that it was a gift for me as well. When my husband is deployed, I lose my teammate and support system at home. I am the only one the kids can come to when they need something, and I have to be "on" all of the time. With these stories, I can pop in one video and be able to make dinner uninterrupted, or I can use the videos to have Rex tell the kids their bedtime stories while I tidy up and do the dishes before tucking them into bed. Sometimes, I read a book myself for a rest. Those little thirty-minute breaks can really help a spouse recharge when she is alone.

Like any mom, there are days when I still feel like I'm failing my family. But when I take a step back and look at the kids, I know I'm doing something right. United Through Reading is a piece of that. It helps me do my job of keeping our family connected, even when Rex is oceans away.

A few Christmases ago, when Rex was deployed, we had a tough holiday season. It was our third year in a row not having Rex with us, so we were all feeling pretty down. When I had the kids write their Santa letters, the only thing they put on their lists was for Daddy to be home. I had to tell them there was no way that Daddy could be here for Christmas, so they would have to come up with a few other ideas. Christmas came, and we had an "okay day." The kids were happy with their presents, but we all agreed it wasn't the merriest of Christmases since we didn't have Rex home.

The day after Christmas, we walked down the street to check the mail. We all got excited when we saw a small package with the postmark from the USS Dewey. As soon as the kids saw the United Through Reading sticker on the back, they took off running for the house to watch Daddy read to them. They were all piled on the floor watching Rex with big smiles. Louanna, our six-year-old, turned around, and with the happiest look on her face, said, "We got Daddy for Christmas!" Immediately, I got tears in my eyes. I agreed with her. The one thing the kids wanted more than anything I could not give them — but United Through Reading did.

While the program made a big difference that Christmas, these stories have been there for us on more than one holiday. With Rex deployed two-thirds of our son's life to date, we're not sure what we'd do without the stories that keep us reading together. For the kids, it gives them a piece of their daddy. They ask to watch them over and over again, and each time, they smile as soon as Daddy's voice fills the room.

~Veronica Boblett

36

Tender Mercies

*Happiness isn't complicated. It is a humble state
of gratitude for simple pleasures, tender mercies,
recognized blessings, and inherent beauty.*
~Richelle E. Goodrich

Salty tears stung my tired eyes. I couldn't bring my husband home for Christmas, but I was determined my six-year-old son would get his other wish — a new bike.

Wiping my eyes, I studied the instructions and surveyed the assortment of bicycle parts scattered on my bedroom carpet. Never mind that it was Christmas Eve and midnight was an hour away.

"You can do this," I said.

Not that I had a choice. Since my husband's deployment with Desert Shield, I'd learned to do many things on my own. Assembling a bike would be simple compared to raising kids. Right?

I grabbed a wrench and the bike frame while Christmas carols played softly in the background.

Eight weeks earlier, I'd been blindsided when I met with my son's kindergarten teacher. She had more on her mind than his academic performance.

"You do realize children aren't allowed to bring stuffed animals to class? And yet your son brings his elephant every day."

"I don't see the harm," I countered. "He keeps King Tusk in his cubby hole."

"Yes, but…" She looked over the rim of her large framed reading glasses. "Mrs. Foster, is your husband in the military?"

What did King Tusk have to do with my husband's job?

"My husband's a pilot in the Air Force Reserves. His unit was activated last August. Why do you ask?"

The teacher spread Jonathan's artwork on the table. "That explains why your son keeps drawing camels and Army tanks during his free time. Does he talk about his dad?"

I shifted in my chair. "He knows his dad transports military troops and cargo to Saudi Arabia. But we don't talk about what's happening. You know, Iraq's invasion of Kuwait and what happens if they don't withdraw."

"Maybe Jonathan knows more than you realize," she said, sounding more like a family counselor than a teacher. "Perhaps he's worried and draws these pictures as an outlet for his emotions."

I picked up one of his drawings and studied the desert landscape filled with soldiers. Using brown and green crayons, my son had captured an image that reminded me of the evening news.

"You're right," I said, blinking back tears. "That explains it."

However, I didn't mention that one night when I tucked Jonathan into bed, he had asked me if Daddy was going to die. My stomach lurched. I wanted to hold my son and assure him that everything would be all right. That Daddy would come home soon, and we'd go to Sea World again.

Only, I didn't know if that was true.

I'd grown up in an Air Force family during the Vietnam War. I'd lived on base and seen black smoke rising in the distance after a cargo plane crashed at the end of the runway. My schoolmates and I had worn POW/MIA bracelets with the names of soldiers who'd never come home.

No, I wouldn't promise my son that Daddy would live.

"Mrs. Foster?"

I looked up and waited for her to finish speaking. Instead, her eyebrows went up expectantly.

What did she want me to say? Did she want me to describe the ballooning pressure to maintain a house and yard, and raise two children while my husband was gone? Maybe she needed to know that we didn't live near relatives. My friends at church were my local support network. Or maybe I could tell her that trusting the Lord — no matter what happened — consoled me when I lay awake at night on the verge of a crying jag.

I didn't know what the teacher expected. But the silent gulf between us disappeared when she touched my hand and said, "I'll make an exception. Jonathan can bring King Tusk to school."

Thank God for tender mercies.

The memory of that conversation warmed my heart as I tightened the last bolt on my son's bicycle. Walking the bicycle downstairs, I parked it next to the Christmas tree. Strings of multicolored bulbs crisscrossed helter-skelter within the pine-scented branches. I chuckled, remembering how the tree had fallen twice before I had been able to tighten the bolts in the tree stand to the trunk.

Now the tree and the bicycle stood upright. Grinning, I gave myself two thumbs up. And then I filled the stockings and added the wrapped gifts beneath the tree.

The wall clock chimed twice by the time I dragged myself upstairs. My body ached from fatigue, but also for my husband's arms. I hated for him to be without family on Christmas. Hated the thought of him not seeing the children's animated faces as they unwrapped their gifts. Videotaping would never do it justice. And back then, Skype and FaceTime didn't exist.

Had I known my husband would be home by June, the night would have seemed less cold. Instead, I warmed myself with the anticipation of our children racing downstairs.

Pausing at my son's bedroom, I peeked inside. The nightlight cast a golden glow on his peaceful brow. His lips curled in a half smile. And tucked in next to my son lay his cherished friend — King Tusk.

Thank God for tender mercies.

~Karen Foster

37

Fly

Sometimes you don't realize your own strength until
you come face to face with your greatest weakness.
~Susan Gale

Hand in hand, they walked toward the airport terminal. When they got to the gate, the U.S. Navy sailor bent down, fervently kissed his wife, and then briskly walked away... wanting to put this deployment behind him.

As he disappeared into the plane, his wife heard sobbing in the not-too-far distance. Holding her head high, not wanting tears of her own, she slowly turned around to find the crying source.

A few feet away, she saw a young couple — a soldier and his girlfriend — standing in the corner. Fear was in his eyes as he desperately tried to console her with promises of coming home safely and forever love.

The sailor's wife walked over, wrapped the girl in her arms, and then told the soldier that he should leave, that his girl would be taken care of.

As he walked away, the upset girl looked up at a face not much older than hers and said, "You can't possibly help me. You have no idea what this feels like."

The Navy wife, her heart overflowing with sorrow, said calmly, "I don't have any idea what you are feeling. I won't try to understand. But I do know what it feels like for me to watch a loved one walk away."

Curious, the girlfriend calmed her crying enough to ask, "What does this feel like for you?"

"There are no words to describe this," she said. "Just an analogy that might help. To me, it feels like I have been pushed off a cliff. As I'm falling, the wind takes the air from me and makes my chest ache. I'm confused as to why I was pushed and angry at myself for choosing to live so close to the edge.

"I try to slow down the fall, but soon enough I accept that I am falling. Eventually, I hit water, shocked at the reality of how cold the water is. My chest hurts, my head is dizzy, my body is cold, and I decide that I don't want to live... I don't want to feel this way anymore. I start to drown, hoping that this pain will quickly end.

"It isn't long before I realize that I am in shallow water and have to choose. I have to choose to continue to let myself drown, or to straighten my legs and somehow find the strength to swim upstream to shore. That is what it feels like to me."

As the soldier's girl listened, she felt she could relate. She had difficulty breathing, her heart hurt, and she wanted something, anything, to take away the pain. She looked into the face of the woman who understood so well and asked another question. "If it hurts this much for you, then why are you so calm, so put together?"

That Navy wife was me. And I had just had an epiphany. I smiled at the girl and I said, "I have been pushed over that cliff many times by the big man (the one with deployment orders) and finally decided one day that I didn't like him pushing me. This time, as I watched him walk toward me, I knew there was no way around the fall. So I turned around, faced the chasm, and jumped. I embraced the feelings to come, but this time something was different. This time, I learned to fly."

~Shannon Patterson

38

The Military Wife

It takes a strong person to be a soldier. It takes
a stronger person to love a soldier.
~Author Unknown

As we struggle to regain the closeness of American family life,
    it may be a good time to recognize the military wife.
While their spouses are often deployed around the world,
    fighting the good fight,
the military wife must continue on alone through the day and
    into the night.
I have some experience on this subject; I truly know where
    it's at,
like so many of my friends, I grew up with the title:
    "Military Brat."
It can be taken for granted, and often neglected,
    as they employ organizational skills, so clearly perfected.
She becomes Mom, Dad, tutor, coach, disciplinarian, cook,
    the skills she achieves could quite easily fill a rather large
    book.
Car repairs, gardening, nurse, good friend, family banker,
    I remember my mom being a bit overwhelmed but these
    responsibilities never sank her.
She would take us to school, football practice, and was skilled
    at shooting hoops,

after much serious thought, I finally figured what sustained her
were her military wives' groups.
They bonded together, if one was in distress or let out a yelp,
the others would respond to ensure that she always had
help.
Always yearning for their spouse's return, they deserve full
respect,
always functioning at high levels, while never quite sure just
what to expect.
As a nation, we know the importance of reconnecting to our
family based lives,
a start would be to acknowledge the achievement of military
wives.
When we appropriately salute our brave troops for the
commitment to our freedom, the sacrifices they make,
let us remember the military wives who, day in and day out,
always give more than they take.

~Michael Kincade, Sr.

Military Families

Patriotism in Action

39

Keeping Troops Connected with a Guitar

Music was my refuge. I could crawl into the space
between the notes and curl my back to loneliness.
~Maya Angelou

I'll never forget a trip I made to the Marine Corps base in Quantico, Virginia, in April 2008. We traveled there for a Jack Daniel's/USO Toast to the Troops event where volunteers stuffed care packages for our men and women serving overseas. I had the honor of talking with some of our wounded warriors in the tent before taking the stage to perform. One of the young men I met had lost both his legs on the battlefield. During our conversation, he shared with me that one of the things that encouraged him throughout his difficult rehabilitation was one of my songs, "International Harvester."

I was kind of taken aback because at first listen, it's not exactly an emotional or particularly inspirational song. Then the young man revealed he had grown up on a farm. When he heard that song, all he could think about doing was getting his legs fixed so that when he got back to those fields, he could climb up on his own tractor and get back to work. For him, that song was home.

I felt my heart go straight to my throat as I was reminded of just how powerful a force music can be for our men and women in uniform.

Having served ten years of active duty in the Army as a 13 Fox Fire Support Specialist, I've experienced the way music can keep one's spirits up when serving our country far from home. I remember being in Panama in 1989 for Operation Just Cause. After the invasion was over and rebuilding efforts were underway, we were riding around and listening to an artist by the name of Skip Ewing. I might have been in a foreign land surrounded by the sights, sounds and pressures of a full-scale military operation, but the moment I pressed play on that CD player, it felt like I was cruising a country road back in Tennessee. To this day, I can still remember every single word to every song on Skip's album. And I'll never forget them.

When I served in South Korea, Sawyer Brown came to perform on a USO trip. Even though we were only miles away from the most heavily militarized border in the world, for those few hours the hundreds of soldiers watching in that audience — including me — felt like we were home.

As an artist, I've gone to the Middle East to perform almost every year since 2001. I remember on that first trip, we were still sweeping up broken glass at the airport in Kandahar.

At one of those early shows, I came off the stage to find a gentleman waiting for me. The fact that he had a full beard let me know that he was one of the soldiers at the tip of the spear, doing very dangerous things in very dangerous places. It turns out we had a mutual friend. The bearded soldier shared with me that every morning before our friend flew on a mission — and every evening when he got back — he would play a song I had released back in 2000 called "Paradise."

Now as a writer, you are constantly incorporating things that are happening or have happened in the world around you. Having spent a large part of my life in the military, it continues to find its way into my music.

For the chorus of "Paradise" I wrote: "Once I was a soldier and not afraid to die. Now I'm a little older and not afraid to cry. Every day I'm thankful just to be alive. When you've been where I've been, any kind of life... is paradise."

It's a song that touches on a subject that can be hard for those back on the home front to understand. Our men and women in uniform wake up every day knowing that it could be their last. Yet they put their lives on the line — and are proud and honored to do it — because they know they are fighting for the freedoms of the United States of America.

As my conversation continued with the bearded man, he grew quiet. Then he pointed off into the distance and singled out a rocky peak on the horizon. He let me know that our friend had lost his life in a helicopter crash on that very mountainside. And the morning he died, like every other morning, he had played my music. I was stunned. We both sat there and cried for a minute before I had to get myself together and take the stage again.

I have been in public service my whole life. I like helping people. It's a big part of who I am. To this day, when I return to the States after doing a trip to visit our troops, I go home wishing I could do more. And for a long time, I never felt like I was helping anyone as an artist. But after hearing that story in Kandahar, I realized as entertainers we have to go above and beyond to do whatever we can to take care of those men and women. There is no question they go above and beyond anything we can comprehend to take care of us.

Thoughts of my conversation in Kandahar popped into my mind again as I finished talking with the young man who couldn't wait to get back to working the fields on his International Harvester. The power of the stories he and his fellow soldiers shared on that day reminded me that I might not be able to do a lot for these men and women, but I can sing songs, and that can take them home.

I wrote another song that day. I scratched out the lyrics on a piece of notebook paper, taped them to the mic stand and sang "Let Me Take You Home" for the first time that night. It's a song that's not part of any album. I wanted it to be special for them. And I am honored and humbled to play it live for men and women serving our country as long as they'll let me.

~Craig Morgan

Go Ask Max

Brothers and sisters are as close as hands and feet.
~Vietnamese Proverb

I drove the longest three miles of my life the day I took my daughter to the recruiter's office. I bit the inside of my cheek to hold back tears when she signed a contract giving six years of her life to her country. I spent the next three months waffling between pride and terror, while my family acted oblivious to the big red "X" on the calendar.

Rayne, my daughter, is sandwiched between two boys. Her older brother had left home for college a few years earlier. Her younger brother, Max, didn't seem fazed by the idea of becoming an only child. In fact, he looked forward to using her room as his den.

The weekend before she shipped out, we went to Sea World for our last family outing. We settled in to watch the dolphin show, everyone squished together on the steel benches. I couldn't help my melancholy mood. *How long would it be before we were back together as a family? Why was I the only one upset by her leaving home?*

A booming voice filled the stadium. "We at Sea World Orlando would like to take a moment to recognize the men and women who serve and protect our country. We ask all current and former service members to stand...."

Rayne whispered, "Mom? What should I do? Can I stand up?"

"I don't see why not." I smiled, trying to show my support.

My beautiful daughter rose, with her shoulders back and head held high, as the crowd applauded. I bit my cheek again. When our national anthem blared, my vision blurred, and I could no longer hold back the tears. Try as I might, I couldn't wipe them fast enough. My kids rolled their eyes and teased me, but I couldn't stop the flood of emotions. In that moment, I understood how much joining the Navy meant to her.

Rayne left for boot camp later that week. As soon as we pulled away from the recruiter's office, the boys asked for lunch. Once again, I wallowed through my emotions alone. I didn't understand their apparent apathy. Maybe a sister passing into adulthood didn't hurt as much as a parent saying goodbye to a child. Maybe the promise of first dibs on movie choices, one hundred percent of your parent's attention, and no more sharing a bathroom with a teenage girl softened the blow.

I cried in the bathroom every day for weeks after she left. I thought I did a good job of hiding my tears until the day I received a call from Max's teacher.

"I would like your permission to send Max's letter to President Obama." The teacher seemed excited, but I had no idea what she was talking about.

"May I see a copy of the letter?" I asked, curious to see what my son had written that would interest the President.

Dear Mr. President,

I am a middle school student in Florida. Recently, I had to do interviews asking people what freedom meant to them. I got a lot of answers, but I want to share what freedom means to me.

My sister, Rayne, has been serving in the Navy since last September. I miss her every single day. I am also proud of her. I think that my family is serving in the military, even though we didn't sign up! We are sacrificing my big sister. I like using her room to play video games, but I would rather have her home. She's cool most of the time. My mom cries sometimes. She tried to hide it from me and Dad, but she misses Rayne.

I worry where she will go after sonar training in San Diego. I see news about wars and fighting, and I pray that Rayne will not have to go to those places. Can you make sure she is okay?

My sister fights for our freedom, even your freedom, President Obama. Because of people like her, Americans can feel safe that we will always have a democratic government. We studied the Bill of Rights this year in school. This is what freedom means to me.

Because people volunteer, I can go to the church, school and activities that I choose. I can say what I want to say about the government and my country without being thrown in jail. When I am older, I can bear arms to protect myself and my family. I can gather with others to hold a rally, and vote for the people I want to represent me in the government.

These things don't mean much to most kids because kids don't have a lot of rights. To me, knowing that these things will be there when I am an adult is important. So when I miss my sister, I try to remember all of the things she fights for. Some days, I feel selfish and want her to come home. Some days, she says she is homesick and wants to come home too, but she can't. Everyone in my family has made a sacrifice.

One day I hope to serve in the Air Force like my aunt, or in the Army like my great-grandfather and my dad, or in the Marines like my grandfather, or in the Navy like my uncle, great-grandfather, and sister.

Sincerely,
Max H.

They say that wisdom and truth come out of the mouths of babes. I have to agree. My eleven-year-old son summed up his feelings about his sister serving in the Navy better than I could articulate my own. As Max said, we didn't sign up, but our family made a sacrifice for our country. I will never forget the pride in my daughter's eyes the first time she stood up to be recognized for her service. Likewise, I will never forget the freedoms she swore to protect... and if I do, I'll ask Max to remind me.

~Kathryn M. Hearst

Remember the Littlest Veterans

I'm a nomad... a gypsy... an Army Brat. Put me
on an airplane, send me anywhere. That's
where I belong... anywhere.
~Marc Curtis

Every Veterans Day, all across America, patriotic music is played, parades march down Main Street, speeches are given, and small flags stand silent sentry on military graves. We pause to honor generations of veterans from wars past and present. We are deeply grateful for their service and sacrifice.

But there are others who have also served bravely — often overlooked on Veterans Day. They are the sons and daughters of soldiers, airmen, sailors, and marines. We call them military brats — they are the children of warriors. And they, like their warrior fathers and mothers, have paid an enormous price to protect the freedoms and privileges that most of us take for granted.

I am one of them. I was born in Orange, California, on the Fourth of July — an auspicious birthday for a military brat. My mom and I sailed to Japan when I was just an infant to join my dad who was fighting overseas. I didn't see U.S. soil again until I was three years old.

I spent my formative years moving from base to base — from Texas to Montana, from California to Virginia, from Germany to Illinois, from Dover to Puerto Rico. I was at home nowhere... and at home everywhere. I learned to make friends quickly because I knew I would lose them quickly. We were like traveling gypsies, moving from place to place, packing and unpacking... only to do it all over again six months or two years later.

Such a lifestyle has its advantages, of course. I was able to see the world, live in Europe, learn a foreign language at an early age, taste exotic foods and see interesting places that many people only dream of. I had exciting adventures and enjoyed wonderful experiences — all courtesy of the U.S. government.

But I paid a price, too — loneliness, wrenching departures from beloved friends, changing schools umpteen times, and sometimes living in places I didn't like.

The biggest price I paid, along with the other kids, was enormous anxiety. Death was always lurking in the background, but no one ever talked about it. When you are the child of a warrior, you never know when your daddy (or mommy) is going to be called to fight a battle somewhere — or might be killed in training exercises or plane crashes, even in peacetime.

My dad was a pilot in the Air Force, and I can't tell you the number of times I lay in my bed at night, overhearing my mom as she called the control tower to ask for Major Gallagher's ETA (estimated time of arrival). I worried, *What if my daddy doesn't come home? What if his plane crashes?* When I was eight years old, my best friend lost her father when his plane crashed into the side of a mountain — and it wasn't even during a war. I knew if it happened to her, it could happen to me, too. It could happen to any of us military brats. We all grew up with an acute awareness of the precariousness of life — fearing that our warrior dads and moms could be killed anytime, anywhere.

So on Veterans Day, let us honor not only the brave men and women who dedicate their lives to protecting us, but also the brave boys and girls who die a thousand little deaths waiting for their daddies and mommies to come home.

Military brats serve their country, too, and they pay a price every day of their childhoods. They are the littlest soldiers — the youngest veterans. Remember them. Thank them. Hug them.

~BJ Gallagher

For You

The cement of this union is the heart-
blood of every American.
~Thomas Jefferson

My grandfather sat tall and proud on that beautiful Thanksgiving Day. Our entire family had gathered for the dinner, and I saw he was scanning the room for danger, his habits as a soldier continuing to this day.

I watched as my sister pulled up a chair next to Grandfather. As everyone ate and conversed, her little voice chimed in, asking, "Would you ever go through the war again?"

Silence filled the room. The sounds of eating stopped. This was a topic no one had dared broach. Our grandfather had gone through unspeakable horrors in the military, and the trauma and fear in his eyes had never gone away.

"I would do it all over again for *you*," he answered.

~Hannah A.

My Cap and I

*The test we must set for ourselves is not to march
alone but to march in such a way that
others will wish to join us.*
~Hubert H. Humphrey

I spotted the cardboard carton near the doorstep the minute I pulled into my driveway. A smallish box, it only contained one item — a ball cap. The surge of adrenaline that I felt reminded me of times when the mailman delivered something that I sent off for as a kid. But this was better than any magic decoder ring.

I took the box inside to rip it open. It looked exactly like the picture in the online catalog: jet black with the words VIETNAM ERA VETERAN in yellow, and an embroidered red and yellow National Defense Service Medal on the front. Should a sixty-something guy be this excited about a baseball cap?

No single incident or epiphany caused me to want this cap and proclaim my service to my country. Decades before — in the 1960s — we servicemen did not announce our participation in any military activities. Times change, as do attitudes. I was ready to let people know I had proudly served.

Having talked to other veterans over the years, and seeing them wear black caps similar to my newfound prize, I realized it is okay to be patriotic. Proclaiming one's past commitment and sacrifice is all right. Declaring this fact is just that — a fact. But it is information I *now want* people to know about me.

Wearing a head covering is not something I do much, so I didn't intend to wear the cap every day. I decided I would pick and choose when to wear it. Each time had to be for something exceptional.

Not long ago, my cap and I found the special occasion that cemented my pride in serving my country. When a young man from Loveland, Colorado lost his life in Afghanistan while serving in the Army, many people in the community expressed an interest in showing their support for the family. I knew my cap and I must take part, and we did.

As I drove through town, I saw small clusters of individuals of all ages, many with American flags, lining the curb and sidewalks along the route from the church to the cemetery. This unorganized, spontaneous yet heartfelt show of appreciation and support stretched for miles from the cemetery to the church. My cap and I joined them. I stood with other roadside observers, waiting for the funeral procession to pass by.

The caravan turned on to the street where I stood. A steady stream of local law enforcement cars and motorcycles flashed their red and blue lights, followed by black leather vested Patriot Guard Riders with their Harley engines roaring and Old Glory snapping in the wind. Lastly, the somber gray hearse and accompanying funeral party passed my cap and me. I stood at attention.

Feelings flowed through me — a mixture of patriotism and pride. By standing there watching, I shared my feelings in public. It felt good.

My cap and I watched with reverence and respect. People held their hands over their hearts or let their American flags dip in honor of the young soldier as he passed by. I gave a somewhat rusty salute, my fingers touching the brim of my cap. Yes, a tear may have been in my eye, too, for a military brother I did not even know.

My heavy heart gave credence not only to my pride for this brave warrior, but also to my service to my country. Ordering my cap was a good decision.

~Bob McDonnell

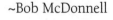

44

In the Presence of Greatness

*The greatness of a man is not how much wealth he
acquires, but in his integrity and his ability to
affect those around him positively.*
~Bob Marley

The day wasn't extraordinary in any way. Same talk of snow, same dismal December grays and browns smudging the Ohio Valley background as if painted by the hand of a melancholy artist.

Usually, I am a positive person, turning over challenges to discover those precious gems of hope buried beneath. But today was different. Perhaps it was the dark news broadcast over the radio as I drove along the highway. Perhaps it was because of the next radio station I turned to, which was idolizing celebrities and their designer wardrobes.

Whatever had me depressed, I needed to shake it off fast. Within minutes, I'd arrive at the local library to somehow lead and inspire my writers group.

"Shh… here's the teacher," one of the members joked as I entered the library.

I smiled, but didn't take my eyes off the new guest sitting beside one of my regular members. Dressed handsomely in black trousers, a grey dress shirt and vest, he was the definition of refinement. He smiled somewhat nervously at me when I walked over to him, and as I held out my hand for an introduction, he immediately stood, took off his hat and brought it to his chest. That's when he captured my heart.

Now, everyone who knows me knows I love bygone eras. On those rare occasions when I have time to watch television, you can bet the channel will be turned to a 1950s black-and-white movie, where men were debonair and the women — classy. And a gentleman rising to his feet in a lady's presence might not seem like a noteworthy act, but it was for this man. His careful movements showed his advanced age, but with painstaking effort, he'd acted on gentlemanly principles that reflected a time when those principles were still being taught in the home and society.

I sensed that I was in the presence of someone completely different from those in my usual social circles. And I wasn't letting go.

"I'm Karen Garrison," I said, meeting his eyes. "Or you could call me my Italian name, Karina."

"Bill Apesos," he said, and we shook hands.

He placed his cane beside his chair after we took our seats, and throughout the meeting, I focused on Bill a little more than the others, gently trying to draw out the deep scars that seemed just below the surface of his eyes. It was as if he had so much to share, but the awkwardness of being new perhaps inhibited him.

But then, whether it was the warm interest of the other members, or perhaps just the fact that this was a divine appointment, something remarkable happened. Suddenly, Bill opened up. As he did, no one heard the activity outside the room or the ticking of the old fashioned clock on the wall. We only heard Bill. And all of us journeyed back with him in time.

He told us stories about World War II that seemed long suppressed. Perhaps they were waiting for an eager audience, like our group. He started with a humorous story of how he and his brother wrote war letters back and forth, infused with secret codes to identify their locations in different parts of the world. Every word exuded the fierce love of brotherhood.

It's amazing how identification has a strong impact on one's life. Identifying with someone else's experiences allows the door to open to things that otherwise might escape one's notice. That night, I identified with Bill. As the youngest of five, I thought of my own siblings — of our childhood pranks and all the trials of growing up, and our strong family bonds.

For Bill and his brother, the hopeful promises of what awaited them after the war encouraged them to press on through the atrocities of combat. That is, until one fateful night, when Bill learned his brother had died.

When he finished his stories, I couldn't find my voice to move the class forward, and looking at each member's face, I knew that they were internalizing what had just happened. We'd heard of loss, love, and grace under pressure. We had seen the brutality of hundreds of bodies of fellow countrymen strewn along foreign shorelines. This wasn't some Hollywood war movie production, but the true spirit of America — personal and intimate as only a surviving veteran could tell.

With pounding hearts, we had parachuted with Bill under the cover of night to help his fellow servicemen. Our eyes had become ninety-year-old eyes, and through them, we watched, felt, and heard the events of the past unfurl like the American flag in a wounded soldier's hands.

So now, after Bill finished speaking, none of us knew exactly what to say. Many of us didn't even want to try.

Finally, Bill sheepishly lifted a notebook and handed it to me. I opened it and flipped through, appreciative of the handwritten poems scrawled on the pages. No typed words, no iPad, no computer — only Bill's quiet contemplations about his life experiences scrawled by his own hand.

How I valued that.

I thought of the radio station earlier that had spoken of celebrities as if they were something remarkable and worthy of admiration, and I knew that many people would most likely pass this elderly man on the street and think of him as just that — an elderly man.

But for me and this class, we knew differently. Bill's remarkable generation was dying.

I met and kept his gaze. This time, I didn't hold back my tears.

Reaching for his hand, I cupped mine over his weathered fingers — fingers that had tended to the wounds of many, comforted those in need, and still wore the wedding band from his late wife. Yet, here he was, a humble man declaring he was neither a coward nor a hero.

A bridge of understanding and the universal emotions of the human spirit closed any generational gap between us. After all, what are age differences between people when grief and pain, blended with the heights of love, are shared by every person?

Smiling, I squeezed Bill's hand. He, and so many others like him — American servicemen and women who have seen the best and worst of human nature, who have had to draw within themselves the courage to do the unthinkable, to witness the unimaginable, and to somehow survive the memories in order to lead a productive life — are all around us if we'd only stop for a moment to recognize and speak with them.

Bill looked at me, and I knew then that Hollywood might have its celebrities stepping out on red-carpet runways, and Nashville its iconic musicians, but I didn't need to admire any of those so-called stars. I knew without a doubt that not only was I sitting in the presence of a real man, but I was sitting in the presence of true greatness.

~Karina Garrison

45

Just Two Marine Moms

Darkness cannot drive out darkness; only
light can do that. Hate cannot drive
out hate; only love can do that.
~Dr. Martin Luther King, Jr.

The war in Iraq was in full swing. One of my sons was a Military Police officer stationed in a very dangerous camp. His younger brother became a Marine fresh out of high school. He was stationed with the last Marine unit in Ramadi, a place fraught with bombings.

As anyone can imagine, my stress level was high, and my resentment ran deep toward people to whom I had never given a thought before 9/11.

One day, I was in a local market when two Muslim women were shopping. I swallowed hard and tried to keep my emotions in check when I noticed the purse one of the women was carrying. It had the U.S. Marines Corps emblem stamped on it, and on the bottom, clear as day, "Marine Mom" was printed in the traditional red and gold of the Marine Corps.

I was stunned. I had never thought there would be Muslims fighting in our armed forces, and I swallowed hard. I walked over to the woman and said to her: "I like your purse." She smiled shyly and said, "Yes, my son is a Marine."

I told her my sons were in the service, both in Iraq, and my younger son was a Marine. She leaned over to me and whispered,

"They are doing the right thing. Our sons will be okay." I smiled and thanked her, telling her I would pray for her son.

As I walked away, I felt a tremendous peace come over me. All the hate and resentment that had been building up was suddenly no longer there. For that brief moment, we were not two women of different cultures or religions. We were just two Marine moms comforting one another.

I think back to that day often, and I know that God made that encounter happen. It was what I needed to let go of a heavy burden — the burden of hate.

~Candy Storey

46

Finding True Patriotism in a Fallen Flag

The American flag is the symbol of our
freedom, national pride and history.
~Mike Fitzpatrick

I was a new Airman attending technical school in Monterey, California. I was assigned to Charge of Quarters (CQ) duty on July 4, 2008. An hour into a very long, minimally manned shift, we got a call. The base flag's straps had snapped in the extreme wind of the early morning, and the flag was falling.

Another Airman and I drove to the site to check things out. A maintenance man, who happened to be on base and made the call, was attempting to lift the flag off the ground. The flag was unbelievably large, and the pole stood in a field off to the side of the road.

My fellow Airman, the maintenance worker, and I each took a corner of the flag and held it off the ground. It was extremely heavy and a difficult task for the three of us alone. My co-worker called our sergeant to inform him of the situation, and he said he would make some calls and be there to assist as soon as he could. We were already feeling the extreme weight of the flag in our six arms and knew this was not going to be easy, but we never questioned the task that had fallen to us. Then we began to take turns using one hand to make calls and texts to friends and colleagues to try and acquire assistance.

We were not incredibly confident that we would be successful in gaining ample assistance on the early morning of July 4th. It was a Friday and the first day of a three-day holiday weekend. Most of our fellow students would be taking advantage of the time off for the holiday and be sleeping in. Many would already be headed to the beach for the weekend Fourth of July festivities and a much-needed break from the intense studies and duties we performed daily.

The sergeant arrived about an hour after we began. He was frantically trying to find someone who could fix the straps so we could raise the flag. His attempts were mainly answered with voice mail that informed him of holiday closures and promises of response on the next business day. Another hour passed, and the sergeant took a corner to aid our aching arms as much as he could. He had exhausted all options, and now the only thing he could do was wait. He continued to check his phone frequently, hoping for any response or instruction. The four of us continued to hold Old Glory as high as our aching arms could. We ensured she didn't touch the ground, but our muscles were exhausted. The sun was also rising higher, and it was getting hot.

We saw a car pull up, and two Airmen in civvies started to walk toward us. Without instruction, they each took a spot and bore some of the weight of the massive flag. They were friends of friends (who were actively headed back from the beach to help) that we had contacted. They informed us that they had contacted a few more of their friends who were now on their way as well. About a half hour later, a few more cars pulled up full of Airmen coming to assist us. With the added people, the flag was still incredibly heavy, but much more bearable than before. As more people arrived, we were able to hold the flag out more evenly, which aided in the weight distribution.

We stood, mostly silent, arms shaking, brows dripping from the heat of the sun for more than four hours. Finally, our sergeant got the call that instructed us to do our best to fold up the flag as no one was open on the holiday that could repair the broken straps, and no Honor Guard was currently available. None of us were trained in the Honor Guard and had no idea how to properly fold the flag. We did our best and folded it as neatly as we could. Afterward, we all shook hands and went our separate ways. Many headed out to celebrate our country's independence with beach barbecues. Some returned to their dorms for some much-needed rest. I returned to my Friday duties.

Throughout the remainder of the day, I thought about how those of us who held that flag off the ground never asked why or gave up on a task many would have deserted. We were not trained for this. They did not teach us in Basic Training to keep the flag off the ground.

I learned something that hot July day. Seeing many young military members come together for a task many would consider futile taught me that true patriotism is shown in the selfless actions of those living in a country they love. The irony that this all happened on Independence Day was not lost on me. I think about it every July 4th with a smile on my face.

My arms may have ached for days, but I had never been prouder. That gargantuan flag had always been there, but it flew higher in my eyes after that day. I never once passed it again without a smile and the newfound appreciation that I had gained for all that it represented. On that day, I learned the meaning of true patriotism, and that is something I will never forget.

~Cassandra Burns

47

Up Close and Personal

Patriotism is a thing of the heart. A man is a patriot
if his heart beats true to his country.
~Charles E. Jefferson

Eyes fixed straight ahead, a troop of young men and women soldiers marched through Hartsfield-Jackson Atlanta International Airport on their way to Fort Benning, Georgia. Carol Lee and I, two senior citizens, sat in comfortable chairs and watched. We had twenty minutes to wait before our flight departed. The company guidon bearer crisply snapped out: "Just back from Iraq! Company A!"

People shouted and whistled their gratitude. Smiling travelers set down suitcases, purses and packages in order to vigorously applaud. American soldiers being shown appreciation and respect for serving their country brought tears to our old eyes. We stood up and joined a crowd of travelers watching the soldiers in Army colors march over to waiting trucks.

It was quiet again when they left, until a second company, looking sharp, marched into the rotunda. *Step, step, step* echoed through the building until we heard, "Company... halt!" Soldiers stood ramrod straight until the company commander said, "Fall out." A large crowd of waiting families scrambled to find their loved ones. We saw plenty of girlfriends and wives kissing their soldiers, and lots of proud parents and young children too.

But the soldier who affected us most was the one I'll call Mommy

Soldier. Her parents were there, along with a little blond girl wearing a big green bow in her hair, a fluffy white dress, little socks, and black Mary Jane shoes. She was about four years old.

When Mommy Soldier turned, smiled, and opened her arms, the little girl stopped, put her feet together, and tried to salute with her left hand. No one cared that she didn't touch her eyebrow, or that it was the wrong hand. People watching felt a rising compassion for that family and began to cry. We certainly did.

"Come here, precious!" Mommy Soldier called. The girl flew into Mommy's arms. Mommy kissed and hugged her baby and said, "I'm gonna miss *you!*" Mommy Soldier held onto her daughter tightly even as she hugged her parents. Grandpa and Grandma got involved in the goodbyes and promises to write, honoring their Daughter Soldier as civilians have always honored outbound soldiers. When word came that it was almost time to "fall in," the civilians backed off.

Mommy Soldier's tears flowed as she patted her daughter's blond hair, wiped her tears, gave her one last kiss and then, reluctantly, handed the girl to Grandpa. Mommy Soldier stood erect, eyes forward. The guidon bearer barked, "On their way to Iraq… Company B!" On the command "Forward… march," Mommy soldier, looking sharp, left with her company. The little girl's salute was wasted. Only Carol Lee and I noticed it as the crowd cheered, applauded and whistled at the departing soldiers.

As the airport got back to business as usual we held our positions, too emotionally drained to move. And we weren't the only ones with tears in our eyes. But it wasn't over. A heavyset man appeared in the center of the terminal and burst into "God Bless America" *a cappella.* While his high tenor voice filled the space, travelers again got teary-eyed during "land that I love, stand beside her and guide her." The airport became as quiet as a library. Carts stopped beeping. Cash registers went silent. We had heard "God Bless America" hundreds of times before, but no one had made it sound more beautiful. "Through the night with the light from above!"

By the time he sang "from the mountains," I didn't dare look at Carol Lee. I knew what she was feeling, that her whole face was wet, and she would soon have to sit down. I was pretty much the same way.

"To the prairies, to the oceans white with foam," the man sang. Nearing the end of his performance, when he hit the high notes, the stranger might have been showing his musical range as he sang, "God bless America, my home sweeeeet home." Then, in even higher notes, using the acoustics of the building and really showing off, he finished with "God bless America, my home sweeeeet home!" and a lot of people wept openly. I might have been one of them.

And then the stranger left. People were asking, "Who was that guy?" and "Where did he go?" They wanted to thank him.

I doubt that anyone had heard a rendition of that Irving Berlin song so well done before. As the lyrics were dying out over the sobbing civilians, Carol Lee and I found our comfortable chairs and pulled ourselves together.

When our flight was announced, our visit was over. We had attended a wedding of some friends of Carol Lee's in south Georgia. We had visited with my old Navy buddy and his wife in Atlanta. We had stayed at a charming B&B where we had to pray with strangers before each meal. And, more importantly, we had gotten in touch with America.

We drifted over to our departure gate, where we boarded the plane and headed toward California and our safe "home sweet home," close to an ocean "white with foam."

~John J. Lesjack

Chapter 6

Military Families

★ The Faces of the Forces ★

48

This Ain't Goodbye

*You've got to get up every morning with determination
if you're going to go to bed with satisfaction.*
~George Lorimer

It was a brisk 36 degrees, the fog was low and there was condensation on each blade of grass. We were doing physical training with our battalion commander on our first day of Infantry Officer Basic Course. He called it "The Five Day Sore." It was brutal. Immediately after we were dismissed, the guy standing next to me yelled out to the crowd, "Does anyone play golf?" The crowd chuckled and gave him some funny looks.

"Hey, does anyone play guitar?" I shouted out immediately after. "Yeah, I do!" said the same guy. We exchanged numbers and agreed to meet up later that night. His name was Justin.

"I hope he can play. He's in the Army. Crap. He probably sucks," I said to myself while walking to my car.

Later that night, guitar in hand, I headed down the street from my apartment to Justin's place. We didn't know how to get started. "Well… uh… have you written any songs?" he asked me.

We stayed up playing guitar, exchanging original for original until the wee hours of the morning. Besides the fact that Justin seemed to have this HUGE grin that excessively showed his teeth when he sang, this guy was extremely good. He was better than me. He had written some great songs, and he could freestyle and improvise-sing with the best of them. "I'm not going to lie," Justin said, "I thought you were going to suck. I mean, why would anyone good join the Army?"

After finishing basic and Ranger School, we showed up at Fort Carson wide-eyed and bushy-tailed, only to deploy weeks later to Afghanistan. Luckily, we ended up working in the same location, so every night after patrol we would climb up on top of a building, watch the mortar illumination rounds and helicopters fly overhead, and play guitar.

During 2015, after our deployment to Afghanistan in 2014, we were already ramping up to head back overseas after not even a year of dwell time. This was a problem for our music. How were we supposed to get out there and play to promote our music if we released it? At the end of 2015, with countless hours spent driving to Denver to record until 3 a.m., only to have first formation a couple of hours later, we had seven songs and a music video recorded, an online presence on all platforms, a music publishing company, and affiliations with the various royalty and copyright agencies we needed. But we still didn't have any time to do a proper release that would make an impact.

After a lot of head scratching, I started reaching out to military friendly organizations to see if they could help us reach a wide audience. After a shot in the dark e-mail to what seemed the best point of contact on the USO's website, I received an e-mail back from Gayle Fishel. Little did we know that the USO was celebrating their 75th Anniversary.

The USO flew us out to Washington, D.C. for the USO's 75th Anniversary VIP Celebration in February of 2016. We were to play our song "Hometown Hero" as an opener for Craig Morgan, and in front of some of the highest-ranking officials in the military, celebrities, and major corporate leaders.

After an interview with the USO, we proceeded to a "mystery event" that Gayle was suspiciously excited about, stressing that we "have to go to it."

"Go ahead and just hang out in here. Make yourself comfortable, and we will start in just a minute," Gayle told us as we walked in to a conference room. Justin and I had a feeling we knew what was going on. All of the USO personnel started to pull out their phones and aim them at the door. In walked Craig Morgan.

"Holy crap" I muttered to myself as I nudged Justin, "Dude, that's Craig Morgan… it's freaking CRAIG MORGAN. Be cool. Be Cool."

We stood and awkwardly started the conversation to try and find some common ground. We hit it off. We were joking, laughing, and having a ball. I quickly said to Justin in a side comment, "We need to get Craig Morgan to hang out with us later and write a song." Justin then proceeded to challenge Craig Morgan to a freestyle battle: "Hey Craig, I hear you can freestyle a song."

"Yeah, sometimes when we play shows we have the crowd give us three words and we freestyle a song using their words," said Craig, "It's usually a huge hit."

"Well, what do you say we hang out after the show and have a competition?" Justin asked. Craig agreed and shortly after we were ushered into the event.

We took the stage and performed "Hometown Hero" after an introduction from the actor Dennis Haysbert, with our families cheering in the front row. Craig Morgan approached us afterwards. "You guys killed it!" he said, before taking the stage himself. Justin and I took a stand at the front of the crowd to watch him perform.

After being blown away by Craig's vocal ability, we went back downstairs to the conference room. We were worried that he wasn't going to come as it was getting late, but lo and behold he walked through the door with his guitarist and was ready to write. He set his glass of wine down on a table, pulled up a chair, looked at us thoughtfully and asked "So what you got?"

We were dumbfounded. "Well shoot… uh… we can show you some titles of half-written songs," I said, frantically trying to find an answer to a question that we hadn't thought about. We were the dog who had caught its tail. We were so focused on getting to this point that we hadn't actually thought about what the heck we were going to do.

I pulled out my phone and started reading the list of song titles to Craig. "Sippin' on the Simple Life," I finally read aloud.

"Oh, that's good. I like that. Let's hear it. Damn, that's a good title. Hey, Mike did you hear that? Oh, that's good," Craig exclaimed to his guitarist while clapping his hands.

We all ended up having a few drinks and staying up until two in the morning while we finished the song.

We had completed our first co-write. With Craig Morgan.

We got the whole thing on video, and throughout the whole process Craig and his bandmates kept saying, "This is a hit! This is a hit! We are going to get into the studio next week and cut this!"

Justin and I flew out early the next morning and went back to reality. We were awestruck. "What the heck just happened?" Justin asked me, "I think we can really make it in music. I really think we have a chance to make it." We went back to work the next week with that thought, and less than a month left before deploying back to Afghanistan.

After releasing our song "Hometown Hero" in conjunction with our performance at the USO's 75th Anniversary, we decided to release an old song I had written called "I'm Gonna Miss You" for Memorial Day. We scheduled the last available times at the studio, and I was in the vocal booth recording at eight o'clock the night before I was leaving for Afghanistan.

With both of us stationed at opposite ends of Afghanistan, we stayed up late at night with a whiteboard and drew out a huge timeline of the shots and scenes we needed to create a music video. With the music video slated to publish and ABC News steady on the trigger, we fired. The video launched the Friday before Memorial Day weekend. ABC News, The Howard Stern Show, Good Morning America, Fox News, CNN, HLN Morning Express, numerous news stations in major cities, radio stations, newspapers, and every major blog and online news source was publishing and covering our story. "Army Rangers Release Memorial Day Song From Afghanistan" Google's Trending News and all the headlines read. "I can't sleep at all. I can't stop checking our Facebook page," I texted Justin. "This is insane! Our video views are climbing 1,000 views a minute!"

We woke up that Saturday to find we were over 400,000 views on our video. There was no stopping the video. It had gone *viral*. That next week, when things had simmered down, we clocked in at over four million views.

With a newfound sense of determination, I decided that I was going to repeat my formula for success with the USO. I started searching on Wikipedia for the names of the producers of the biggest artists in country music. Through a stream of tweets I contacted two-time Grammy Award–winning producer Nathan Chapman.

"I thought this was some kind of prank," said Nathan through a choppy FaceTime feed. "I sat there and had to tell my wife 'Hey babe, these guys contacted me from Afghanistan and asked if I'd re-produce their song.'" After remotely managing the production of a music video and staying up all night for two months straight calling over 200 radio stations, enlisting the help of University of Georgia students, and contacting all the old connections we made with our Memorial Day release, we secured airplay on twenty-seven radio stations nationwide.

We have since returned from Afghanistan, and Justin and I are now scheduled to be separated when we leave Fort Carson, Colorado. Who knows what the future holds or where we will go? All we know is we will never give up and we will never quit. We've made it work before and we will continue to make it work. Dreaming. Hoping. Wishing. This Ain't Goodbye.

~Andrew Yacovone

49

Nail Biter

A deep sense of love and belonging is an irreducible
need of all people. We are biologically, cognitively,
physically, and spiritually wired to love,
to be loved, and to belong.
~Brené Brown

I pulled the last inch of Scotch tape off my forearm and laid it gently on the folded corner of the bright crimson wrapping paper. The Navy officer in front of me picked up his blue cap and asked, "Do you have gift tags by any chance? The little 'to and from' kind?" I showed him our selection — tiny, ice-skating penguins or a vintage Father Christmas — and handed him a candy cane shaped pen.

This was my third holiday season wrapping presents for the patrons at the Marine Corps Exchange aboard Marine Corps Air Station Cherry Point. I volunteered for the Enlisted Spouses' Club, and our supplies came through donations. Any funds we raised by wrapping presents would support our scholarship fund benefiting military spouses and children in our community.

The evening rush was ending and soon I would be able to pack up my supplies and head home to my Marine and our dog and cat.

Then I noticed him. This man had passed by my table more than once while I was wrapping the gift for the Navy officer. I watched him walk to the rack of clearance chocolates to my right, and to make conversation, I asked, "Is there anything good over there? I can always go for cheap treats!"

The man tilted his head back and looked straight up, then quickly dropped his chin to his chest and turned bright red. Then, shaking his head tightly, he said, "Girl, no. Nothing!" He looked up at me, and we both laughed for a minute. He cautiously approached my table, placing a single fingertip on the tablecloth and dragging it along slowly until he reached my peppermint jar. He stopped directly in front of me, and I could sense he felt nervous, but not because of me. He looked out of the far corner of his eye, as if trying to spot a secret follower.

"Would you like a peppermint?"

"Oh, yes, please!"

He appeared to be maybe nineteen or twenty years old. He fumbled with shaking hands to open the plastic wrapper. His nails showed signs of a compulsive nail biter, and I noticed he had a wedding band on his left hand.

"Do you have anything you need wrapped? Perhaps a gift for your wife or a Secret Santa swap at work?"

He popped the mint in his mouth and asked me about the Enlisted Spouses' Club. Who could join? What rank did his military service member need to be? How much did monthly dues cost? Did we have any guys in the club? What type of socials did we host? Did we have any other community service projects planned? Around question number three, I realized he was asking because *he* was interested in joining. We had only had one male spouse previously, and we constantly sought new members — male or female. When the club initially began, it was known as the "SNCO Wives Club." But as more women joined the ranks of the military, their male spouses started looking for a club to join, and our club became the "Enlisted Spouses' Club."

As I told him about our ideas for the next year, another young man walked up to my table and tapped my new friend on the arm. He said, "It's almost closing time. We need to go." My meek friend sighed and looked at me with tears in his eyes. He thanked me for the mint and the conversation, and promised he would look into the club later at home. I reached out and gently touched his wrist, stopping him from leaving. "Hold on, let me get you my e-mail address."

I reached around my table of gift-wrap clutter, tossing aside bright bows and fuzzy pom- poms. I found my pen and began to write my information on the back of a flyer. He whispered back and forth with the second young man. I could not hear their words, but I could feel the air around us thicken. There is a stigma associated with spouse clubs as catty, rumor-breeding cesspools, good for nothing more than gossip and coffee. We had worked diligently over the past three years to shed this reputation. We had formed a new social network for the spouses at Cherry Point. *All* the spouses. Now my fingers shook as I wrote, praying this other young man would not make fun of my new friend for showing an interest.

I smiled as I reached across the table to hand him the flyer.

"You guys take gay spouses too, right?"

He wiped a stray tear from his cheek while the young man next to him studied the floor intensely.

"Of course we do! We're here for *every* enlisted spouse, no matter what. Now if your husband is an officer, you'll need to contact the Officer Spouses' Club."

I leaned over and tilted my head to the side to make eye contact with the second young man. He cleared his throat, looked deep into my eyes and smiled a little corner-of-his-mouth smile. I gave him my biggest holiday grin. "So, is this your husband?"

The three of us talked past closing time. My new friends helped me pack up my paper, bows, ribbons and tape, and then walked me to the front doors of the Marine Corps Exchange. A manager pulled out her giant ring of keys and let us out into the starlit parking lot. This couple had met many people since arriving in North Carolina, but they still lacked real friends. That night, they had found me. With hugs and a "see you later," we parted ways in the chilly December night air.

~Angela M. Young

50

How My Life of Service Served Me

Don't take counsel of your fears or naysayers!
~Colin Powell

I remember it as if it were yesterday. My mother retired from her civil service job in Washington, D.C., and announced that we were moving back to her small Virginia hometown. Lying in my bed that night and looking up at the ceiling, I wondered how it happened that I'd be entering the twelfth grade in a new school.

Being the new girl in my senior class was hard. Although the girls were standoffish, the boys were a little too friendly. As if living in a small town where I didn't know many people wasn't bad enough, graduating and working a dead-end job day after day seemed desolate.

One day, flipping through a magazine in the break room of the shoe factory where I worked, I saw an ad for the Air Force. It showed a young, African American woman in a crisp, blue uniform, sitting in front of a console with numerous knobs and gauges. I knew this was my answer.

I tore out the prepaid card and filled it out. I dropped it in a mailbox on the way home, and then completely forgot about it. That is until the day an Air Force recruiter called me.

"Carol, telephone!" my younger sister yelled. "It's some sergeant!"

"Who is this sergeant?" my mother asked. "What have you done?" She was thinking it was the police, and horror of horrors, I was on my way to jail.

Three days later, the recruiter brought the military entrance exam to our house. Before I knew it, I was on an airplane bound for basic training in San Antonio, Texas. I was twenty years old.

"Put out that cigarette," barked the drill sergeant to a guy who had just lit up. With his crisp uniform and straight military bearing, he brooked no argument.

"All of you pick up your baggage, and then form a single line!" the sergeant continued to bark. *Oh man, Carol, you have done some stupid things in your life, but this is the stupidest thing you have ever done,* I thought to myself. Still, there was no turning back.

"I am an American Airman," began the Air Force creed. This was both "our promise to country and colleagues." The promise, however, didn't mention that I would spend six weeks on my hands and knees cleaning grout from restroom tiles — with a toothbrush. Nor did it mention I'd spend six weeks sleeping on the floor.

Initially, it was to save time each morning. Secondly, it was to not mess up my military bunk after finally learning how to make it, where the sergeant bounced a quarter on it to test its tight, four-cornered facade. After all, there was no way I could make it up, shower, dress, eat and be in formation on time. Other women did similar things, including sleeping partially clothed at night in order to get a head start.

Lined up according to height, we marched everywhere in formation. "Forward, march! Hut, two, three, four," called out the drill sergeant, as we marched across the base compound. Marching in my men's size five combat boots (the smallest standard issue available), my voice rang out with the others. "Over hill, over dale, as we hit the dusty trail, and those caissons go rolling along." Surprisingly, despite the physical demands of basic training, I thrived.

When I entered the Air Force, there were only a handful of women. We were part of a new breed of airman, albeit with breasts. We didn't seem to fit what people thought military females looked like or acted like. This pretty much allowed me to set my own standard of who a military woman was and what she could do.

It's no exaggeration to say that the military changed my life. In fact, it wasn't until then that I discovered what a truly sheltered young woman I had been. In my squadron, I discovered many women didn't have the same basic value system that had always been instilled in me.

Little by little, I found myself moving away from much of what I was raised to think, feel and believe. Away from home, the opportunity to try new things was tremendous. Pierce my ears (something my overly strict mother frowned upon). Dye my hair? Smoke a cigarette? Yes, yes and yes!

I'd like to say my joining was about serving my country or making a difference. After all, military women have performed all sorts of jobs, from code breakers to photographers and a host of others. The truth is, I went into the Air Force to escape an overly strict childhood and the lack of career prospects. I also went in because of the naysayers: the women who came to my mother's beauty shop and questioned why a nice girl like me wanted to go into the service.

Their horror stories abounded! "My niece went into the Army and came home with a lot of problems," said old Ms. Johnson, a lady with blue hair. Mrs. Smith knew a lady whose granddaughter went into the Navy and came home with a husband who had been dishonorably discharged and abused her when he drank.

Consequently, I stayed on active duty the first four years to prove to my mother and those women that I *could* do it. The second four years, I did it for myself: for the travel opportunities, educational benefits and much more. Lastly, I stayed in because I finally discovered that the Air Force was not just a job, and it was way more than just an adventure.

Before the military, I'd lived a life unscripted. In truth, the military guided my life's trajectory. The skills I learned — time management, the ability to make quick decisions, resolve problems, to motivate and lead others — have all been transferrable to my subsequent careers. Likewise, the Air Force inspired fearlessness. Thus, I'm unafraid of changes, be it new ideas, locales, or situations.

Not only did it provide me the opportunity to travel, I experienced things I'd never experienced before. Like getting up too close for comfort to buffalo in South Dakota. Like eating octopus tempura and living to tell about it.

More than a mere slogan, the Air Force's "Aim High" became my own personal mantra. Using the military GI Bill, I obtained not one but two degrees, allowing me to venture into new territory as a leader.

When many people learn that I served for over twenty years, they are frankly surprised. "I can't believe you were in the service," they say. "You look so feminine, so soft." My love of pink, perfume and all things girlie aside, life has demanded that I be strong. Then they thank me for my service. "Thanks so much," I reply. Still, I chose that life, and I was honored to have served.

~Carol L. Gee

51

Army Strong: We Move On

The soldier above all others prays for peace, for it is the soldier who must suffer and bear the deepest wounds and scars of war.
~General Douglas MacArthur

Ted slept soundly on a lazy Sunday afternoon. It was time to wake him. Gently, I touched him on the shoulder, saying his name softly. In the next breath, I felt his hands around my neck. As quickly as it started, it was over. His hands dropped to his sides, leaving no marks on my neck, only on my psyche. To this day, I recall his words, "Never stand too close or touch me to wake me up..." and to this day, I don't.

Then one day we were walking up a tree-lined street as a car backfired. It didn't strike me as unusual, so I kept walking. Ted dived face down on the sidewalk. As people stared, he slowly got on hands and knees, and then stood tall beside me, apologizing for his behavior.

Like many wounded warriors, Ted rarely talks about his war experiences. One time I noticed a sad look on his face and I asked what he was thinking about. He described "riding shotgun" on a helicopter that was moving severely wounded men to an aid station. The pilot was shot and died instantly. The co-pilot was severely wounded. Ted climbed from behind to the front seat, pushed the pilot aside and took over the controls. Never having flown himself, he managed to bring the copter down in a bumpy but safe landing. Few people know this story as it was lost in the chaos of war.

All these incidents occurred in the mid-1960s. At that time, I didn't see that Ted was a wounded warrior. You may wonder why. It may be because I was an Army brat whose father served overseas during World War II. He returned to us with war wounds no one could see, carried deep inside, wounds not acknowledged by either the civilian or military communities. I lived within this Army family, learning to hide human weakness, to ignore fear and just move on. In the early 1960s, I finished my Bachelor of Science in Nursing with help from the Army student-nurse program. After graduation, I moved from being an Army brat to being an active-duty Army nurse working in a stateside Army medical center where I cared for severely wounded survivors of the Vietnam War.

Along the way, I met Ted. Years later, after he had served two years in Vietnam, we married. Ted left the Army and earned his Master of Social Work, re-entering the military as a Medical Service Corps (MSC) officer. His aim? To help men and women who, like himself, carried both visible and invisible wounds of war.

Shortly after Ted started his life as an Army MSC officer, we received orders to go to Tehran, Iran. We saw it as a wonderful opportunity to experience a culture different from ours. Ironically, the Iranian Revolution hit full force ten months after we arrived. I made the decision to leave Iran with our three-year-old son as military families were evacuated to escape the dangers of the revolution. Along with the other men, Ted watched our bus pull out into the steely cold just before the sun rose over the Elborz mountain range in northern Iran.

During the revolution, Ted holed up with a group of men from his unit, watching the unfolding revolutionary drama from a high apartment. When it was time for the U.S. forces to be airlifted out of Iran, he and the sergeant who worked with him drove toward the rendezvous point. As they drove, young revolutionaries fired warning shots across the front of their Paykan car. He slammed on the brakes. Their captors separated Ted from his sergeant. Ted's captor was untrained in how to use a sophisticated assault rifle. With the safety disengaged, he shoved the rifle up under Ted's armpit and ordered him to drive. This Ted did, praying they would not hit a bump causing the gun to discharge. After a brief interrogation at a remote location, he was driven to the Tehran Hilton hotel to meet up with other military being evacuated out of Iran.

Ted's Iran experiences exacerbated the trauma he had experienced during the Vietnam War. While we did not recognize it, he began to experience more signs of Post Traumatic Stress Disorder (PTSD). We thought it was "just" depression. As military folk often do, we dealt with it and just moved on with our lives. Ted completed twenty-plus years of exemplary military service as he continued to have occasional episodes of kicking out and punching violently in his sleep, sometimes knocking things to the floor and screaming, "Get away from me!"

For fifty years, I have lived with Ted. When we married, we had high hopes for a bright future. He has always been a gentle, loving man who helps others with their difficulties. At the time we married, we did not know how deeply he carried the wounds of PTSD. When people say, "Thank you for your service," on Veterans Day and Memorial Day, I know they mean it. I also know most do not understand the heavy costs of military service.

Yes, Ted still carries those deeply buried wounds. Yes, there have been times when his depression overwhelmed him, and we, his family, had to find ways to live with his physical presence but emotional absence. Yes, I am proud of him and us. Most importantly, I would do it again... and again... And, yes, it scares me when our six-year-old grandson stands proudly at attention, giving a cock-eyed salute, saying he wants to be a soldier "like Grampa."

Today, my feelings confuse me. I feel tears deep inside because I know I am proud, happy, and sad all at once. I have a deep understanding of the sacrifices and the strengths of those who serve in the military and the families who stand with them.

For me, life is a double helix, people spiraling together with never ending moments of sadness, anger, and grief for what has been lost, but also full of love and caring and hope. We have learned to say "yes" to life, knowing it may be difficult, but it is interwoven with deep love and compassion for one another and others. Somehow, we get through. This is what carries us forward individually, as a couple and as a family. It's what makes us strong.

~Carolyn L. Brown

52

Into the Unknown

Her lips on his could tell him better
than all her stumbling words.
~Margaret Mitchell

My husband and I sat on the screened-in back porch at his grandmother's house, enjoying the sound of thunder and the smell of rain. We had been married for six months and were just eighteen at the time. He worked at a local Pizza Hut, and I was a waitress at a nursing community. My husband had just told me that he had known since he was a young boy that he wanted to join the military. He said he wouldn't be happy if he didn't join.

I felt my heart crack a little, thinking of the things and the people I would be leaving behind. I loved my husband very much, and it was what he had to do for his life. It was his calling, and I knew I would go anywhere with him.

He left for basic training six months later. It was one of the hardest nights of my life. For the first time, I was alone. I didn't know when I would hear from him again. I got a call at about 3:00 a.m., and he quickly gave me an address to send mail. I jumped out of bed and wrote down the address he gave me. He told me he loved me, but had to leave again. I cried myself to sleep. I wouldn't hear from him for another two weeks.

I heard from him less than once a week. But I wrote anywhere from two to ten letters a day. Writing those letters helped me to cope.

I made my own envelopes when I ran out — in bright neon colors and even decorated them. I would douse them in his favorite perfume.

He later told me his drill sergeants and friends made fun of him because he always had stacks of letters. Later, he told me they got him through the hard times he experienced there.

We fell in love again in a new way. We wrote back and forth, and spilled our love over the phone and onto paper every chance we got.

One afternoon, halfway into his training, I was driving on an old back road in our town, and it was raining very hard. As I approached a curve, a woman driving in the opposite lane took the curve too fast and entered my lane. I turned the wheel as quickly as I could, avoiding what would have been a head-on collision at 60 miles per hour. It wasn't a very reliable car, and my brakes locked. My car started spinning out of control. All I could think of was my husband. I thought about how I wasn't going to see him again. I closed my eyes and let it happen. There was nothing else I could do.

My car wrapped around a tree on the passenger's side. The windshield shattered, and my chest collided with the steering wheel as my head hit the window next to me. The car was totaled, but I was alive. By sheer chance, my husband called me as I was being put into an ambulance. He needed information from me for paperwork. I told him that I had just been in an accident. He instantly panicked and asked if I was okay. I told him I really didn't know. We got off the phone, and I was rushed to the hospital. Later, he told me that as soon as he got off the phone, he felt his world shatter, and he started crying in front of everyone around him. He thought he might never see me again.

Miraculously, the only injuries I sustained were badly bruised ribs, whiplash, and glass in a few parts of my body. My husband was informed, and he sent flowers the next day. He stayed at boot camp and I spent the next month recovering.

And then boot camp was over. I would be moving to California after my in-laws drove me to Texas to see my husband graduate. I watched my mother cry as we drove off. It was incredibly difficult to say goodbye, but my place was beside my husband.

We arrived in Texas, and on yet another damp day, I watched from the bleachers as my husband graduated with honors. He was prepared now to serve his country, and I couldn't have been prouder. Our eyes locked for the first time in months, and everything else faded away. He walked to me as quickly as he was allowed. I can only assume his heart was racing as fast as mine. Our hug began our life together in the military.

Everything felt right. I was so far away from everything I knew, but embraced in his uniformed arms, I knew I was home.

~Taylor Jackson

53

The Things You Learn

We have the right, and the obligation, to tell old stories
in our own ways, because they are our stories.
~Neil Gaiman

I joined the Army in the summer of 2011 right after high school. Many of my friends joined, and my sister convinced me that having loan-free college tuition was the best route to go.

I've spent almost six years in the Army and have learned more in those six years than I ever thought possible. I would not trade these experiences for anything in the world. They have helped make me the person I am today.

One of the first things I learned is that most people in the military don't know what to say when people tell them "Thank you for your service." Personally, I have no idea what to reply or how to act because I'm just doing my job. I do not see myself as a hero. Soldiers who lost their lives or were deployed deserve the recognition more than me, but in the end I just say, "Thank you," and move on. Many people in the military feel the same way.

Another thing that I have learned is the strength of the friendships that we make in the military. These friendships will last a lifetime. I have met people from very different backgrounds with different interests and lifestyles. Seeing each other almost every day from 6:00 in the morning until 5:00 in the afternoon is a sure way to get to know each other. This is even truer while on deployment. However, the flip side is we also get on each other's nerves very quickly. But it's all part of being a family. We are willing to do anything to help each other out, whether it's financially, emotionally, or just helping each other get into or out of trouble.

The military has changed me physically and mentally as well. When I first joined, I was a skinny 107-pound kid. Now, I'm still young but I'm 145 pounds, and I feel a lot different. That's only the physical part, though. I have changed a lot mentally, too. I feel as though I grew up faster than my peers who went to college. Since I received a decent steady paycheck, I began paying for all of my own groceries and bills, and learned to save money on my own. I also used to be shy and had hardly any self-confidence. Just a few years later, I am still shy, but I tend to come out of my shell more easily and make friends quickly.

The value of mail was new to me as well. On deployments, care packages are a soldier's best friend. While I was in Afghanistan, I always looked forward to mail. I worked twelve hours a day, seven days a week. I had a day off every other week, but after about two months I was drained and tired of going to work every day. So I found solace in the little things, like the mail I received. I got packages from many companies and programs that sent snacks, hygiene items, clothing, and various other things. Each box was a great surprise. I have never seen such an outpouring of support for troops as I did on deployment.

The USO was also a huge distraction from the tedious day-to-day activity. I spent many a night in the big tent that was the USO. I had heard of them before, but never actually visited them until deployment. Everything was free and catered toward military. They were a lifesaver in Afghanistan when I could go there and call home or just read a book in their comfy chairs. It made me forget about the stresses of work. It was a simple thing, but I will be forever grateful.

There is a lot of travel involved in the military. Aside from a small number of people, most soldiers will travel to many places. If someone told me when I was in high school that I would travel to Europe, Afghanistan, South Korea, and all over the United States, I would have said, "Yeah, right." But, in the end, they are all great places that I will always carry with me. I learned so much about other cultures and how they do things. Some places were better than others, but they are a part of me now, and that makes me happy. I am now in South Korea and have some of the very best friends that I could ever ask for.

Of course, there are times when I become frustrated. In the Army, we have a job and get paid, but we can't do everything a civilian can. I can't wear my uniform and protest anything. I can't just quit my job, and I can't call in sick. Some of these things may seem small, but they are things that most civilians can do without any problems. If I want to go on vacation, I have to submit a form requesting leave. If it's not approved, there is nothing I can do about it. I can't say, "I quit," and I can't just not show up without consequences. If I am sick, I have to go to the doctor and get a note saying I can have time off from work.

In the end, even though the job may be tough at times, I still enjoy doing it. I am grateful for the many friends I've made in my tours of service, and I am happy about how the Army has changed me and, in my opinion, made me better.

~Jonathan J. Cervantes

54

Always with Me

*Loneliness can be conquered only by
those who can bear solitude.*
~Paul Tillich

My family didn't believe me when I told them I was going to join the Navy after I graduated from college. They thought I was playing one of my practical jokes. The day before I left for boot camp, my family gathered together and cooked some of my favorite dishes to make sure I was sent off properly. I can still visualize us sitting around the table, sharing jokes and stories. As time passed, they all hugged and kissed me, and let me know how much they loved me before they departed for the evening.

The next morning, my cousin dropped me off at the Military Entrance Processing Station (MEPS) in Raleigh, North Carolina. The last words she spoke to me were "It will be alright," referring to boot camp.

Boot camp was a unique experience, but I made it through. Then I transitioned into rate training for storekeepers (now called logistics specialists) in Meridian, Mississippi. Afterward, I reported to my first duty station, Logistics Support Group Two at Little Creek, Virginia. I was stationed there for two years, but it was not until my second duty station when I really leaned on my family. That's when the "ride-along" began. I was truly excited about exploring the world. Being a country girl, I knew I was stepping into a new realm.

I could not wait to get to Manama, Bahrain, and start working at the Fleet Mail Center. This was the first time I set foot out of the country. Little did I know that I would be stepping into a "hot oven" when I walked off the plane. I was really overpowered by the desert heat. I thought North Carolina was hot, but it was like comparing apples to oranges.

With the time difference and my work schedule, communication was difficult. This was before videophones and all the technology that we have today. Therefore, many silent days and nights passed until I was able to talk with my family. I realized my friends were now my family, and I had to learn to socialize with my peers. Mingling with my co-workers did help pass the time, but my next assignment was a little more of a challenge.

I was able to spend time with my family before reporting to Naval Mobile Construction Battalion Eleven (NMCB 11) in Gulfport, Mississippi. At the time, NMCB 11 was already deployed to Afghanistan, and I knew I had to go once my leave was up. I was extremely scared, and my family could sense it. They remained strong for me in my time of fear and weakness. They did an excellent job at masking it in the beginning, but once I left for Mississippi, I knew they were just as worried. The casual, every-other-day phone calls increased to almost a call every hour from them, constantly checking to see how I was doing. It made me happy, just as it did when I deployed to Guam. It also gave me peace of mind while I was in-flight to theater.

Long days and nights in Afghanistan can take a toll on a person. I remember one morning getting up before everyone else and walking to the USO to call my family. The director was there, and she asked me how she could be of service. I said I needed to make a phone call. Normally, we were only allowed ten minutes on the phone, but I guess she sensed I needed more time than usual. I called everyone I knew who was not in bed, and I just poured my heart out. Even though I was in a panic, they remained calm and encouraged me with words like "Just hang in there," "You'll be home soon," and "It's almost over." Later that day, I received a huge box, which contained all my favorite snacks from childhood. I was so overwhelmed that I shared the snacks with my co-workers. They were just as grateful, too. Oreo cookies are not easy to come by in the desert.

I'm very blessed and grateful that I have returned safely after each deployment. I know there are many of our sister and brother sailors who were not able to return. Being a single sailor, at times, I felt as if I was wandering this world alone. It was emotionally challenging at times, especially leaving or returning from deployments. I completely understood why my family was not able to be there physically, but seeing everyone else's loved ones waving, cheering, and hugging them as they welcomed their sailors did pluck the emotional strings. Mentally, I had to stay strong and just focus on how I was going to get home so I could rest. I knew I needed to get plenty of rest before getting on the road to drive thirteen hours back to North Carolina.

Once I reached home, it was like old times. Many times, I experienced or saw something that I wanted to share with my family, but only words or pictures would do. I am sure they felt the same. For my eyes and ears were theirs, and their eyes and ears were mine. We may not have been able to be with each other, but we were always together in spirit.

No matter where I went, for whatever length of time, my family was always there, supporting me since day one with loving letters, drawings, and popcorn and cookie care packages. Most importantly, they prayed for me.

If I never said thank you before, I do now. Thank you for the wisdom you shared, for being my strength when I was weary. Thank you for being there every time I came home, and making me feel missed and loved. You could never be replaced, and I will always love you all.

~Laquita Brooks

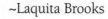

55

Adopt a Soldier

*Sometimes the most beautiful thing is precisely the
one that comes unexpectedly and unearned, hence
something given truly as a present.*
~Anna Freud

Another school year was beginning. I had thirteen excited
first graders eager to learn and ready to fill my classroom
with giggles, tears, and everything in between. I realized
that I had a uniquely small class size and got excited
about the special projects we could do. One project that I had been
particularly interested in was adopting military members as pen pals
for my students.

I began by sending out an e-mail to our school district employees
asking for names and contact information of any military members
they knew of. I was able to gather four different contacts and sent an
e-mail to each one asking if we could "adopt" them.

I only had one reply: Captain Denisar, who was deployed to
Afghanistan. Since six-year-olds' attention spans are rather short, and
many of the students were just learning how to read and write, I thought
it would be best to correspond through e-mail. Captain Denisar quickly
became a reward system. If students practiced and could read a book
fluently, I recorded it and e-mailed it. If they finished a writing assignment, I would scan it and e-mail it. If students were misbehaving, I
caught myself saying, "What would Captain Denisar think about that?"

We also used the information Captain Denisar included in his e-mails as learning opportunities. As we communicated with him, we learned more about him. He was twenty-nine, a year older than me, wasn't married, and didn't have any children. I quickly found that we had a lot in common.

At one point, I learned that one of his soldiers had been killed in action and noticed it was taking a toll on him. We started to lighten things up by recording songs and jokes, and sending art projects and care packages. He was so appreciative of the communication and looked forward to being included in the everyday drama of first grade. The communication between my classroom and Captain Denisar continued when he returned stateside. We even sent a banner down to welcome him home! Even though he was home, we continued to communicate with him, as my students had gotten quite attached. Communication dwindled some as he re-deployed, but he promised that he would make a trip to our small town in Illinois to meet my class when he could.

The school year was beginning to wrap up when he contacted me in April about coming up to visit in May. For the first time, we began talking on the phone to coordinate his visit, and somehow our conversations on the phone started getting longer and turning more personal. Before long, our phone conversations turned into a daily event, and Captain Denisar became just Brad.

As the day of his visit approached, I began getting nervous that this man who had stolen the hearts of my students — and was sneaking into mine — wouldn't live up to the hype and the chemistry that was so present through e-mail and phone calls. Did I mention that Brad's father was my school superintendent (my *boss*)? So I was a tad worried that if things didn't go well, it could affect my reputation within the school system. His dad and I drove to the airport together to pick him up, which was somehow not awkward. And before too long, Brad was there, walking toward us in the flesh. We hugged, and as we headed to baggage claim, he turned to me and wiggled his ears. As crazy as that sounds, I wasn't anxious from that moment on. I knew he was exactly the man I thought and hoped he was.

The next morning, he came to the school and stayed all day. I had planned a huge day with my students. Because he was deployed for an entire calendar year, we wanted to catch him up on the holidays he missed. We went all out with an Easter egg hunt, exchanged valentines, had a Thanksgiving dinner for lunch, and sang "Happy Birthday" with a cake for dessert. We wore costumes and had a haunted house for Halloween, and exchanged Christmas gifts. Brad brought an Army T-shirt for each student with his or her name on the back, and we gave him a school T-shirt. We ended the day with a school assembly at which Brad told all the kids about being in the Army and serving in Afghanistan. He showed pictures and answered *a lot* of questions.

We spent the entire weekend together and had dinner with my parents, his best friend, and his father. Things were great. But one week after Brad's visit, I got a frantic call from him telling me that his father had just had a massive heart attack. He didn't know anyone else to call who was in close proximity to his dad. I was the first person to the hospital and met Brad there. He stayed with me for two weeks until his father was able to leave the hospital and recover at home.

The day after the heart attack, we were driving back to the hospital after being up most of the night, and he looked at me and said, "This is it. You're the one." I was speechless for the first time in my life. Things moved quickly. I was able to meet his whole family, who lived all over the country, as they came and took turns helping his dad through the recovery process. By the end of June, we had booked a church, and I purchased a wedding dress. Then we picked out rings. He asked my father's permission for my hand in marriage, and then he proposed. It was not quite in the traditional order.

We were married on January 1, 2011, just seven months after his visit to my classroom, in the church that I grew up in. It was the same church in which his parents had taught Sunday school before he was born, just miles from his grandparents' farm where he visited as a child. It was a beautiful winter wedding with a large military presence and the beginning of my life as an Army wife. Never in my wildest dreams did I imagine that adopting a soldier would lead to a lifelong commitment and the love of my life.

~Katie Denisar

56

Home

Life is a succession of moments. To live
each one is to succeed.
~Corita Kent

I've been asked many times why I support the USO, and the answer is surprisingly simple: The USO is home to me. When I say that, civilians look both confused and understanding to some degree. It's hard to explain in any other way, and *home* is truly what the USO provides when one is overseas.

The example I fall back on is chairs. If a service member is lucky, he might have office-type chairs. If he's not so lucky, he gets concrete or dirt. Being on a surgical team, I was lucky to have an office chair. When I was trying to "be" with my family virtually, I was never able to take that physical step with them because I was in a funky office chair, and not on the couch or recliner next to them.

This is where the USO comes in. They have chairs like we have back home. They have couches or recliners to actually relax in and have a small semblance of being home. I talked to my family almost every day while I was deployed, but I never truly felt *there* with them unless I was at the USO on a couch in the back.

That little slice of home may not seem like much, but it is truly life changing. I was able to read to my kids at the USO, and they could talk to me in a place where I lost some of the constant fear of attack or concern that patients might be coming in. I could forget, even for a moment, where I was and just "be" with my family.

This was never more important than after the birth of our youngest daughter. As a father of three beautiful, healthy kids, I wasn't prepared for an NICU baby. I especially wasn't prepared to be 12,000 miles away when it all happened. Our fourth baby, Alexandra, aspirated meconium when she was born, and she came out blue and in dire need of oxygen. She was rushed to the NICU, and I was told I could not Skype there. That rule changed the next day after a few conversations with administration. I spent the next ten days at the USO whenever I had time so I could talk to our precious baby in the NICU. I cried and I worried, but I got to see her and stay up to date on her progress.

I got to be a concerned and doting dad, not a soldier, for a few minutes each day. That couch in the back room must have had an imprint of me by the end of those couple of weeks. It helped me "be home" for a moment each day. I even got to be one of the first soldiers to participate in a program the USO launched where I got to send a care package home to my wife and our new baby. I was able to give a gift at no cost to me and be a good dad that way, too.

All of these moments helped change my life. They brought me closer to my family and home. Every moment gave me enough reprieve and rest to get through a few more days of the grinding monotony that is deployment. Every time I stepped into the USO, I was a little more connected to the real world back home, a little more normal. The staff and volunteers create an atmosphere where you can let your guard down and just "be." It's not the same as sitting on my couch at home, but if I've got to be away, it's the next best thing. The USO is home. It's that simple.

~Beau McNeff

Chapter 7

Military Families

★ ★ Ready to Serve ★ ★

57

To Change Your Dreams

Men's best successes come after their
greatest disappointments.
~Henry Ward Beecher

M y husband and his pilot-training classmates had made it through six months of grueling training in the aerobatic T-6 trainer plane. They had studied, taken tests, flown daily, taken more tests, studied more, and passed check rides (in-flight tests of their skills and knowledge).

Every moment of those six months led up to a specific ceremony that would determine much of their future career in the Air Force. This ceremony, called Track Select, was when the class would split between two new training planes. One group would go on to fly the T-38 in preparation for flying fighter jets after graduating from pilot training. The other group would fly the T-1, which would provide the foundation for flying larger, heavy aircraft.

The T-38 track was the one that most of my husband's classmates wanted. Only a few top performers would be assigned to it. The rest would go the T-1 route.

My husband had his eye on the T-38 prize, and we knew it would be close. He had performed well, but he was not at the very top of the class. We truly did not know how this ceremony would unfold, which was a very public ceremony with many members from the base community and his family present. He was nervous, and I was nervous for him.

The moment came when his dreams would be realized or crushed in front of everyone. He was called up to the front. The MC told some jokes, and there were some laughs and stories told about his T-6 experience. Finally, the MC clicked to the next PowerPoint slide, which revealed which trainer he would progress to.

T-1.

My heart was crushed for him. He tried to maintain his composure, but it was still clear the result was not what he had hoped for. I truly didn't know how he would handle this experience. Everything he had been working so hard for had been taken away with one PowerPoint slide.

After a few days of grief, he decided something. Rather than be bitter or angry, he chose to re-evaluate his dreams for the Air Force. He began to look at the different aircraft options available to him. He considered their various missions, places where they were stationed and what the deployments would be like. He spoke with instructors about their experiences and what they liked and did not like about each aircraft. He embraced this new outlook wholeheartedly. He was determined not to make the same mistakes he had made in the T-6. He was completely focused on being the very best T-1 pilot he could be.

His dedication paid off. At the pilot-training graduation ceremony, each new pilot is given his official Air Force aircraft assignment as well as the location for his duty station. He was awarded not only his first choice of plane, but also our first choice of station. He had achieved the number one spot in his group. To say I was proud would be an understatement.

Looking back on the experience, I am so grateful that we had to weather this particular storm. Not only are we now in a wonderful community that supports our family but my husband loves the plane and mission that he flies.

We also learned a very valuable lesson about being flexible. The one consistency of military life is its fluidity. I always remind myself that though we might be asked to rank our preferences for our next base assignment or whether we would like to try for a specific opportunity, the needs of the Air Force supersede all. This life requires humility, acceptance and resilience. On the days that I struggle with the reality of our military life, I recall these times in pilot training. I try not to think about my husband's face when his dream was crushed. Instead, I recall his look of determination when he decided to create a new dream.

~Kathryn Taliaferro

58

Citizen Soldiers

We join all right thinking men in wishing for our state
and nation a long period of peace and prosperity,
but… we know that we must always be prepared…
~Colonel Hogaboom, regimental commander of
Mississippi Rifles (1923-1941)

Duty, honor, country. That motto was daily forged into my husband's very marrow at the United States Military Academy at West Point. The words are bedrock. Their embodiment by leaders of character help ensure our country's continued freedom.

As a military wife, those three words took on new layers of meaning as my husband, Scott, left active-duty military service, joined the civilian work force, and became a Citizen Soldier in the Army National Guard. The National Guard of the United States is part of the United States reserve armed forces components. They are under the dual control of the individual state government and the federal government, and serve as part of the first line of defense for the United States.

Though I had been an active-duty Army wife living in Baumholder, West Germany, and Fort Benning, Georgia, the transition to wife of a Citizen Soldier was challenging for different reasons. "Is it guard weekend already?" I would ask as Scott would dash in, weary from work, and pull out his pre-packed Army duffle and fresh uniforms. I would sigh. His civilian job was hectic enough, with many hours of unpaid overtime. Our three sons were young: eleven, six, and two.

Scott had recently formed a Boy Scout troop and many of his free weekends were invested in the troop. He also had church activities and responsibilities.

"Yes, it comes around quickly each month, but a man's gotta do what a man's gotta do," he would respond with humor and a quick, reassuring hug as he moved to load his military gear into his dad's old white Ford farm truck. I would hand him his packed supper, which he would eat during the four-hour trip to Tupelo, Mississippi, the location of his unit. Then we would gather for family hugs beneath the oak trees in our front yard and wave our Citizen Soldier down the lonely county road.

The years ticked by, as did the weekend drills and summer two-week drills. Scott continued his civilian job in the oil and gas industry and continued his scout leadership as well. And then, when he was almost fifty and within six months of military retirement, he received deployment orders: eighteen months, with twelve months in Iraq.

The call-up was historic. The Mississippi Rifles, the 155th Infantry Regiment, is Mississippi's oldest National Guard unit, established in 1798. Now they were assigned to the 2nd Marine Headquarters Expeditionary Force in Fallujah, Iraq. The Mississippi Rifles were briefed that it was the second time in U.S. history that a militia was assigned to a Marine Headquarters, the previous one being Mississippi Rifles' participation with the Marines during Tripoli two centuries ago.

After five months of training at Camp Shelby, Mississippi, and in the Mojave Desert of California, the difficult night of actual deployment arrived. The boys and I said our goodbyes in the frightening dark of a January 2005 night at Camp Shelby. The soldiers, surrounded by piles of duffle bags and military equipment, gathered around buses, hugged their families, and boarded for a year's separation. I had decided I would not cry on the hour journey back to Laurel, Mississippi, but the van was deathly silent, each son dealing in his own way with the heavy weight of his dad's departure.

I looked out at the bright, full moon as we drove and silently prayed for the protection of all these brave Citizen Soldiers leaving full-time careers, families, extracurricular volunteer responsibilities, church responsibilities, and their beloved Mississippi behind. We turned our family focus to our school, scouting, competitive swimming, and home duties to "make Dad proud." The boys dug in with courage and tenacity.

The Mississippi Rifles also proceeded with bravery in embracing a two-pronged mission: combat operations and nation-building. Their primary assignment location was a region near Fallujah and Baghdad. These Citizen Soldiers were perfectly suited for their missions as they came from all sectors of industry: policemen, highway patrol, full-time elections officials, pastors, attorneys and judges, teachers, oil and gas professionals, farmers, business people, and entrepreneurs.

The nation-building portion of the deployment was particularly hopeful as it would mark the first time in Iraqi history that elections were held. First came the constitutional elections, followed by the national elections based on that constitution. Scott was Brigade Elections Officer and oversaw a sector with six hundred polling sites and two million voters. The Mississippi Rifles ensured the printing of the constitution in the Iraqi newspaper for readership by the Iraqis prior to their voting. They also helped facilitate safety during all voting by providing physical barriers and protection.

While the Mississippi Rifles were away throughout 2005, Hurricane Katrina struck our state, creating devastation for much of south Mississippi, including our town of Laurel. The Mississippi Guard, normally deployed for state disasters, was thousands of miles away. Some of the Marines from Camp Lejeune, whom the Mississippi Rifles had just replaced in Iraq, took their posts in Mississippi and Louisiana following the disaster, and seventy Mississippi Rifle soldiers whose homes were destroyed by the storm were sent home for a couple weeks.

Though Scott was not home for Christmas that year, our Christmas tree was covered with yellow ribbons, American flags, and red, white, and blue miniature lights that could be seen from our front living room window. We left the tree up until his homecoming in early January and tied large yellow ribbons on our oak trees in the front yard as we marked off the days until his return.

Homecoming day, January 2006, arrived, and dozens of friends joined us at Camp Shelby to welcome the returning buses with the Citizen Soldiers, about to set foot again on Mississippi soil. As they unloaded, I thought with tear-filled pride, *Our Citizen Soldiers, America's backbone ever in the backdrop, faithful in war, faithful in peace, now home. Thank you, Lord.*

~Beth Jeanine Wiggins

59

Stranded

Semper Paratus (Always ready)
~Coast Guard motto

I stood at my window and squinted through binoculars as I brought the small island into focus and searched for my daughter and her husband on the sliver of beach. Waves churned into white caps, and the knot in my stomach tightened.

"Do you think I should call the Coast Guard?" I asked my husband.

"Naw, they'll be fine," Jim grunted from behind his newspaper.

"But they could be in danger," I persisted. "We are the only ones who know that Laura and Geoff took the canoe and are camping on the island. What if they can't paddle back in this storm?"

"You're overreacting," Jim mumbled as he turned to the sports page.

Was I being a drama queen? What if they were in danger? Should I call for help?

The day before, when the couple arrived for the weekend, Laura proposed a plan to Geoff. "Let's take advantage of Florida's sunny weather and paddle the canoe to that spoil island in the distance. We can take a tent and sleeping bags and stay overnight." Her eyes twinkled with excitement as seagulls squawked and lazy sailboats moved along the calm Intracoastal Waterway. Within the hour, they were on their way, and before long the green canoe was a speck on the beach.

By morning, the weather had changed. Dark clouds hung low in the gray sky, and stiff winds stirred the water.

"Something is wrong. They should have returned by now," I said.

Jim lowered his newspaper. "Look, they'll be fine. But if it will make you feel better, give the Coast Guard a call."

Feeling foolish, I looked up the number and dialed.

"Hello. My daughter and her husband took a canoe to a spoil island yesterday, and they're camping there. The water looks too rough for them to paddle back."

"Well, ma'am, there is evidence of a front moving in. Keep an eye on them, and if conditions worsen, give us another call."

I squinted through the field glasses again and suddenly spied Geoff as he pulled the canoe away from the surging surf. He paused, massaged his chin, and looked toward the binoculars.

Notify the Coast Guard again, urged my inner voice.

"Hello, I just called about the couple stranded on the island closest to the Causeway Bridge. You told me to call back if things got worse. They're worse."

"Yes, ma'am, the wind has increased several knots during the last hour. We'll dispatch a rescue boat and arrive at the island in about twenty minutes."

"Thanks… and hurry!"

I watched four men in a small orange and black boat land on the beach. Minutes later, they loaded Laura and Geoff and their camping gear, lashed the canoe to the side of the boat, and then scrambled into the craft.

The boat thrashed about in the choppy seas. Waves crashed over the bow and drenched the huddled passengers. The experienced rescuers fought stiff winds as they maneuvered the boat to our dock and secured it.

"I was worried about you!" I yelled over the storm as I rushed to my daughter with outstretched arms.

"We were worried, too!" said Laura as she shivered inside my hug.

The officer in charge staggered against a violent gust of wind and approached us.

"Are you the lady who called us?" he shouted.

"I hope you don't think I over reacted," I yelled into his ear.

"You didn't overreact! There is no way that couple could have paddled the canoe upwind, against those waves. If you hadn't called, and they had tried to get back, they would have capsized and died of hypothermia within minutes. You did the right thing by calling the Coast Guard!"

The blood drained from my face as I listened to his solemn words.

After a hot shower, Laura snuggled in her pink robe and sipped hot chocolate. "Thanks for keeping an eye on us, Mom. We never would have made it back alive if you hadn't used your good judgment and called for help."

As I put away the binoculars, I was overcome with gratitude for the brave men and women in the Coast Guard who risk their lives daily to rescue others.

~Miriam Hill

60

A Soldier Ahead

Your body will argue that there is no justifiable reason
to continue. Your only recourse is to call on your spirit,
which fortunately functions independently of logic.
~Tim Noakes

In 490 B.C., the soldier Pheidippides ran from a battlefield outside the town of Marathon, Greece, to Athens bringing news of a Greek victory over the Persians. Legend has it that Pheidippides delivered the momentous message *"Niki!"* (victory), then collapsed and died.

This was to become the inspiration for the Marathon.

Today, two and a half miles have been added to the Marathon. Unlike Pheidippides, who, after shedding his packed gear, still wore up to forty-eight pounds in weapons and uniform, the average marathon walker does it in nylon shorts, a tank top, and running shoes, with a total average weight of three pounds, usually finishing in less than eight hours.

My brother, Cpt. Van Allen Zallee, did his 26.2 in under seven hours, wearing his Army Combat Uniform (ACU), boots, and his standard Expert Infantryman Badge (EIB) ruck (35 pounds) in the Portland Marathon, to let people know that the Guard was here, doing the job of keeping Americans free and safe.

Keeping pace with 1,700 civilian walkers, Captain Zallee was the only man in uniform.

The majority of the 6,500 Guard members in Oregon don't get

paid to do their physical training, but they get up early anyway before heading off to their jobs to run, hit the gym, and keep themselves physically prepared.

Still, the second half was hell. Van was hurting the whole way. At one point, I asked him how he was doing. He said, through clenched teeth, "Every step hurts." I asked if he could make it, and he replied, "I have no choice."

Mothers came up to Van along the route, giving him hugs, telling him about their boys in the Middle East. Grandmothers cried as they hugged him, thanking him for serving.

When they asked why he was doing this, Van replied that it was to let people know that the Guard was out there training. "We always are," he told them. "Sometimes, you just don't know that the guy running through your neighborhood before dawn is running to stay at his best for the next call to serve."

Another mile would pass, and someone would ask how much his ruck weighed, and then a few seconds later one would hear, "But… why?" Then he would tell them the same thing he'd said fifteen minutes earlier, "To let you know the Guard is out here training for you, ma'am."

When you walk a marathon, you start with thousands and soon end up in a small group, all keeping the same pace.

Strangers.

Faces and names that became friends by the end of the day.

Flo gave him salt at Mile 18. Walter, a Vietnam veteran, kept crying out, "You can do it, Ranger!" And even though, as Walter put it, he "hadn't worn a pair of Uncle Sam boots" for two decades, they were brothers that day.

While resting at the finish line, stretching his legs and rubbing shoulders that had supported his pack for the last seven hours and twenty-six miles, several walkers came up to Captain Zallee and thanked him. They told him that they'd wanted to give up when their legs ached and their feet burned with blisters, but as long as they could see "that soldier" ahead, they knew they could make it.

"At that point," Zallee would laugh, "I'm just really happy that I didn't quit."

Military historian Edward S. Creasy, in his classic book, *The Fifteen Decisive Battles of the World*, wrote: "The day of Marathon is the critical epoch in the history of the two nations. It broke forever the spell of Persian invincibility, which had previously paralyzed men's minds."

Now, as we find ourselves in another "epoch" battle, it's more important than ever that the men and women of America (and the world) know that the American military is here, that it's prepared, and that it's ready and able to fight for their freedom…

There will always be a soldier ahead.

~Perry P. Perkins

61

Trainee Childers

*Success comes from knowing that you did your best to
become the best that you are capable of becoming.*
~Coach John Wooden

I never knew what I could do until I went through basic training
in the U.S. Air Force. Imagine being eighteen, fresh out of high
school, never having left home, and suddenly being uprooted
and sent to a different state, with no means of contacting family
and friends. From my first day off the bus to my graduation day, I
endured challenges I never knew I was capable of overcoming.

Two months may go by in the blink of an eye in the "civilian
world," but in basic training, two months is an eternity. Every day,
my fellow brothers and I would reminisce about where we were from
and the first thing we would do or buy after graduation. In a place
where literally everybody is screaming and pushing you to your limits,
those short talks each day were like therapy to us. Being able to vent
to people who know 100% what you're going through is something
special and rare outside of military life.

Every evening, when our instructor handed out mail, the tears
would flow, even from grown men. I had friends who had left kids
behind, hoping to be a better provider for them after graduation. They
shed tears of joy and pain as they received pictures of their families
and kids.

Sunday church was my get-away. The instructors weren't allowed
to enter, so for one hour a day we were free from all the chaos. Every

Sunday my fellow trainees and I would gather at the altar and just cry, thinking of our families and loved ones. Thinking back on it now, those were beautiful moments. Normally, those kinds of bonds with people aren't formed in such short amounts of time, but when one lives with somebody for two months and spends literally every waking minute with them, those bonds just sort of come naturally.

Every day, my motivation was getting to see my father again. During every mile we ran, every hardship we endured—even while being tear gassed—the thought of seeing him again was what kept me motivated. I was only eighteen, and I wasn't married with children, so being able to hug my father was the most blissful thought I could imagine.

After eight long weeks, it was finally time for the coining ceremony and graduation. I had only been able to speak on the phone to my family twice for fifteen minutes the entire two months I was gone. After what was the proudest moment in my life—receiving my Airman's coin and shaking my instructor's hand—I was finally able to see my family. As I waited for them to find me, I anticipated the moment I would see my father. When I finally did, I was surprised I wasn't in tears like I had imagined. In that moment, I realized I wasn't the kid who left for training two months prior. All the hardships I had endured had molded me into a man, and judging by the smile on my father's face, a man he was proud to see standing before him.

Spending the weekend catching up and visiting with him and the rest of my family was just as blissful as I expected. To be able to say I had done something that few people my age have done meant the world to me. I was an American Airman.

~Jesse Childers

62

Full Circle

Don't simply retire from something;
have something to retire to.
~Harry Emerson Fosdick

ebruary 16, 1991, was a cold, stormy day that delayed a young soldier's flight from San Francisco to the Republic of South Korea for twelve hours. The soldier was starting his new life in the Army, and this was the farthest he had ever been away from home.

As the soldier sat at the gate pondering what to do or where to go, an older man approached him. The gentleman, named Adam, was wearing a Vietnam Veteran hat, a USO shirt, and a warm smile. Adam asked the young soldier if he knew what the USO was. He explained that the USO had been special to him and his buddies by giving them a break away from the daily horrors of Vietnam.

Adam invited the young man to the USO center at the airport. The soldier followed quietly, not really knowing what to expect. At the center, Adam turned to the soldier and handed him a phone, encouraging him to call home and let his parents know what was going on. The hours passed quickly at the USO, and soon it was time for the soldier to depart.

The flight was long; the country was a strange mix of smells and sights. His new unit swiftly whisked him away. He was introduced to his sergeant who explained that the rest of the week would be full of briefings, classes, ranges, and an orientation to what would be his new home for the next year. After explaining the do's and don'ts of the new unit, the sergeant told the young man to follow him. The sergeant led the man on a brisk walk to a nearby building. As they drew near, the soldier noticed something a bit familiar. Emblazoned on the doors was a large sign reading "USO." For the next year, the USO became a home away from home for the soldier.

The soldier enjoyed the Army life, and so began his journey. Over the years of changing duty stations, the soldier could always count on the USO as being a place to relax while traveling through airports. The young man rose through the ranks to sergeant, and soon learned he was on orders to go overseas once again. He found himself in war-torn areas like Bosnia-Herzegovina and Kosovo, leading young soldiers. The sergeant ensured his soldiers were able to get away from the daily routine of patrol and guard duty by visiting the USO. The service members were able to enjoy soda, hot dogs, and other snacks that gave them a break from the dreaded Meals Ready to Eat. Phone card competitions — when soldiers competed in trivia games in order to "win" coveted cards to call home — were prized the most.

The soldier continued to rise through the ranks of his Army career and found himself in places that most people only read about — Baghdad, Iraq, and Mihtarlam and Kandahar, Afghanistan. Each place offered something familiar: a USO to get away from the stress of combat. Even when this soldier was deployed to areas that did not have a USO center, the USO still reached out to him and his soldiers, whether it was through performances by Toby Keith and the Lt. Dan Band, or care packages.

Soon, this soldier was at the end of his career. Retirement was odd. One day, he was making decisions, giving guidance, and sharing a type of bond only soldiers know; the next, he was sitting at home with no decisions to make and no guidance to give.

Once again, this now retired soldier would learn that life is one big circle. Exactly twenty-five years to the day after he first encountered the USO, that soldier is paying it forward. That soldier is me. And I have the honor of managing the USO center at Pōhakuloa Training Area — a remote and desolate location on the Big Island of Hawaii — where we provide a home away from home to the young men and women of our Armed Forces.

~Jody Brissette

63

How to Say Goodbye

Man's feelings are always purest and most glowing
in the hour of meeting and of farewell.
~Johann Paul Friedrich Richter

I kept an eye on my watch as noon passed, then 12:30, and soon 12:45. It was almost 1:00 p.m., almost time to load up the buses and head out. The past few weeks had been a whirlwind of exercises, rehearsals, briefings, and other tasks, all meant to prepare us as soldiers of the Army National Guard's 29th Infantry Division for our deployment. Despite all the training we had completed, there remained one outstanding topic that hadn't been covered — how to say goodbye.

My family and I had found a spot on the curbing in the Fort Belvoir, Virginia parking lot to sit and enjoy the lunch that had been provided for soldiers and their families immediately after our official departure ceremony. Our meal was about as "American" as it gets. Slow-cooked and finely chopped barbecue with the perfect amount of sauce. Piping hot baked beans with bits of bacon and spices mixed in to awaken the taste buds. The coleslaw was crisp and cool, just as it should be. The food was outstanding, but the swirl of emotions amongst my group as we ate our meal made for a rather bittersweet atmosphere.

Both of my parents, one of my sisters, two of my grandparents, and even an uncle from Georgia were there with me. My other sister had watched the ceremony and now joined us for lunch via FaceTime from her home in California. I felt happy and fortunate that my family was healthy enough and able to travel the distance to Belvoir to be with me, but I felt bad for them, knowing how sad they were.

My thoughts raced as we ate, and I wondered what my family was thinking. There were awkward silences and an element of emotional uncertainty floating about. I knew that my granddad and uncle were excited for me as both men are veterans. As a child, I remember my granddad in particular recounting some of his many stories from his time in the service. I could tell that he was excited about the grand adventure I was about to embark on. He knew that I would be having the opportunity to experience what few others in our society do. Soon, I would have my own stories. His composure and quiet demeanor told me that he was not worried. My grandmother, on the other hand, was worried — a lot. I'm thankful she was able to manage those fears and be strong and resilient that day as this made my pending departure easier.

12:50. It was time for me to go. Everywhere I looked, I saw soldiers saying goodbye. Husbands struggled to console their wives, and departing wives hugged their husbands, knowing that they would be separated for up to a year. Birthdays would be missed, along with anniversaries, weddings, Thanksgiving, Christmas, Easter, and Fourth of July fireworks. Siblings, boyfriends, girlfriends, children, and friends all watched as the buses began to fill up. I turned to my family and told them, "Well, I'll see y'all when we get back. Love ya." I hugged everyone and made my way to my assigned bus to join my new Army family.

Shortly after 1:00 p.m., our convoy of eleven buses began to move. We were escorted by members of the Patriot Guard Riders, a group of veteran motorcyclists. They donned big VFW jackets covered with patches from units they had served with and insignia from wars they had fought long ago. I am grateful for their quiet professionalism and continued service. They spoke not a word to us nor sought to be recognized for their actions. Their bikes were rigged with the largest American flags, along with red, white, and blue streamers making it clear to anyone who looked our way that they were leading the most noble of processions.

Our families gathered along the roads and waved us off with small American flags. As we exited Belvoir's main gate and turned onto the Fairfax County Parkway, the post police raced ahead with sirens blaring and lights flashing, holding traffic at the intersections. Our buses continued through all of the red lights without delay as motorists traveling in the opposing direction waved out their windows and honked their horns. Some even stopped in the middle of the road, got out of their cars, and gave us two thumbs up while nodding their heads in respect. Though they may not have known what unit we represented or where we were going, they knew somehow that we were soldiers and we were leaving.

As we rounded the curve of the on-ramp for I-95 northbound, our Fort Belvoir police escort was relieved by an arsenal of mounted Virginia State Police troopers parked just to the south of our merge point. I couldn't believe that the troopers had actually stopped traffic on this major East Coast thoroughfare for just a few buses. The police followed us and guarded every entry and exit point between the Parkway and Washington Dulles International Airport. The highway was like a ghost town as there was not a single car in sight that could possibly hinder our movement.

When we arrived at the airport, our buses pulled directly onto the tarmac, and we set to work unloading and staging our gear for the flight. The Boeing 737 soon arrived and taxied into a parking spot, its wingspan looming over us like tiny ants as we stood watching. Almost immediately, we climbed the stairs to board the massive jet and took our seats. There was no ticketing, no long security lines, and no pat-downs — just the occasional barrel of an M2 .50-caliber machine gun to step over as soldiers walked down the aisle to find a seat. Our flight was marked by the best crew known to man, as they offered us four rounds of drinks (non-alcoholic, of course) and a slew of Oreos, chips, peanuts, pretzels, and coffee. They truly went to great lengths to make us feel comfortable and welcome.

As we descended the stairs of the plane at our destination, a colonel greeted each of us, offering a firm handshake and a hearty "Welcome!" So began the next chapter of our deployment. "29, Let's Go!"

~Matthew W. Mawyer

64

Serving Those Who Serve

The purpose of human life is to serve, and to show
compassion and the will to help others.
~Albert Schweitzer

Some young people enlist in the military to figure out what they want to do with their lives. Others make serving a life goal that they pursue intentionally. Such is the case with my son, Gabriel, who spent his childhood playing war games. As a teenager, he was a member of the Civil Air Patrol. Completing his Search and Rescue training, becoming a certified First Responder, and reaching the rank of Lieutenant (when he achieved his Billy Mitchell award) were just some of his early accomplishments. Although his best friend had accepted a commission into the United States Air Force Academy, Gabriel's desire was to begin serving right out of high school as an enlisted Airman. He intended to work his way through the ranks as his grandfather and great-uncle had before him.

During his Basic Military Training, he developed a pretty severe case of bronchitis, but was still able to graduate without being held back. We knew he was disappointed not to have achieved honor graduate status, but were not really surprised when the honor graduate from his flight stopped by to chat with us while we were enjoying lunch after the graduation ceremony.

"Gabriel really helped me through this whole basic training and made it possible for me to achieve this award," he shared. It is very much in my son's character to help others reach their goals — even if his own aspirations end up on the back burner.

Over the next two years of his active duty, he was proud to have been "coined" five times by a variety of his superiors and to have attracted the favorable attention of a three-star general at Maxwell Air Force Base in Alabama. In the fall of 2012, he was excited to find that he was being deployed to the Middle East. He had always enjoyed traveling and experiencing different cultures.

We knew that he had been experiencing some grave health issues, and growing up in a military family myself, I understood the seriousness of the call I received. He was being medically evacuated to Landstuhl Regional Medical Center for treatment.

I began to make the arrangements necessary to get to his side as quickly as possible. The Colorado Springs area, where we live, is a military town surrounded by Peterson Air Force Base, Schriever Air Force Base, Fort Carson, the North American Aerospace Defense Command (NORAD), and the United States Air Force Academy, and it seemed that everyone I encountered that day was filled with compassion and understanding. At the credit union, the teller seemed upbeat and interested as I made my withdrawal.

"Big plans for the weekend?" she asked kindly.

"Heading overseas," I replied with tears brimming in my eyes.

"Where to?" she countered.

"To see my son in Landstuhl…" The "Germany" caught in my throat, and I couldn't say more.

Immediately assessing my situation, she replied, "I was born at Landstuhl. Quite a complicated delivery they tell me. All the best doctors in the world are there, and I'm sure he is getting the very best care possible."

Words were impossible for me, but as I completed my transaction, she spoke encouragingly again. "I'll be praying for you both."

How thankful I was that she seemed to know the situation was dire and didn't ask for details that I couldn't share.

Within twenty-four hours of the initial call, I had boarded a flight to Germany. While on the plane and waiting in line for the lavatory, the man behind me asked amiably, "Where are you headed?"

"To Landstuhl," I replied, almost choking out the "visiting my son."

"I spent some time there many years ago," he replied reflectively. "I'm glad you are able to go. The doctors there are all top-notch. Thank your son for his service for me."

After the plane landed in Frankfurt, we waited to get off the aircraft. Finally, the pilot announced, "There's been a delay with the plane sitting at our gate. We will disembark here, and shuttles will take you from the tarmac to the terminal." As I boarded the shuttle and sat down, the woman behind me asked cheerfully, "What brings you to Germany?"

"My son has been admitted to Landstuhl," came my vague reply. After a quiet moment, her husband leaned forward and put his hand on my shoulder.

"Would you mind if we pray for you? I'm a retired military chaplain..." I nodded my consent, not trusting that I could actually form the words to reply.

When we arrived at the terminal, the chaplain asked, "Is anyone planning to meet you at the airport?" Shaking my head, the realization dawned that while my focus had been on getting to Germany, I had neglected to make plans for getting to Landstuhl or for where to stay once I arrived.

"Follow us," the chaplain directed. "We'll get you through customs and take you to the USO."

Falling in line behind them, we arrived shortly at the USO. A spot on a van headed for Ramstein Air Base and Landstuhl was secured for me, and along the Autobahn, I marveled at the serene landscape filled with vibrant autumn colors and dotted with white farmhouses, all with identical red roofs. Appearing to be generations old, yet as if ordered to uniformity, they all looked indistinguishable. Maybe my mind simply couldn't process differences, but I allowed the scene to lull me into a calm.

The van driver dropped off each of the other passengers before me when we arrived at the gate of Landstuhl, obviously the last stop on his route.

"Do you have your orders?" he questioned me.

"Oh, I'm not in the military," the words stumbled out. "I'm here to see my son who has been admitted to the hospital."

"Didn't you get an e-mail with instructions from the Red Cross?" he inquired.

"No, I didn't even think to wait for that," I admitted. "I just got here as quickly as I could."

He seemed mildly surprised, but since there was no one else to drop off, he came with me to the gate. After explaining the situation to a few different people, a passerby overheard the dilemma and offered to sponsor me onto the base. Once through the gate, we walked across the street to the hospital, and he gave me directions to the information station.

I was escorted to the elevators and through long hallways toward my son's room. The large biohazard notice on his door took me by surprise, but the assisting nurse explained that he was in isolation. My belongings would remain in the hall, and everyone entering his room was required to "gown up" — including gloves, booties and hairnet — "as a precaution," they said.

My cell phone battery had died during the trip, so I was unable to call ahead to announce my arrival before I reached his bedside. Nothing could have prepared me. I looked down at my young warrior son — emaciated, yet lying peacefully asleep with wires and tubes attached to his frail, broken body. Could this really be the same young man who had so recently run a ten-mile race through Garden of the Gods? No, this shrunken version of that young man was more reminiscent of his ten-year-old self — the little boy who dreamed of growing up to be a hero.

Suddenly, realizing his nurse was attempting to update me on the specifics of his care, diagnosis, and treatments, I strained to comprehend all that she was saying.

"I'm sorry," she said. "He tried to tell me that you were coming, but I thought he was hallucinating. Let's see if we can rouse him."

She moved closer to the head of his bed and placed a gloved hand gently on his shoulder.

"Mr. Lorrig," she said, giving him a gentle nudge. "Your mother is here to see you."

His blue eyes blinked open a few times, unseeing, and then he was able to focus.

"You're here," he whispered. "I knew you would come."

The next morning, the doctor on his rounds caught me in the hall.

"I'm so glad you came when you did," he shared. "Yesterday, we were not sure he would make it through the night. But I'm glad to see him still here today — and I think he is going to make it."

It was a long month of treatment and recovery until Gabriel was stable enough to return to the United States for continuing treatment. Three years later, he is medically retired, finishing up his bachelor's degree and reaching toward some new life goals.

~Donna Lorrig

65

Behind the Iron Curtain

History studies not just facts and institutions;
its real subject is the human spirit.
~Numa Denis Fustel de Coulanges

I t was cold and gray when I arrived in Frankfurt, Germany, in
December 1981. A few days later, I received my orders for the
American Forces Network (AFN), Berlin — 101 miles behind
the Iron Curtain.

After working a few years as a radio disc jockey as a teenager,
I joined the Army to use my broadcast experience to entertain the
troops — and to travel the world. I hadn't envisioned Berlin, a divided
city during the Cold War. West Berlin was an island in the middle of
East Germany, and following World War II, it was occupied by the
United States, France, and England; East Berlin was occupied by Russia.

For soldiers traveling from Frankfurt to West Berlin, it was an
overnight ride through East Germany on the Army duty train. "Flag
orders" were issued with one's name, rank, and personal information.

At the train station before boarding, a loudspeaker blared rules
for duty train travel through the East: no photography, no looking out
the windows, which had shades pulled down, no throwing anything
out the windows, no exiting the train when it stopped at checkpoints
in East Germany, and no conversing or making eye contact with any
Soviet or East German personnel.

The train's sleeping cars had bunks, so one could sleep during the
ten-hour ride. At some point during the journey, I just had to sneak

a peek out the window. It was pitch black, and I couldn't see a thing. When we stopped at a station, I could see lights and a few people in uniform on the platform as I discreetly peered out the small space between the shade and the window.

Arriving in West Berlin, a woman from my unit was there to greet me. After a quick rundown at our barracks, she showed me to my room. A life very different from what I was used to in the United States began.

In addition to learning my job responsibilities that first day, one of my new colleagues asked me to a concert that night. He'd interviewed the performer earlier in the week and had free tickets.

Unpacking could wait. I wanted to take in as much of this new, strange place as I could.

My new adventure was underway as we rode the U-Bahn (underground subway) to get to the venue. I learned how to read the map and buy a ticket for the U-Bahn, and how to count to ten in German.

After the concert, we met up with German friends of my colleague. I learned a little more German, had my first taste of *Apfelkorn* (a German liqueur made with apples), and made new friends, who warmly welcomed me with their laughter and stories.

I enrolled in German classes, practicing what I learned at stores and eateries. As an added and unexpected bonus, I married two years later. My husband, an Air Force sergeant I met through work, had two children; a year later, we had another one.

I met Germans who loved and appreciated Americans and enjoyed telling their stories. Others protested with anti-American demonstrations.

Along with strudel and sauerkraut, plenty of stress was served. One day, we had a bomb threat at AFN. We were given notice to evacuate, but first we had to check our work area for a bomb. I had no idea what a bomb looked like, but browsed around for any strange object. Turns out, a bomb was found at the bottom of one of our transmitters located at a different site.

On April 5, 1986, there was a large explosion at the La Belle nightclub in Berlin, well known as a popular American hangout. Two U.S. soldiers and a Turkish woman were killed. The blast injured 230 people, including more than seventy American service members.

The following Monday, a co-worker, noticeably shaken, told me he'd been at La Belle that night, leaving shortly before the bomb went off. He realized it could have been him and felt relief, yet grief.

Tension followed as the U.S. retaliated. My kids evacuated school due to a bomb threat. School buses had machine-gun escorts. We were told to check under our vehicles for bombs before turning the key in the ignition. Things eventually quieted down.

In 1987, President Reagan celebrated America's birthday party for Berlin. After his speech at the Brandenburg Gate, he visited the American Air Force base. Three stages were set up for entertainment before he arrived, and I was honored when asked to emcee one of those stages.

After leaving the military, my husband and I stayed in West Berlin, working for a German radio station founded after World War II. Target audience: East Berlin and East Germany, giving them a view of the news from a western perspective. Many tuned in, although it was forbidden for them to listen.

After ground war broke out in Iraq in 1991, my husband and I were taken off the air as a security measure. The kids went to a German-American school, and it was canceled, so they were home, too. I was concerned about them going to any American institutions, but pretty much everything closed for a short while, even the American church.

The night my husband was back on the air, there was a bomb threat at the radio station. He also received some threatening letters. Fortunately, none turned out to be real.

My house was located a half-mile from Potsdam, East Germany. The Berlin Wall was a chain-link fence in this area, so when I jogged near no-man's land, I watched East German guards patrolling, sitting in a tower or driving an Army jeep on a narrow paved strip. I never thought I'd see the day I'd be riding a bike or jogging on that strip.

On November 9, 1989, the most exciting news came. The East German government announced that restrictions on travel and emigration had ended. I witnessed the fall of the Iron Curtain and the Berlin Wall. As a journalist, I helped print and broadcast media in the U.S.

get interviews and do translations.

A refugee camp was set up near my house. I visited regularly, looking for English speakers for interviews. Many told their stories about leaving the East to make a new life in the West. I still have contact with some of the people I befriended during that time.

I joined the military to travel and see the world. If I hadn't joined the Army, I never would have gone to Berlin and stayed for ten years. My travels during that time took me to twenty countries. One weekend, I was invited as a guest DJ at a discotheque in Poland — what a dancing frenzy. I rode a camel in Morocco and went camping near Prague.

It was a wonderful opportunity with many unique, interesting, and tremendous experiences. Had I been asked where I wanted to be stationed, I'd have picked skiing the slopes of Stuttgart or Munich. Glad they didn't ask. If my orders had taken me anywhere else, I would've missed out personally with my firstborn child and historically with a monumental event that, to this day, gives me chills when I say… "I was there."

~Jo Eager

66

Returning the Favor

Unselfish and noble actions are the most
radiant pages in the biography of souls.
~David Thomas

iscipline and respect are two of the core values with which Alex was raised, and they led him to provide help and support to our wounded warriors overseas. His mother told me that from childhood, he dreamed of being in the military. Since he came from a military family, he wanted to follow in his father's footsteps to provide service and protect our country. The military principles of honor, courage and commitment were drilled into him from a very early age.

A few months into his college career, his studies were short-circuited when his mother, who is a friend of mine, was hospitalized with a brain aneurism. As a captain in the United States Coast Guard, Alex's father was away from home on active duty, so, eighteen-year-old Alex became the sole caregiver for his family. He explained that he had to grow up a little faster than others his age.

By the following September, his mother's health had greatly improved. Alex put his college career on hold. Now it was time to start pursuing his personal dream of joining the United States Marine Corps. After he completed basic and combat training, he was moved to the Military Police Academy. Upon graduating, he was stationed for over six years in the Reserve Military Police Company in Lexington, Kentucky. From there he was deployed to Afghanistan in 2010, where he served as part of a security element team that provided transportation for military equipment, supplies, and food.

Alex's life changed forever during a routine mission to bring back a damaged tank. He was riding in a Mine Resistant Ambush Protected Vehicle (MRAP) when it struck an improvised explosive device, an IED. Alex was riding at the top of the vehicle and remembers nothing of the event other than a white flash of light. The next thing he remembers was being in a hospital twenty minutes later.

He could barely talk or see, and he felt as if his back had snapped in two. He had suffered a traumatic brain injury (TBI). Thankfully, he only required hospitalization for seven days, but he spent several more weeks in rehabilitation. He declined the Marine Corps's offer to send him home and chose to finish out his deployment in Afghanistan.

Alex finally came home in April 2011 to open arms and a huge "Welcome Home" party. He received the same support and encouragement from his family and friends he had received from the Marine Corps. He continued working to overcome all the challenges brought on by his brain injury. With much frustration and lots of struggling, he was able to complete his degree in Criminal Justice in May 2011. In this same stretch of time, Alex met and fell in love with his wife, Caroline. He had already accepted an active-duty position with the Wounded Warrior Regiment in Germany. He and Caroline were married just two days before he was shipped overseas.

He felt driven to give back for all the help and reassurance the Marine Corps had given him when he was injured in the line of duty. He not only received the Purple Heart but also the support and encouragement of the entire Marine Corps. He wanted to reach out and advocate for other injured Marines to give them the same compassion he had experienced as a wounded warrior.

In Germany, Alex acted as the first contact for Marines injured in the line of duty. He was their champion/liaison through their initial recovery. Once, he met the plane transporting a double amputee who was so seriously injured he was not expected to live to see his family again. Miraculously, the injured Marine defied all medical expectations and was taken off a ventilator within a few days. Alex and another fellow liaison would sit with him to telephone his family. He could not speak yet, so Alex would hold the receiver to his ear so he could hear his family's voices. The injured Marine would respond by squeezing his fingers. Alex then became the voice of the wounded Marine by speaking his words to the family. He described the scene as being extremely moving.

A few days before the birth of his first child, the Marine Corps let Alex go home to surprise his whole family. The looks of delight and the shouts of joy made it well worth the trip. Alex's wife, Caroline, gave birth to a precious little girl named Charli. It was hard for him to go back to Germany a few weeks later.

There, he felt torn between his family obligation as a new dad and his commitment to the Marine Corp. When the Marines asked him to stay another year, or possibly two, Alex declined. Being with his new family now took precedence.

But how could he balance family life with his desire to serve in the military? He found his answer in the Inactive Ready Reserve (IRR). An individual assigned to the IRR typically receives no pay and is not obligated to attend monthly training periods or participate in any military activities until activated by Presidential Reserve Call-up Authority. Marines in the IRR can elect to drill, train, or return to active status anytime.

Alex wants to use his experiences as a wounded warrior and give back to the Marine Corps for their commitment and support to him during his struggles. A military life remains his dream, and he has indeed found a job where he can assist other wounded warriors with the same exemplary care and support he received when he was injured in Afghanistan. As he puts it, "I'm just returning the favor!"

~Mary Varga

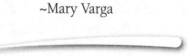

67

A Matter of Time

All men of action are dreamers.
~James Huneker

I knew it was just a matter of time. The moment his little feet hit the floor of the toy department, he went straight for the Army tank with the little toy soldier perched atop. My heart sank. Why not the big colorful beach ball? Why not the coloring books and big box of crayons? What would a barely-three-year-old even know about a tank? I was a good mom! He watched *Sesame Street* and *Blue's Clues*. We went camping and to museums — no tanks there!

But that was just the beginning. As I watched my little boy grow, I watched the destiny of a soldier unfold before my eyes. I taught peace and justice to all my children and in two different Christian congregations. I taught my children to follow their hearts and find their own peace in helping others. Of course, I meant feeding the homeless or caring for abandoned animals (all of which I faithfully modeled).

I knew deep down in my heart that my children would all find their own way. It was obvious in my son's case that service to others meant he would become a soldier. Maybe I shouldn't have indulged him in G.I. Joes and paintball guns. I did feed his artist's soul and his athlete's soul, as well. I tried to foster a musician and a scholar. He showed promise in all of these pursuits, but passion in only one. He never lost his love for that toy tank and little toy soldier.

The day came when he would graduate from high school. I prayed over his college applications, knowing that his academic record would limit his possibilities. When the last of the rejections reached our door, I knew he would be heading out anyway. I begged, pleaded, bribed, cried and cried some more. The day finally came when he left on a beautiful summer afternoon to sign at the recruiter's office. With tears streaming down my face, I said, "Please, Matthew, don't do this."

My baby looked at me with his incredible blue eyes and said, "I'm sorry, Mom, that the thing I want most in this world is hurting you, but I have to do this." The door swung shut, and my heart broke. I was terrified. I had not brought him into the world to die thousands of miles away. It was the "surge" in Iraq, and I knew he would be deployed.

And then something unexpected happened. As I anxiously awaited his return home, I realized that I had known this would happen all along. It was time for me to become the mother of a soldier, the best soldier mom I could be. When my soldier returned, I threw my arms around him and told him I was proud. Scared, but proud, and I would do all I could to support his journey into Army life. He looked at me in amazement — almost in fear that I had lost my mind.

It's a funny time between enlistment and reporting for duty. When my girls went off to college, there was so much to do: shopping for dorm life, haircuts and clothes. With my son, none of these things were necessary, so I had no preparations to work on to help pass the time.

Finally, it was the day when his recruiter would come and pick him up. But I would have none of that. They would not *take* my son from me! I would *give* him to them, so I drove him to the recruiter's office and dropped my son off at the curb.

Once again, I waited. There's a lot of waiting for an Army mom. I'm sure I needed that first call from boot camp more than Matthew did. It was the only phone call I would receive during the thirteen weeks, and I had no idea what to expect. When the phone finally rang, I was in tears before saying hello. He was limited in what he could say, but a mom knows her children, and I could tell that this recruit had already found his way.

The letters started to arrive. How odd to receive a letter from your child in this age of e-mail and social media! I took great comfort in his words. They spilled across the paper with excitement and pride. "I can't believe they are paying me to do this," he wrote.

He received his MOS (job assignment) shortly before graduation. Mortar Man. That's right — he was to be the soldier perched atop the tank. I sighed and thought, *It was just a matter of time.*

The entire family went to graduation. I had given birth to our three children within four years, and we had sat through many graduations and award ceremonies in the recent past. His sisters were strong academically, and Matthew had spent many hours patiently sitting through ceremonies where they were honored. As his ceremony began, we saw one recruit being brought out in front of the others. It was Matthew, the honor graduate of his platoon. His sister turned to me and whispered, "It's Matt's turn." On that beautiful fall day, with the tanks showing off their maneuvers and the graduates showing new bodies and new pride, I watched destiny fulfilled.

~Gloria Orioles Talbot

68

Push Me Higher

Fear can keep a man out of danger but
courage only can support him in it.
~Thomas Fuller

As I sat in the Denver airport, on my way to Oklahoma to speak at a women's retreat, my cell phone rang. It was my husband, Bruce. "Sarah has her commissioning ceremony for the Air Force on Monday, and she wants us to go," he said.

I was stunned. Our oldest daughter, Sarah, was fiercely independent. At twenty-eight years old, in the middle of her doctoral studies in psychology, she had decided that she wanted to help soldiers returning from Iraq with post-traumatic stress disorder. Her husband, Shaun, was all for it. Shaun had served tours in Iraq just before he became an EMT. I was glad he was supportive, but I wasn't convinced that my daughter would be safe in the military while our country was at war.

"I thought they weren't taking her until next fall," I stammered into the phone.

"They aren't, but they're swearing her in right away. She wants us to be there. We'll have to leave early Monday morning. It's a four-hour drive to Sacramento. Will you be up for it after traveling all weekend?" Bruce asked.

"I wouldn't miss it," I replied.

As I sat in the airport reviewing my notes for my talks at the retreat, my thoughts turned toward Sarah. *Where would she be stationed? She* had assured us that her work would keep her out of harm's way, but I knew our daughter. She was the little girl on the swing set yelling, "Push me higher, Mommy. Now, let go!" I knew she would volunteer for hazard duty. I was concerned about her stress level, too, while dealing with so much stress in others. I hadn't shared these concerns with her because I never wanted to be a meddling mother. If she believed she was supposed to help soldiers, who was I to get in her way?

"I need the peace to handle this," I prayed honestly as I heard the loudspeaker in the airport announce that my flight was boarding.

The flight was brief and I soon found myself busy with the wonderful Southern women at the retreat, but my mind kept drifting to my daughter. The second night, after I spoke, the pastor's wife, Ami, approached me and asked, "Is everything okay? You have been very busy speaking and counseling the ladies here, but I think it's my turn to pray for you."

Her compassionate invitation was all I needed. I shared my concerns with her. "I have to confess that I am not crazy about my daughter's enlistment," I offered. "But I don't want my petty fear to get in the way of her call and destiny." Ami placed her hand on my shoulder and prayed that God would give me a sign that would calm my fears. I arrived home late on Sunday evening, drained but fulfilled by a meaningful weekend.

Early the next morning, Bruce and I picked up Sarah and Shaun and headed for Sarah's commissioning ceremony. When every uniformed person in the building had gathered to watch my daughter stand beside the American flag and be sworn into the United States Air Force, I had to fight back the tears.

After lunch, we started for home. Our trip was uneventful until about an hour down the highway when we passed a green sedan driving on the shoulder of the road! We noticed that the driver, an older man, was swerving back onto the highway. As he began weaving in and out of lanes, he clipped a white pick-up truck about four car lengths ahead of us. We watched in what seemed to be slow motion as the truck slammed against the guardrail, sending dust and vehicle parts flying everywhere.

We pulled to the side of the road as my husband dialed 911. Then Sarah leaned forward, tapped her husband on the shoulder, and said, "Are we ready, babe?"

I thought, *Ready? Ready for what?* But before I could ask, Sarah and Shaun had jumped out of our car and run into oncoming traffic. I watched my diminutive daughter's blond ponytail swing in the wind as she flagged down an eighteen-wheeler to tell him about the accident ahead. Then I jumped out of the car and followed her to the crushed pick-up.

There, Shaun was already tending to a three-year-old in the front seat with a cut on her cheek. "I need a cloth or something to put pressure on her wound," he called out.

I rushed back to our car to retrieve a stack of clean napkins that I had accumulated in my glove compartment. All the while, Sarah was calming the driver. Speaking half-English and half-Spanish, she asked the woman for her cell phone and then called the victim's brother to tell him where she was. By the time I returned with the napkins, a California Highway Patrol desk officer from a station near the freeway had spotted the commotion and was on the scene. Clearly out of his element, he seemed to have no problem deferring to Sarah, who was giving everyone orders.

"Do you have a first-aid kit?" Sarah asked the officer. As he handed her the kit, she pointed to the driver of the green sedan. "You need to get that man's keys," she said. "I think he might be deranged. He doesn't need to be on the road." The officer responded immediately.

Sarah dug through the first-aid kit, searching for items she needed to relieve the woman's pain. She kept assuring the victim that an ambulance would arrive soon.

I realized in that moment that I was absolutely useless except to pray, so I moved against the guardrail to get out of everyone's way. As I did, I realized that the sign Ami had prayed for had just unfolded in front of me. I could see clearly that my daughter was not a little girl anymore. She was a grown woman capable of helping people, and I had to let her go so she could do that.

Six years have passed since that day. My daughter served four years as a psychologist in the United States Air Force. Today, she works as a civilian counselor at an Air Force base in Sacramento. She is currently perfecting a protocol that is helping hundreds of soldiers with PTSD. I am proud of my brave and accomplished daughter. I can look at her confident smile and still see the vestiges of the brave little girl on the swing set beckoning, "Push me higher, Mommy. Now, let go!" I'm glad I did.

~Linda Newton

Military Families

Coming Home

69

Getting to Know Dad

It takes a strong person to say sorry, and an
even stronger person to forgive.
~Vanessa Guzman

I knew from a young age that my father had been in Vietnam, and that it had left a mark on him. It had changed him, and not in a good way. I don't remember if this was something my mother told me or whispers I had heard in the family. I just always knew.

As I grew older, I learned about Vietnam in the usual ways — at school and on television — but never from my dad.

My feelings about being the child of a Vietnam veteran took their own path as I grew up. By the time I was a young adult, I was pretty bitter on the subject. I used to tell people I lost my dad six years before I was born. I hated the fact that the children of those who were officially lost in the war had benefits, college scholarships and sympathy. Hadn't I lost my dad, too?

Where was the help for those of us who had to live with parents who brought the war home with them? Instead of embracing his experience, it seemed my dad's time in the service was just a reminder of everything that was wrong with him. On particularly bitter days, I would tell myself that I would never take care of him when he was old, that aging parents would not be a burden on me.

When I was almost forty, I enjoyed a detached, but cheerful relationship with my father. Of his four children, I was really the only one who kept up with him, lived nearby, and tracked him down on Father's Day. We saw each other only a few times a year, even though we lived just twenty minutes apart. I had never been to his house, and he had never been to mine. I had just gotten married for the third time, and he had never walked me down the aisle. But I had come to learn there were things you just didn't expect from him. If I had a flat tire or something like that, I called my husband or uncle, but never my dad.

I did take some interest in his time in Vietnam, mostly because research and documentation were interesting to me. If he wasn't going to tell me, I would just figure it out on my own. I requested his military records and even tracked down some men from his group, reuniting him with one of them in California and getting some great old photos in return. I learned about the Amerasian children and the poor homecoming for those returning from Vietnam. It was a great history lesson.

Then, one July, my uncle called and said my dad had had surgery, and it had gone well. I didn't know he needed surgery or had anything wrong with him, but I made some arrangements at home, packed a bag and headed out for the two-hour drive to the VA hospital. I would probably miss the Independence Day celebration with my kids and husband. On the drive there, I heard on the radio about terrorist threats directed at military bases and other possible targets on this proud American holiday.

I had never been to a VA hospital, but I had heard the bad press. When I walked into this one, I was not pleased. Despite a pretty impressive façade from the parking lot, it looked old and outdated. I was concerned for my father. Would their technology be up-to-date? Would the rooms be clean? Would everything be in working order? I wandered the halls looking for him, and finally found him giving some sweet physical therapists a hard time.

My dad looked twenty years older than he had at Christmas. I had never seen him without a hat, and his hair was thin and messy.

He looked tiny in his baggy hospital gown, and his hands shook as he tried to perform the tasks they requested. One of the women pointed me out and asked who I was. He said I was his daughter. As I watched them finish their session, I found myself holding back tears, overcome with emotions I hadn't expected. The therapists asked me whether his walk was any different. Had his right leg always been weaker and stiff? I didn't know the answers.

Over the next few days, my dad held my hand and cried. He apologized for his shortcomings. He told me about climbing poles to connect antennas during enemy fire, taking some shrapnel in his arm and his friend cutting it out. He talked about his memories of Vietnamese children and how excited he was on his trip home between his two tours. He told me stories about me when I was little. Every nurse, therapist, and passerby either shook his hand or thanked him for his service. Everyone had a story about a son or brother or dad like mine. I slept in a recliner next to his bed. I cut up his food and held a straw to his lips.

When Dad was sleeping, I would kill time walking around the hospital. The walls were covered with stories and history. Lots of people wore yellow ribbons or dressed in red, white and blue. No one was too busy or in a bad mood. Everyone — from doctors to janitors — had a friendly word and a warm smile. Everything was clean; everyone called me "ma'am." The idea that the entire building was full of veterans taking care of veterans was a little overwhelming.

When we woke up the morning of July 4th, I walked down to my car for a change of clothes. Overnight, the parking lot had been transformed, with hundreds of flags covering the equivalent of several football fields. My family and friends had been sending well wishes, many commenting that they felt sorry for me being stuck in such a place for the holiday. But I couldn't imagine a better place to be. No one here cared about fireworks or barbecues, but there sure was a lot of American spirit and patriotism.

I spent three days there with my dad and later had him moved to a rehabilitation facility near my home. It was the most time we had ever spent together. He may not have remembered my birthday or put me through college, but he would have died for me. He would have died for all of us.

~Cherilyn Hindle Hearn

70

Homecoming

The desire for safety stands against
every great and noble enterprise.
~Tacitus

I frantically tore open the envelope. I hadn't received a letter in more than a month. "Please, Lord, please let my son be okay." I yanked out the letter and scanned the contents.

"David, David!" I shrieked.

He ran into the kitchen, "What is it? What's wrong? Why are you crying?"

"He's coming home."

Two weeks later, I sat in the cushioned seat at the airport security area. I hadn't realized until then how much tension I kept inside me.

Three months earlier, I watched the news in our family room and got yet another update on Operation Iraqi Freedom. The news feed across the bottom turned horrifying: "Huey helicopter down — no survivors... Huey helicopter down — no survivors..."

I sat frozen, afraid to move. That was the helicopter Joshua was assigned.

There was no more information than that. There was nothing I could do. So, I called my husband at work. I didn't know if he could talk while working patrol, but I tried anyway.

When he answered, I blurted out, "David, the news said a Huey went down. What should I do? What if it's Joshua's? You know there are only eight or nine out there. I don't think I can handle this."

"It's okay. Try to stay calm. I'm so sorry I can't be there. All we can do is pray. Pray he's okay. I'm being called to an accident. I have to go. I love you, and hang in there. I'll try and call later. Bye."

Pray. That's all I could do? "Please let Joshua be safe." I stopped. *If Joshua was okay, what about the families of those lost?* I added, "and lift up the families of the fallen crew."

Only ten minutes had passed since the news flashed across the screen. An hour later, I talked with an officer. He informed me I had twenty-four hours to wait. I would hear by phone if he was injured, a knock on the door if it was my ultimate nightmare.

Somehow, I made it through the night and went to work the next day. I felt like a machine on autopilot. Students filed in, then out. *One class down, four to go.* I greeted my students and taught my lessons.

Finally, the school bell rang. It was 2:30 p.m. Twenty-four hours had passed with no news. He was okay. I laid my head on my desk and cried — in sadness for the families who had lost their warriors and in gratitude for the knock that never came on my door.

Now I sat in the airport, about to see my boy. I watched as my family talked quietly while they held balloons, flowers, and a large banner with "Welcome home, Joshua" painted across it in red, white, and blue paint. I smiled.

My legs started to ache from sitting. I stood slowly and walked to the arrival-and-departure board.

"He's landed. You guys, he's finally here!"

We all ran back to the exit from the security area. My heart pounded. I wanted to yell to everyone that my son was home.

I strained to see the boy I loved and missed for so long. A sign warned everyone to stay behind the wide yellow line. But when a tall, thin, young man with auburn hair and a big smile came into view, I sprinted down the walkway anyway and jumped into his arms.

Then I stood back and looked into his face just to make sure he was real. It was definitely Joshua, but he looked different. I saw a weariness in his face, and I could feel his bones in my embrace. His smile held a bit of sadness along with the joy.

He slowly picked up his bag as everyone in the waiting area stood and chanted, "USA!"

Arm in arm, we walked back to the others. I found my way to my husband, grabbed his arm, and whispered, "Our boy's home."

~Dianna Beamis Good

71

The Bombs Bursting in Air

*The stronger a man is, the more
gentle he can afford to be.*
~Elbert Hubbard

grew up in Southern California, and my family often made pilgrimages to Disneyland, Knott's Berry Farm, and Sea World. The highlight of those park visits for me was always the evening festivities, when there would be fireworks.

As I grew older and more observant, I noticed that my grandfather would go missing just before the fireworks were scheduled to start and reappear shortly after they finished. I asked my mother about this and was told that Grandpa didn't like to hear the noise of the explosions. They reminded him of the war, so he went inside the bathrooms until they were done. The way she said it seemed to indicate that some in the family felt that Grandpa was being overly dramatic, and that they merely tolerated him excusing himself from the shows.

One summer night, somewhere near my tenth birthday, my family and I exited a ride just in time to hear over the loudspeakers, "In only two minutes, the lights will be dimmed around the Rivers of America, and Disneyland will present their fireworks spectacular in the skies over the park." Grandpa was just in front of me, and when he heard the announcement, he started jogging ahead without a word to anyone. Without really thinking, I took off after him, against the orders of my mother, who repeatedly called after me to stay with the rest of the family. Grandpa, unaware that I was behind him, tried desperately to weave through the masses of people who were stopped in the street waiting for the show to begin.

As he tried to reach the restrooms, the first shell broke in the skies above us. Grandpa startled and shuddered like he had been hit by a shot, then kept moving forward. As shell after shell burst overhead, my grandfather reeled and stumbled, barely keeping his footing long enough to collapse onto a bench nearby. Instantly, I was by his side, and when he looked up at me in surprise, I saw fear on a face that had only shown strength and kindness before. I grasped his hand in mine. It was trembling and seemed suddenly much more frail than I remembered.

Grandpa sunk into my arms. His breath was labored and quick, and he wept soundlessly. I kept perfectly still and didn't utter a word. Absorbed in the show, no one noticed us on that bench as we sat for what seemed like hours… a child cradling a grown man.

When the last volley of the finale had died away, my grandfather straightened abruptly and wiped the tears from his eyes. He composed himself for just a moment, and then put his arm around me and hoarsely said, "Thanks, Smokey." Seconds later, he was on his feet, brusquely declaring that we should find the others and leading me away by the hand. His strong hand once again enclosed all of mine.

Heading off through the crowds, I knew that I ought to never mention this to anyone and that we would never speak of it again. Still, even now, as an adult, when I hear people say that "real men" don't cry, I wonder if they have ever known a real man… ever seen one… as I did on that night.

~Tamara Bostrom-Lemmon

Greeting the Troops

Sometimes the path you're on is not as important as
the direction you're heading.
~Kevin Smith

I was standing in a field watching my son's soccer game one Saturday morning when I looked up and saw a military cargo jet, so big and gray it might as well have been a whale cutting across the sky in a slow, deliberate arc. I could not ignore the shadow the jet was making on the grass or the grumbling it made in the clouds. It had just taken off from across the street, where the Bangor International Airport and Army National Guard base sit. It is the place where international flights bringing troops to and from points abroad arrive first in the United States. It is also the last place on U.S. soil that many troops see before heading overseas.

I hear the jets several times a day, most of them at night, as my house is just one mile away from the airport and base. First, I hear the whistle of the jet engines. Then there is a grumble and a roar. By the time the airplane is flying above my house, I am thinking, almost reflexively, about all the times my own military husband, Dustin, has left and come home again on one of those same gray jets.

For residents of Bangor, the comings and goings of military jets filled with troops is a regular sight. Because this is not a large military community, however, what those jets mean to the families left at home may sometimes be lost. On outbound flights, for example, when the troops arrive in Bangor and wait for the plane to refuel before beginning the next leg of the trip, they have long since said goodbye to their families. They might technically still be in the country, but for their families, they are already gone.

So when I saw the jet flying above my son's soccer game, I spent a lot of time thinking about the wives and children who were now going to soccer games alone because their husband and father was flying above my head. I thought about wives who said goodbye to their husbands at a military hangar early that morning, then returned home to an empty house and a towel still damp from their spouse's shower. A house never seems quieter than in that moment. There are so many reminders (shoes kicked off at the closet door, a book beside the bed, a wet toothbrush) that the person who is now several time zones away was literally just there with you. And then, of course, I thought about the servicemen and servicewomen who really aren't excited to be flying over Bangor, no matter how beautiful this city is, because they already feel light years away from their home and family.

But that's just when I see the jets headed east.

When I see a jet coming the other way, returning to Bangor before taking off again to take the troops home, I feel a rush of excitement. I think about the wife who is counting down the hours until her husband lands at home in California, Colorado, Virginia or Florida. I picture her trying on twenty different outfits to find just the right one, then combing and re-combing her children's hair and realizing how much they have grown or how many teeth they have lost since their dad saw them last. I think about the men and women on the airplane who can't wait to leave Bangor because then they will finally be headed home.

This morning, I joined the Maine Troop Greeters at Bangor International Airport to welcome home a flight on its way to Colorado. One by one, the Greeters and I shook hands with the returning men and women and said, "Welcome home." Then to one of the young men, I said, "Well, I know, you aren't really home yet, but you are close!"

"After fourteen months away, I can't wait to get back on that plane and go home to my family," the man said. He went through the line of Greeters, and then quickly excused himself to a corner of the lobby to use his cell phone. I knew he was probably calling his wife. I remember receiving those phone calls from Dustin: "I'm here! I'm actually in the United States!" he would say. "I just have to get back on this plane for another leg, and then I'll be there to see you!" My heart would flutter so hard, I'd think it was going to jump right out of my chest.

This morning, I knew there was a wife in Colorado feeling the same thing. And I couldn't have been happier for her. I know that later tonight, when I am getting in bed to go to sleep, another jet will fly above my house, and it will be going the other direction.

~Sarah Smiley

73

Because We're Men

*I hope I shall always possess firmness
and virtue enough to maintain what I
consider the most enviable of titles,
the character of an honest man.*
~George Washington

"**T**ake care of yourself out there, Butthead!" That's the last thing I recall saying to my cousin at his going away party the night before he shipped off to Afghanistan to serve our nation, right as the War on Terror was officially underway. It was September 2001, just days after the 9/11 attacks.

I was trying to remain macho in front of my family, and I fought back the tears when it was my turn to say goodbye. I called him Butthead to cover up my true emotions. After all, Alex and I were "men." He was eighteen, and I was fourteen. Men don't express their true feelings, or so I thought. At age fourteen, I wouldn't have dared to say something deep and heartfelt in front of anyone for fear of teenage ridicule.

The next morning, Alex's plane left for the Middle East. Months passed, and the pain sank in more than ever throughout our family. On Thanksgiving that year, when Alex wasn't there to eat his usual three plates of turkey and mashed potatoes and tell jokes, the room felt a little emptier. The vibe of the evening was completely different, and it wasn't long before everyone took notice. The food didn't taste the same as it usually did that cold November evening.

On Christmas, when Alex wasn't there to light up the room with Santa Claus impersonations, I wanted to cry my eyes out. It was like the life had been sucked out of the holidays. The laughter was gone. The joy was absent. I put on a front for everyone and tried my best to cope with these emotions. I was brave on the outside, but scared on the inside. I spent my nights crying myself to sleep, wondering if he was okay or not. Every time I watched the news about the war, my heart sank.

Four long years passed, and Alex's service was finally over. I remember waiting for him with our families when he flew into the Chicago Midway International Airport to take his first step onto American soil in years.

When Alex returned home, he was different. He was a man. Seeing him walk through the airport terminal in one piece made me realize how lucky I am to have such an incredible family, one whose love was strong enough to bring us through this difficult time and bring us all closer together as a result. Although it had been four long years since our paths had crossed, we picked up right where we left off, and things felt just the way they did before. They say that absence makes the heart grow fonder, and I know this to be true.

Despite being involved in combat, Alex had a pretty smooth transition back to civilian life. By the time he returned home, he was twenty-two years old. He immediately enrolled in college and got good grades. He sought counseling for a very minor case of post-traumatic stress disorder, but in general he was coping well. He was just happy it was over, he was safe, and he was home at last.

One day, Alex and I sat down together and talked about his experiences. He confided that he was terrified every day he was over there. He told me horrific stories of how some of his friends had been killed during battle. He went on to talk about near death experiences that he faced. He said that knowing his family was waiting for him to come home was what brought him through so many terrifying days and sleepless nights. He opened his heart and told me things I can't even bear to write in this story.

I had always looked up to Alex, but I now have even more respect for him. We bonded that day like we never had before, and from that moment forward, things were different between us. We were more than just cousins; we were close friends.

They say real men can't express their feelings, but I beg to differ. Real men do express their feelings. Alex and I don't shake hands anymore; we hug. We even say, "I love you, man" to each other at times. We don't say that because he's going overseas again, or because he's going into combat in a third-world country. Instead, we choose to say it because we mean it. We acknowledge it because we're friends. We know it because we're family. We embrace it because we're men.

~Kevin Matthew

74

No Mission Too Difficult

Problems are not stop signs, they are guidelines.
~Robert Schuller

After three years of trying, Mike and I conceived our first child. Between deployments and field training exercises, somehow we were blessed with this pregnancy.

During my first trimester, Mike spent a total of two months in the swamps of southeastern Georgia training for a possible deployment into Kuwait, for what we thought would be a peacekeeping mission. He was home for most of my second trimester. We decorated our daughter's nursery, attended doctor's appointments, and laughed as the little "alien" grew inside of me. Our families lived in California, 3,000 miles away, so we had each other and the Army community family we had developed over the years.

In my third trimester, Mike went to Fort Huachuca, Arizona, to train for a new Military Occupational Specialty (MOS) — military intelligence. We knew this would offer us new opportunities, as Mike wanted nothing more than to be a Warrant Officer and to continue his career in the Army. We also knew it would be hard with him not being present for the birth of our daughter, but we had seen harder days. We could make it through this.

We arranged for my mother to come to Fort Stewart to be by my side for our daughter's birth. The closer the day came, the more anxious I became.

All I wanted was for Mike to be with me, but that was impossible. There was no way for him to leave Advanced Individual Training (AIT) to come back. I had such mixed emotions. On one hand, I was devastated to be away from my husband, and he was going to miss one of the most important days of our lives. On the other hand, I was so excited to meet my daughter.

The big day came. Amber was six pounds, seven ounces, and simply gorgeous. For a few hours, the only thing I could think about was her, but then I wanted Mike. There was no way for him to see his daughter, and it devastated me.

I took her home on a Friday. My mother and I loaded Amber into the back seat of the car. She was so little, so fragile, I couldn't imagine how I could possibly drive slowly enough to safely get her home. As I pulled into my driveway, I robotically unloaded the car, brought my precious cargo inside, and placed her gently into her basinet where I stared into her tiny face and smiled. "Daddy will meet you soon," I told her.

I barely slept that night. Between trying to breastfeed and checking to make sure she was breathing, I was exhausted Saturday morning. While my mom made breakfast, I attempted to get ready for the day while staring at Amber the entire time. But when the doorbell rang, I took a deep breath and prepared for a day of visitors. I picked up Amber and carried her to the front door where I opened it without peeking through first. If I hadn't been holding a baby, I would have jumped and screamed. There before me was my amazing husband. "Mike!" He walked toward us and wrapped his arms tightly around us. "What are you doing here?"

"I drove all night to get to you. I have to leave in the morning to get back in time for Monday," he told me. I didn't care that he was only going to be home for twenty-four hours. My husband drove 1,957 miles round-trip to see his little girl. Mike and I moved into the family room and sat down on the couch. I placed her on his chest, and I watched with tears in my eyes as he took in his little girl for the first time. He breathed in her new baby smell and held her tight.

I couldn't stop watching as he closed his eyes, and together, they fell asleep. She knew at that moment that her daddy's arms would be the safest place in her world.

~Jamie Handling

75

Travels with Rocky

*Once you have had a wonderful dog, a life
without one is a life diminished.*
~Dean Koontz

"**Y**ou don't need a dog," I said to my married daughter over the phone. Famous last words.

Visiting her Alabama in-laws, Launa had just informed me she found the cutest litter of puppies. "They're so fluffy, like little bears. The dad is a Saint Bernard, and the mom is a Great Pyrenees. The puppy's face looks just like the dog in *Beethoven*."

I pictured Cujo. "But you don't need a dog," I replied, trying to speak like the calm, reasonable mother I sometimes am.

After years of pet bunnies, cats, dogs, and horses, I wasn't surprised my daughter couldn't live without a dog. But soon, after spending six weeks in Air Force technical school, my daughter would join her husband, stationed at Aviano Air Base in Italy.

She didn't need a dog!

But she got him, and she named him Rocky. While Launa attended school in Montgomery, he stayed with her mother-in-law. To this day, if you look closely, you can see tiny teeth marks in the legs of the refined Southern lady's dining room table.

School completed, Launa made one final trip home to Pennsylvania. She scheduled a veterinarian checkup, required within ten days of international travel, for Rocky. A few days later, our daughter left for

Italy from Pittsburgh International Airport. Rocky would follow as soon as he received a clean bill of health. A month later, the paperwork was finally in order, and the dog was ready to join his family.

At 126 pounds, Rocky was too big to fly out of Pittsburgh. Rocky would fly cargo, which meant John F. Kennedy International Airport in New York City.

Early one cold November morning, my husband and I drove east on Interstate 80 with Rocky and a giant, collapsed travel crate in the back of our SUV.

I anticipated crowds of people as we approached the largest city in the United States. New York is known for many things — great restaurants, exciting nightlife, museums — but it is not known for being the friendliest city in the world. Driving down the Van Wyck Expressway, we followed signs to Delta Cargo, passing rows of warehouses. We parked. Planes roared overhead. The faint smell of jet fuel hung in the air. I took a deep breath, coughed, and headed toward a single unmarked door. Blaine and Rocky waited in the parking lot, stretching their legs and watering weeds.

Inside, taped to the glass window, a faded bumper sticker had seen better days. *Remember 9-11.* On a bulletin board on the far side of the waiting room was a wrinkled newspaper photo of firefighters in front of the collapsed World Trade Center. Three people slouched in ripped vinyl chairs, glued to a football game on a wall-mounted television. I spotted a battleship-gray steel door marked Cargo Area and crossed the scuffed floor.

I tapped on the door. No answer. Easing open the door, I stuck my head through the gap. A forklift zoomed by, heading for a pallet of boxes. An open garage door to my left showed the back of a hearse, a casket halfway out.

"Can I help you, ma'am?"

I jumped. "We have a dog scheduled for a direct flight this evening. We're a little early."

The tall man in matching blue pants and shirt flashed a bright smile. "Early's good. Let's get started on your paperwork."

I opened Rocky's folder, which contained an international health certificate stamped in the last ten days, travel papers with Delta, and proof of microchip and rabies vaccination. I certified that Rocky had been fed within the last four hours. I also presented a food dish, water dish, bedding, a gallon of water, and enough dog chow for the trip.

"Where's he headed?"

"Milan. My son-in-law's at Aviano Air Base."

"We take care of our troops. Your dog will be fine. Bring him in so we can get ready." Another bright smile.

I headed back to the waiting room where Rocky and Blaine entertained the gathering crowd. Exhausted from his busy morning, Rocky spread out on the floor. My husband worked on the giant travel carrier.

"What kind of dog is he?" The young man kept a safe distance from Rocky. One would swear he had never seen a dog before.

"He's a Beagle," answered my husband, the comedian.

"A Beagle?" The young man turned to his friend and pointed to the 126-pound animal on the floor. "That's a Beagle."

"That ain't no Beagle."

Obviously, his friend was a little worldlier. He wasn't sure what Rocky was, but he knew he wasn't a Beagle. By the time we moved Rocky and his carrier into the cargo area, everybody was chatting like old friends and patting Rocky on the head.

We left feeling good about Rocky's care and with an enlightened opinion of the city.

Launa called the next day. Hearing the happiness in her voice, I realized we had sent more than a dog to Italy. We had sent a little bit of home.

Rocky's adventures continued once he got settled. When he found a convenient hole under the yard fence, he went traipsing through fields of red poppies in search of… well, who knows… margherita pizza, perhaps. The *polizia* offered him a ride to the nearest pound where Launa found him smiling, as if to say, "This is fun. I'll bet you wish you could ride in the back of an Italian police car." My daughter smiled at the officials, paid the enormous fine, and took Rocky back to her little block house across from the gas station with the red and yellow rosebushes out front.

Soon, Rocky found another hole and visited the Italian country-side and his police buddies once again. By the time we visited, Rocky resided indoors, which is probably what he wanted all along. After all, summer in Italy can be hot, and the marble floors were cool.

Four years later, their tour of duty in Italy ended. Time to return to the States. Rocky weighed 148 pounds. How to get him home?

Cargo. Into JFK.

By then, we too were worldlier. Our daughter Kristen now worked in the city, so our trips had become more frequent. We zipped across the George Washington Bridge and down the Van Wyck Expressway. Except for a tiny problem with paperwork, we soon found Rocky, fluffy tail wagging and barking *Ciao, Mamma*.

The young couple was assigned to Ellsworth Air Force Base. Hmm. How to get Rocky from Pennsylvania to South Dakota?

Road trip.

I rented a compact car for our trip west. I drove. Rocky stretched out in the back seat and snored most of the way.

Today, months later, my son-in-law is in Korea. My daughter is completing a one-month reserve tour in North Carolina before taking a three-month assignment in Georgia. Rocky and I — he with a dog biscuit, I with a cup of coffee — relax on the back porch and reflect on our shared adventures. In a way, when a person joins the military, the family does, too.

My husband says we should have named the dog Boomerang because he keeps coming back. That's okay. The military sends my daughter to faraway places, but Rocky brings her back home.

I guess we did need a dog.

~Tanya McClure Schleiden

76

In the Nick of Time

Every traveler has a home of his own, and he learns
to appreciate it the more from his wandering.
~Charles Dickens

Unpredictable doesn't begin to describe our lifestyle when my husband was flying C-5s. By choice, we lived in a rural area of Dover, Delaware. We could have lived on base, but we always made it a priority to try to live out in the community so that our family could integrate and experience "regular" life as opposed to base life. So we were living on a small farm complete with sheep, chickens, the occasional pot-bellied pig and Amish neighbors.

I learned early on that life would be very different here. Four-day missions turned into month-long excursions with little or no direct contact with my husband. Well-meaning base personnel would call and give us updates that frequently led to tearful disappointments when missions would change, and children who were bouncing with anticipation would have to be told it would be another week... at least. Eventually, I asked them not to call unless they knew for a fact that his plane had crossed that golden line over the ocean that meant it couldn't turn back.

It was situation normal when my husband announced that he would be leaving the day after Thanksgiving for a four-to six-day mission. No big deal, status quo, so we got our Christmas tree early, enjoyed Thanksgiving with friends, and then said our goodbyes. By this time, the farewells barely left a ripple in our days, and we got on with whatever we were doing. Our children were young and homeschooled, so this meant diving into projects and keeping a fairly normal schedule.

This also meant I was on 24/7 duty, and it was getting critical after about two weeks. He wasn't back, and I hadn't had a second to do my Christmas shopping, let alone bake all the goodies my children were dreaming about. Three weeks in, it looked like we were going to be on our own for the holiday. This realization landed me on the front porch of our nearest Amish neighbor, tearfully asking if they would please watch my youngest while I ran out to get everything I needed for Christmas.

Mattie was a beautiful Amish woman, probably in her sixties then, and more than happy to take him in for a few hours. This is someone who helped me chase my sheep when they snuck out of their fence on more than one occasion, taught me about Rhode Island Reds, and shared eggs, canned fruits, baked goods and the occasional recipe. I thought she hung the moon. I tried my best to return these favors, but I was more the type who had to explain that I had baked them a beautiful pie, which had looked great until my youngest son accidentally sat on it.

Over the course of December, I received a couple of calls indicating that my husband might or might not be on his way — which I did not relay to the kids. I wanted to avoid any unnecessary heartbreak. We went ahead and made sugar cookies and a gingerbread house with full gumdrop trimmings, and planned our traditional Christmas Eve dinner of homemade bread and New England clam chowder. The gifts were wrapped and ready to be placed under the tree on Christmas Eve.

Christmas Eve morning, the phone rang. It was a ham radio operator letting me know he had a MARS (Military Auxiliary Radio System) patch call for me. It was my husband letting me know that they had crossed that golden line, and he would be home. I knew he wouldn't call unless he was positive, but I also knew better than to say anything because things change when you least expect it.

I proceeded with our normal Christmas Eve activities. Christmas music and sugar cookies fueled the day while the smell of baked bread filled the house. I put the finishing touches on the table and our soup as the kids played out the Christmas story in the living room. They couldn't wait to take their baths and get into their Christmas pajamas so we could have dinner and read *The Night Before Christmas*.

We sat around our carefully set farm table and said grace, prayed especially for Daddy, and dug into our favorite meal of the year. From where I was sitting at the table, I could see our front door clearly, and there framed in the window stood my husband — tired, scruffy-faced and still in his flight suit. My heart skipped a beat as he raised a finger to his lips to keep me from saying anything. I held my breath as he knocked on the door. Three heads snapped up from their bowls, and our home erupted with shouts of "Daddy's home! Daddy's home! He's really home!" They were at the door before he could get it fully open and were all over him in a second.

We laugh about our "Hallmark Card Christmas" now, but the feelings are still fresh — even twenty-five years later — and all that joy wells up in my heart all over again. Being a military family has its challenges and hardships, but it can have its sweetness, too. I won't pretend it was easy being the one left behind, to hold down the fort or whatever phrase we use to describe the day-to-day. It could be downright hard, but it made those homecomings all the more significant and memorable.

~Susan Mulder

Chapter 9

Military Families

★ The Lighter Moments ★

77

Letters from Boot Camp

*And none will hear the postman's knock without a
quickening of the heart. For who can bear
to feel himself forgotten?*
~W.H. Auden

I knew how he'd play it. When I landed in Killeen, Texas, he wouldn't be among the people crowding the exit gate, anxious to greet their arrivals. He would choose to blend in, to hide in plain view. In the continuation of a game we had been playing for two decades, he would test me to see how long it would take me to spot him, a real soldier this time, not a boy dressed in camo from the military surplus store. My trip to his permanent duty station in Texas was his belated Mother's Day gift to me, and he would make me work for it.

His big grin hadn't changed, and our conversation picked up as if we hadn't been separated by 1,500 miles. As he drove us to the gate at Ft. Hood, my soldier handed me his wallet to retrieve his military ID. The shaved head, tired eyes and zombie-like expression in that photo taken at boot camp in no way resembled the tanned, lean and confident man who had greeted me at the airport with a giant bear hug. Boot camp and training were both well behind him. He was regular Army now, and he carried it well.

I had expected a lot of life changes to hit me in my fifties, but I don't think I was fully prepared to become a new MoMM at that age. That's when I joined the ranks of Mothers of Military Men. Although my rational brain had been preparing, my completely irrational heart still couldn't comprehend what had happened the day we dropped him off with his recruiter. We had said our goodbyes at a highway interchange and delivered him into the hands of strangers.

We knew it would be months before we would catch even a glimpse of him again. I told him that day that I could accept that he was leaving; I just couldn't accept that he would no longer be here. Of course, that made no sense to anyone else, but it seemed like a perfectly logical reaction to me.

Until then, nearly all of our son's big memories had been sewn together by our family's shared experiences. Friends, girlfriends, sisters and even dads don't get what mothers understand. When we send our children off to boot camp, it is the giant, irreversible step out the door and off the map into a world in which we will no longer have a critical role. No matter how close we remain in our histories and our hearts, I knew our two worlds would have new epicenters from that day forward.

He, of course, was fine. It had been his dream to enter the military, and he had been preparing for it in some way nearly his whole life. But boot camp is the training period for new MoMMs, too. I had to practice doing what we do best: waiting. I waited at the mailbox and by the phone for that treasured first call from Fort Sill, Oklahoma. I waited out the days until graduation knowing that boot camp was simply military kindergarten for families waiting at home. It was the thing we needed to prepare us for the next longer separation, the bigger unknown and deeper letting go.

I think on some level my grown kid knew his mother still needed some handholding, and he was great about writing home from boot camp when the opportunity arose. The envelopes arrived stuffed with single sheets ripped from a spiral pocket notepad, notes he scribbled while he stood in line for chow or any of a dozen other hurry-up-and-wait activities that constituted his training days. I've kept them all for his grandkids to read some day, because whatever else might have been changing about him, his sense of humor was still intact. We gained insight when he sent home notes like these:

Day 3: Good evening. I am writing this after lights out so I am in ninja-mode, also known as under a blanket with my red light.

Day 10: It's long and busy days here. Up at 0400 and lights out at 2100. The yelling, a.k.a. the "motivation," is not as bad as they show in the movies.

Day 12: My left boot came apart. I have tough feet. Most of our platoon does not. Am making friends by giving away my moleskin.

Day 14: Did gas chamber today. Wanted to cough up a lung and snot ran out of our noses in buckets. Best thing is, they got it all on video.

Day 15: I have forgotten how to eat slow. My spoon is my friend. It is like a mouth-sized shovel.

Day 21: It was good to live by a farm. The latrines on the range reek. There are 44 soldiers in our bay with various levels of hygiene. For the most part, it doesn't bother me.

Day 22: All the males got bad sunburn yesterday. Our near-bald heads look like big tomatoes on top of our ACUs (a.k.a. our uniforms).

Day 28: Sleep in the Army. Though not officially against the rules, it is strongly recommended that you don't. You don't have to have the discipline to stay awake. The Army does that for you.

Day 31: Carrie Underwood lied. There IS enough wind in Oklahoma. They could make a fortune bottling it and selling at a slight markup. "And for your cooling pleasure, we have a well-aged 2013 Afternoon Gust, bottled March 2nd at the east range of Fort Sill, Oklahoma."

Day 33: Good news, bad news, good news. I ran at the head of Bravo group again today. Bad news: I've been ordered to run with Alpha from now on and they run farther and faster and I vomit at the end of the run. Good news is that being pushed that hard will make my final PT test a breeze. P.S. It's 30 days till Family Day.

And so it went. Since boot camp, communication between us now feels more like conversation, and his scribbled notes have been replaced by more frequent calls and texts, holiday leave and the occasional special visit. I get more information from him while it is still news, but those letters from boot camp are solid gold. That's where I retreat to remind myself that although my son might be committed as a soldier now, I will always be his MoMM — and nobody outranks that.

~Mitchell Kyd

78

One Day, You'll Laugh About This

Hindsight provides new eyes.
~Wayne W. Dyer

It was just an average Monday. I had gotten my kids off to school that morning without incident, which was a monumental victory in my opinion. As lunchtime neared, my phone rang. Glancing quickly at the caller ID, I saw that it was the elementary school my sons attend. I answered immediately, and the nurse's voice came through with a frantic edge to her voice.

"Mrs. Chovan? I've got Noah here… I'm so sorry; he seems to have accidentally eaten some fish! It wasn't on his allergies list, so we didn't know not to give it to him, but now we don't know what needs to be done!"

The hesitation in my voice must have been mistaken for concern because she rushed on, "He's not swelling up that we can tell yet, but I'm sure you'll want to come down. Does he have an EpiPen at home? Or what does he need?"

I was confused. "Why? Why would he need an EpiPen?"

At this point, I imagine the nurse thought I was the worst mother in the world. She nearly growled at me: "He's allergic to fish! He told us! He thought it was chicken but it was fish, and he's allergic!"

And then when I laughed — a deep, full belly laugh — she was probably ready to have me committed as a lunatic. But I honestly couldn't help it. They told me I'd laugh about this someday, and that day had come.

To understand why I was laughing, I have to take you back to the timeframe between May 2011 and May 2012. This was the year my husband, Matthew, was deployed with the Army to Afghanistan. My older children, Harley and Ben, handled the deployment very well, but Noah, four years old, did not.

Matt had deployed before, but Noah had been too young to remember. This time it affected him in surprising ways. His appetite decreased significantly, and he would break down crying in the middle of the day or wake up screaming in the middle of the night. He wouldn't sleep in his own room, insisting instead on sleeping on Matt's side of the bed in our room. He often slept with pictures of Matt or in his old T-shirts. He talked frequently of death or destruction. He complained of body aches constantly, specifically in his heart. Anytime he would speak with Matt over the phone or through Skype, he would be physically sick afterward. At best, he would complain of a stomachache; at worst, he would throw up violently and then cry himself to sleep.

In November 2011, Matt was nearing the halfway point in his deployment and he would be home for Christmas. As a fun distraction for me and the boys, I decided to make a trip home to Florida to see our family for Thanksgiving and Ben's birthday. On Ben's birthday, we all sat down for a quick lunch, at which we served fish. In the middle of lunch, the computer began to ring with a Skype call. It was, of course, Matt.

We all quickly abandoned our lunch and went to talk to him, and we closed out the call about an hour later. We resumed lunch, and Noah sat quietly at the table. Soon he whispered softly that his stomach hurt. "Maybe you're just hungry, pal," I urged him gently, pushing his plate a little closer to him. He took a small bite of fish, and then his eyes went wide. I knew that look. Every mom knows *that* look. I leapt up, grabbed him and rushed into the bathroom. We made it just in time, and he spent the next several minutes purging the little bit of lunch he'd had. Afterward, he looked at me pitifully and said, "I must be allergic to fish, Mom." At the time, I didn't disagree. Perhaps

I should have, but explaining to a four-year-old that he wasn't allergic to fish — he was just having an intense reaction to his father being deployed — is easier said than done. So I murmured a noncommittal "hmmmm" and let the moment go.

Time passed, and things slowly returned to normal. Matt returned home safely in May 2012. Noah went to see a therapist, which helped him immensely. Over the next several years, we faced many more military life challenges, but no more deployments. And we all moved on from a troubling time in our lives. Noah's aversion to fish remained, but it wasn't a huge issue. I am not much of a fish fan, so we didn't eat it that often, and when we did Noah just didn't have any. Though we all remembered the issues he had while Matt was gone, we had all forgotten that Noah attributed being sick that day to a fish allergy.

Until the school called. Until that day when Noah, now eight years old, accidentally ate a fish stick thinking it was chicken and then told his school nurse he was allergic to fish. Four years earlier, if you had told me I would laugh about that day or that year, I would have told you, "There's no way this will ever be funny!" But laugh I did, as did the nurse when I explained the story to her. And Noah did as well when we sat him down to explain that he's not actually allergic to fish.

And so, because of this situation, I know these things to be true: I will never forget my children's heartbreak over missing their father, particularly Noah's, as his was the most evident. But when another deployment comes, and inevitably it will, I know that the hard times will not stay hard. The pain will turn to joy again in time, and the things we thought we'd never look back on fondly will become fodder for memories that we will never give up. The difficult times belong to us as much as the good times do. And with any luck, one day the difficult memories will not be the whole story. They will just be the background of a happy ending.

~Jacqueline Chovan

79

The Peach Connection

We are not cisterns made for hoarding; we
are channels made for sharing.
~Billy Graham

I n the spring of 1969, I arrived in the Vietnam War zone soon after completing a stateside small unit, leadership training program. As an untested infantry squad leader, I was put in charge of a dozen men who had been in-country from four to six months. Since they had previous combat experience and I had none, the pressure on me to effectively take control was enormous. However, I did not have long to wait for the opportunity to prove myself because my company had just been ordered to take part in the famous battle for Hamburger Hill.

Upon arrival at the assault staging area, it was assumed that we were going into battle immediately, so we were instructed to leave all non-essential gear behind and only take our weapons, ammunition and a single canteen of water. However, I decided to bring along a small C-ration can of sliced peaches just in case I got hungry along the way.

As we slowly moved into our assault position, the formidable terrain and thick vegetation caused significant delays. Other units ran into the same problem, causing the assault to be postponed until the next day, and requiring us to spend the night at the base of the contested mountain.

When morning arrived, everyone was hungry because it had

been nearly twenty-four hours since we last ate. As I casually opened my can of peaches, I wrongly thought that other soldiers had also brought food along for themselves. That was when some of the guys began staring at me. They *all* wanted peaches. Since the tiny can could not realistically feed a dozen men, I decided to just get it over with and quickly eat the fruit. No one said anything, but their cold stares confirmed that I had made a mistake. Instead of acting like a leader, I disappointed them by only thinking of myself.

A short time later, we were given the order to assault the mountain. The moment our troops moved into the battle area, we immediately came under heavy fire. As enemy bullets pinned down our skirmish line, I looked for a way to escape. To my left was a small ridge that still had enough vegetation to provide us with some cover. I leapt to my feet and ran to the ridge while yelling to my squad, "Follow me! We're going up this way!"

I led the charge up that ridge like a madman, pushing branches aside, jumping over abandoned enemy positions, and ignoring bullets nipping at my feet. When I reached the crest of the hill, I decided to set up a defensive position. However, when I turned around to tell my squad, I was alone. They had let me run up the hill by myself.

About thirty minutes later, the battle ended, and my guys finally made their way to my position. As they gathered around, I scolded them.

"Why didn't you guys follow me?" I yelled. "That ridge had plenty of cover! If we had been all here together, we might've made a difference!"

No one answered as they sheepishly looked at each other, knowing full well that they should never let a fellow soldier charge the enemy alone. Then one of the men broke the silence.

"We didn't follow you because you didn't share your peaches."

Everyone laughed, including me.

I learned a good lesson that day. In a dangerous place like a combat zone, refusing to share something as simple as peaches can get a guy killed. To prevent that from happening again, I needed to find a way to make up for my selfishness. Before long, I would have the solution.

The most welcome diversion from the war came in food packages from home that were filled with cookies, fruit cakes, seasonings, powdered juices, and a variety of canned goods. One package from my mother contained a seven-ounce can of apple juice. It was the first real thirst quencher I had had in over two months, and it was so refreshing that I wrote a thank-you letter to the manufacturer.

I described briefly how miserable infantry life was in Vietnam and explained how the juice was such a welcome change from drinking water from rice paddies and rubber bladders that I wanted to purchase a case to share with my squad. About two weeks later, I received a complimentary carton of twenty-four cans with a letter from the manufacturer stating that the gift was their way of showing support for the troops. What a fantastic surprise!

Infantrymen like us often felt forgotten, so something as simple as a can of apple juice was a real treat. It not only revitalized our taste buds, but also restored some lost faith in the folks back home.

Then I got an idea. If I sent the same kind of letter to other food suppliers, I wondered if I would be able to get more free items. So I sifted through the garbage for names and addresses and began sending requests at two-week intervals.

It did not take long for the goodies to start rolling in. In the coming months, I received peanuts, pretzels, fruit nectar, canned berries, sardines, steak sauce, and more. As a joke, I asked a tobacco distributor for cigar prices, and I was sent a box.

My squad members began calling me "Operator" because I reminded them of the Sergeant Sefton character portrayed by William Holden in the 1953 movie, *Stalag 17*. However, unlike Sergeant Sefton, who as a prisoner of war was somehow able to live comfortably while his comrades suffered, I shared everything that came my way to help make our situation a little more bearable.

Naturally, my squad was curious as to how I was able to obtain cases of hard-to-get provisions, but I just told them that I had an uncle who worked in a food distribution warehouse. If the guys had known the truth, they might have tried the same thing, and it would not have taken long for manufacturers to catch on and stop sending the freebies.

I took advantage of some very generous people, but my scheme only proved that even during the unpopular Vietnam War, the American spirit of appreciation for our military was as strong as it had always been. Those of us who benefitted were certainly grateful.

~Arthur Wiknik, Jr.

80

Wolf Man Howls into Manhood

Other than dying, I think puberty is
probably about as rough as it gets.
~Rick Springfield

ilitary families struggle with stressors not faced in the civilian world. "Normal" families often have a two-parent support system; military ones rarely have that luxury. Deployments and Temporary Away Duty (TAD) frequently send one parent or both away from home. Even routine deployments can last several months or even years, while others occur in combat for indefinite periods.

Spouses accept dual roles and responsibilities, emulating "single parent" personas, and then readjusting as a family when the service member returns. However, there is just so much that one parent can do when two are needed. Our family has endured many TADs and four combat deployments, two to Iraq. Each one had a different purpose, timeline, and characteristics — all of them stressful.

Scott, my husband, was a Colonel in the U.S. Marine Corps and Commanding Officer (CO) for CLB2, the Combat Logistics Battalion in Al Asad, Iraq, from 7 February 2005 until 7 September 2005. My son Will and I lived at Camp Lejeune, North Carolina. While Scott was commanding overseas, I was commanding at home as wife, mother, middle school science teacher, and Key Volunteer Advisor to the families of CLB2.

The families left behind were my priority. Each spouse had a point of contact for unit information at home and away. If there were problems with the paycheck, housing, medical, or other items, someone helped solve the problem. Through the Key Volunteers and Family Readiness Officer, we set up family days, support groups, and events to keep morale strong. My roles were to make sure things ran smoothly on the home front, provide support and assistance, and only intervene if needed. It was an honor to serve my Marine Corps extended family.

I'm sure most families thought the CO's wife never had difficulties during deployments, but it was quite the opposite. After a major storm, my car suffered an electrical shortage when it flooded out. It was towed to the garage, and after two weeks, I received a $750 bill. A week later, driving Scott's car, the battery died in the bank parking lot. Even with the hood up, standing around looking stranded, no one helped me. After an hour, I flagged down a high school student to jump the battery and then asked him to follow me to the auto center.

These were mere annoyances. What I wasn't prepared to handle was my son's emergence into puberty. My only child was transforming into an alien. Scott was gone, and I freaked out.

Months earlier, a short, pudgy, high-pitched, Pokémon-playing little boy had lived in our home. Then suddenly, his voice changed from tenor to bass — and everything in between — and hormones poured from glands that should have remained bottled until Dad came home.

At fourteen years old, Will began the journey into manhood moments after Dad left for Iraq. When he had a question or something to discuss, I tried not to answer like a science teacher. Will grew about four inches, and outgrew all his shoes, shirts, and pants were too small. He got hairy, and his nickname became "Wolf Man." Every day, I e-mailed Scott about the trials and tribulations of raising a male teenager. Scott gave me advice, but Dad at home would have been better, especially for Will's question: "How do I shave?"

It was late August, and school was scheduled to start in a week or so. Shaving couldn't be put off any longer. People stared at Wolf Man, and even my family harassed me. Will was eager to shave, not realizing that once the act began, he would be different. People's expectations would change, and he would no longer be my little boy. That was frightening.

Off we went to Walmart. Will found the shaving aisle. We stood there forever, looking at all the paraphernalia. We were overwhelmed with the products and the variety of items. There were plastic and metal manual razors, with pivoting heads, multiple blades, and bins filled with the electric varieties. Some razors bore flat heads with screens and rotating blades that swiveled, resembling some kind of kitchen tool. One of these razors would be cutting my baby's face, not a potato, but which one?

We picked up each package to study the specifications and promises, totally confused. "I wish your dad was here," I lamented. By divine intervention, a man's voice broke our concentration, saying, "Do you need some help? I couldn't help but notice that your son is in need of a razor."

For a split second, I thought *Hallelujah*, and then my pride kicked in. As a Commanding Officer's wife, I help others with problems, not receive help from another Marine. Then Will's face flashed before me. I was way over my head. "Yes, thank you."

The following minutes blurred by as the young Marine explained the functions of each razor and what lotion or foam was needed to get the job done. Wolf Man was mesmerized. He took in every word as gospel until another voice stopped the lesson. "John, leave these people alone. They don't need your help."

Turning to the Marine's wife, Will said, "Actually, I do." I was so proud of him. John continued for several moments longer, giving more instruction, and with a satisfied look on his face, he patted Will on the back and said, "Good luck." Then he walked away.

Will was delighted with his new information and placed the recommended plastic manual razor and accouterments in the cart. "Just to be on the safe side, I think this electric razor might be the best one for you," I said, as I added that to our arsenal. Now, both of us felt prepared.

We returned home anticipating the historical event and headed to my bathroom. This was one of those pivotal moments; I wished I had a video camera to record the event, not only for me, but also for Scott. When we got to the bathroom door, Will told me he wanted to do this by himself, and another panic attack hit. *My baby was going to shave!* He closed the door, and I left to pace in the kitchen.

Minutes that felt like hours later, the Wolf Man joined me, proclaiming, "I need Dad here, so I will wait until he gets home." Apparently, neither of us was emotionally strong enough to handle such an act. My teenager made the right decision.

A couple of weeks after school started, Scott returned home for good. The first thing he did when he got home, still in desert cammies and boots, was shave the Wolf Man. With this momentous act, the male bond became stronger. This milestone was one of many in Will's journey toward manhood, and thankfully I didn't have to go through this one alone.

~Helen B. Aitken

81

The Best Crab Cakes I Never Ate

You got to go down a lot of wrong
roads to find the right one.
~Bob Parsons

The Army/Navy football game is a highlight of my family's year. Attendance is mandatory for the five of us, and we've attended every game, with just a few exceptions, for more than forty years.

For those who choose to attend, the alumni associations of West Point and Annapolis hold a special tailgate. Half a building near the stadium is decked out with Army black, gray, and gold, and the other half with Navy blue and gold. Then each tailgate is grouped or "tabled," usually by graduating class year.

Often, the big game is played in Philadelphia, but occasionally it is played in another city. One recent year, it was played in Baltimore. At the Baltimore tailgate location, there were large areas to accommodate a big crowd that was divided into class years. The rooms for each side had many alcoves. I hurried ahead of my family and quickly snagged a table with the correct year. I waved my umbrella and my family quickly found me. We set our perimeter and settled in for the tailgate. I was then sent to find the wonderful crab cakes that are a specialty of Baltimore. There were no more crab cakes on the Army side. Undaunted, I decided I was going to the other side to find the crab cakes.

One of my assets is that I can find anything for anybody. Radar O'Reilly from *M*A*S*H* has nothing on me! My liability, however, is that I have no sense of direction, and I usually get lost. It is fortunate that I married a man with an internal GPS — he never gets lost — but finding stuff stumps him. We make a good team: I find a sought after item, and then he finds me.

This day, as I set out on my recon for crab cakes, I was determined not to get lost. I followed a group of Navy fans to the other side of the building, keeping a careful eye on our Army alcove. Though clearly on the wrong side, in my Army fan attire, the Navy folks welcomed me to their buffet. Alas, no crab cakes remained. I was about to leave and return to the Army side and my family when I spied a waitress carrying a tray with crab cakes. She had five crab cakes, perfect for my party of five!

I nearly swooned.

She disappeared through a swinging door, and like Alice following the White Rabbit, I followed. I caught up with her at the catering room and asked breathlessly about the crab cakes. Yes, I could have them, though the lettuce on the plate was a little wilted. She told me she was simply clearing tables and straightening up. Because there were no more crab cakes available, she was removing the nearly empty platter.

Securing my prize and giggling maniacally, I hurried back up the rabbit hole. And guess what? I came out somewhere else!

Clutching my precious platter, I searched for aid in finding my family. Seeing an Army Military Police officer in uniform, I followed him, looking for our alcove. Then I stopped in my tracks, nearly bumping into the policeman.

For many years, a very rich person has sent a train to Walter Reed National Military Medical Center. This person arranges for wounded warriors and medical personnel to attend the game. I had blundered into this group. The Military Police officer said to me, "Ma'am, you cannot come in here. It's private…"

Just as he said it, I saw through the doorway four soldiers with scars and prostheses — young, brave, and so glad to be out of the hospital.

One young man, missing an arm and a leg, said to his comrades, "See? Crab cakes!"

He said to me, "Ma'am, we were told there were no more crab cakes. So I prayed for crab cakes, and here they are."

Not skipping a beat, but feeling a divine nudge, I said, "Soldier, your prayer has been answered. Here's one for each of your buddies and two for you because you asked." I placed the platter on their table, spun around, and left.

Shortly thereafter, my exasperated family found me in the main hall, without crab cakes. "Why can't you be where you are supposed to be?" they asked.

Little did they know that, for once, I had been exactly where I was supposed to be.

~Anne Oliver

82

Field Mice

Languages are not strangers to one another.
~Walter Benjamin

My husband, Mike, a Captain in the Air Force, was stationed with the 617th Air Support Operations Squadron in Mannheim, Germany, while his younger brother, Joe, a 1st Lieutenant in the Army, was stationed in northern Germany with the U.S. Army's 2nd Armored Division. Joe met a woman named Petra while stationed there and eventually left the service. Petra, a nurse and German citizen, wanted to be married in Germany, so our family was coming over from the States for the wedding.

We all came in on different flights at different times. My mother-in-law, Sara, and her sister, Nancy, arrived before us and were given a tour by Petra and her brother, Tomas.

Petra and Tomas had learned to speak English in school, and their English was great, but not perfect. It was good enough, though, for Sara and Nancy to strike up a conversation with Tomas as they drove through the industrial areas, past the railroads, over the river and through sections of country on the way to Osterholz-Scharmbeck.

Tomas pointed out highlights along the way, and Sara and Nancy managed to follow along with his accented English. Sara pointed out the farmers' roadside stands and told Tomas that we also had them in Vermont. Tomas was thrilled to hear that, now having found something in common, and he went into great detail about how he and his family would stop and buy field mice from the farmers. They would spear them and slowly roast them over a fire, dribbling butter and salt on them until they were cooked to a crispy perfection.

Sara and Nancy looked at each other. They were starting to worry about what would be served at the wedding.

"Tomas, you cook field mice over the fire?" Sara asked.

"Oh, yes. When it comes off of the fire, it is so tasty," he said with a flourish. He put his thumb up against his first two fingers and brought them to his mouth, making a smacking sound as one would do when explaining delicious food. He showed the act of eating the mice off the stick and then licked his lips, saying, "Mmmmmm."

Nancy was horrified. Sara thought her sister was going to throw up in the back seat.

"Tomas, you're joking with us, aren't you?"

He looked at Sara in all seriousness. "No! It is wonderful. Do you not eat field mice?"

Nancy immediately responded, "No, we don't! How could you?"

Now Tomas was confused. He could see they were not happy about what he had told them. He did not want to offend his sister's new relatives.

Sara asked Tomas if he was spelling mice, M-I-C-E. In his accented English, he said, "No, we spell mice, M-A-I-Z-E."

Nancy placed her hand over her heart in relief. Sara started laughing, which confused Tomas even more.

Sara didn't want to offend Tomas and explained, "Tomas, we pronounce M-A-I-Z-E differently," and she said the word in English.

"What is MAIZE then?" he asked.

"Corn."

"What did you think I said?" he asked.

"MICE."

"What is mice?"

Sara explained, "Field mice are small, furry creatures with pointed noses, small pink ears and long tails that run in the fields and eat corn after it has dropped. Sometimes, they invade homes for food and shelter. They do damage and spread diseases. In the United States, you can find them in older houses, leaving droppings on counters."

"Ah, that is a *MAUS* in German!" he said, now understanding what had happened.

That story was told over and over throughout the weekend. Petra's father, Hans, would yell, "Field mice for everyone!" as we drank toasts.

It was a nice icebreaker and a way to bring strangers together.

I am not sure Aunt Nancy ever got over it, though, as she was very choosy about what she ate during the wedding.

~Kristine Benevento

83

Every Peach Has a Pit

*Never let the fear of striking out keep
you from playing the game.*
~Babe Ruth

I almost didn't show up for our final softball game. It was ninety degrees outside, and if I'd stayed home I could have sipped iced tea, watched TV, and waited for the oscillating fan to blow a cool breeze my way. But something made me put on my peach colored T-shirt, pin up my hair, and grab my glove. I owed it to the team.

We called ourselves the Peaches, after the Rockford Peaches, who played in the All-American Girls Professional Baseball League from 1943–1954. We were all Navy wives playing against other Navy wives on the diamonds at the Naval Submarine Base in New London, Connecticut. That evening, when I walked into the dugout, my teammates cheered.

"You make nine, Mary!" Beverly said. "Now we've got enough to play. We were ready to forfeit the game."

"Where is everybody?" I asked, as if it never occurred to me to stay home.

"I guess they thought it was too hot."

With only the minimum number of players, Coach had no choice but to put Rose and me in the game at the same time. Heaven help us. Rose and I were the weak links. At the beginning of the season, I'd known so little about softball that I'd bought a right-handed glove for practice, even though I was right-handed. Coach rolled his eyes when he saw me throw with my left hand. I returned the next week with a left-handed glove, but my right-hand throw wasn't much better. Rose's skills were just as bad, and she knew it. She referred to herself as "Charlie Brown."

During tryouts, Coach didn't exclude anyone from the team. I overheard him say, "If they have the guts to get out there and play, let 'em play." I was sure he was talking about Rose and me. Rose was the one with guts. What I had was a husband on a submarine deep in the ocean. Softball kept me from worrying about him, at least for a little while.

That night, Coach entered the dugout with his whistle dangling from his neck and read the lineup. "Judy: first; Valerie: second; Shelly: short; Beverly: third; Mary: left; Nina: center; Rose: right." He looked up from his clipboard. "Be alert, girls. When you're standing out there, think about what you'll do if the ball comes to you."

I must have scowled, for Coach said, "Don't be afraid of left field, Mary. It's just like any other position."

"Sure it is." Right-handers had a tendency to hit balls to left field, and chances were good that most of the opposing players were righties. I trotted out to the field and prayed the ball wouldn't come to me. Ever since a ball hit Beverly in the eye, all my instincts told me to duck when a ball came my way.

We were playing against the Furies. The women wore red T-shirts and black shorts, and they'd brought a sea bag full of aluminum bats. Not plain silver aluminum, but neon pink and green. Rose and I usually taunted the other team's batters from the dugout with "Batter, batter, swing!" But now our entire team was in the field. Ann, our pitcher, accidentally hit the Furies' first batter in the arm, so that woman walked to the base.

The next Fury was up to bat. Crack! A red shirt ran toward first. *Where was the ball?* It started as a flying white streak and transformed into a giant snowball coming right to me. My heart leapt. I took two steps forward, raised my arm, and spread my fingers in the glove.

The ball thudded on the ground behind me and kept rolling. I turned and ran after it. A metallic ping rang out as the ball hit the chain-link fence. I finally caught up to it and threw it to Valerie. Too late. The Furies had made a two-run homer.

I didn't have time to dwell on my blunder. Ann pitched again, and the ball smacked against the Furies' bat. It soared toward me, this time in a low arc. I stepped back and held out my glove. The ball hit the ground in front of me, bounced up and struck me in the jaw. *Ouch!* My teeth clanked together, and my head jolted, but still I scrambled after the ball. When it was almost within my grasp, I slipped and did a split in the grass. Nina ran past me and recovered the ball. By then, the batter had circled all the bases — another home run.

Coach blew his whistle to call a time out. "Left field, are you all right?"

Everyone turned around and stared at me. Without realizing it, I'd been holding my aching chin. I dropped my arm to my side and yelled, "I'm okay!"

The Furies eventually made three outs. The bases were loaded, and we had two outs by the time I was up to bat. My first hit was a foul ball, but the next one was good. I ran to first, reaching it just before being tagged.

"Safe," the umpire said, but no one heard. Furies and Peaches began to shift positions.

"I'm safe!" I shouted.

With surprised looks, everyone switched back. Coach nodded to me. He seemed proud I'd stood my ground.

We scored two runs before Rose struck out. Back in the field, the balls slipped by me, and the Furies slaughtered us. I was drenched in sweat and bitten by mosquitoes.

Coach blew his whistle and stopped the game. *What now?* He walked toward the pitcher's mound, where Ann hung her head low and rubbed her eyes. Coach leaned in close to her and patted her back.

I waved to Rose in right field, and Rose waved back. When I pointed to Ann, Rose shrugged. She didn't know what was going on either. I ran to Nina in center field. "Why is Ann crying?"

"She thinks it's her fault we're losing."

"Her fault? It's not her fault!"

"She's got it in her head that it is."

I returned to left field, wondering if I'd been acting like Ann, putting the blame on myself. Maybe the balls I'd missed would have been impossible to catch even for the best players.

When the game resumed, a lefty up to bat whacked the ball to right field, and like a pro, Rose caught it. Later, when the outfielders ran into the dugout, Rose cried, "Mary, did you see me? I caught the ball!"

"I saw you!" I said. "You were great!"

By the top of the seventh inning, the numbers 26 and 7 lit up on the scoreboard. The Furies won, but the Peaches had put up a fight. The teams shook hands and said, "Good game!"

A sailor in uniform walked down from the bleachers and hugged one of the Furies. Seeing them brought me back to reality — my own husband was out to sea. Somehow, I forgot to miss him the entire time I was playing softball. It put losing in perspective. This wasn't the World Series, and we weren't trying to get into any Hall of Fame. We were just a bunch of Navy wives waiting for our husbands to come home.

~Mary Elizabeth Laufer

84

Combat Teddy

A bear grows more alive with age. No one
with one ounce of sensitivity could ever
consign a bear to the dustbin.
~Johnnie Hague

I pick him up and clutch him to my chest, and many frightening memories come flooding back. But he's a comfort — and I can imagine to some extent how invaluable he must have been on his mission in the Middle East so many years ago.

"I bet you've seen things that most people pray they never have to witness, Combat Teddy!"

Yes, I'm talking to a stuffed teddy bear. But he is not an ordinary bear. Combat Teddy has seen firsthand the horror of war.

When my twenty-one-year-old son, Darren, was deployed in Saudi Arabia during the Persian Gulf War with the Army's 82nd Airborne, he wrote home telling his sister how lonely he was. Jacqui decided a teddy bear would be a perfect companion for her brother.

Jacqui and I went shopping and picked out a huggable, eighteen-inch plush bear, and packaged him very carefully for his long trip. Before sealing the box, Jacqui tucked in a note instructing her brother to take good care of both the bear and himself, and to make sure they both returned home safely.

The following day, she took the bear to the post office and sent him on his way to the Saudi Arabian desert. We were delighted to learn that he arrived safe and sound.

Dear Sis! I received the teddy bear today. All the guys are jealous, but they love him. We've named him Combat Teddy because he's going to fight this war with us. I promise you he's in good hands.

We were able to follow Combat Teddy's adventures during Desert Shield through vivid descriptions in Darren's handwritten letters, complete with hand-drawn sketches. Here are excerpts from several of his letters:

Today we played basketball here in the desert. The basket consisted of an old piece of wood and a piece of metal bent around. We made a net out of parachute retention straps. Glad I'm 6'5", because it's easy for me to dunk.

Combat Teddy is with me constantly. He fits perfectly into the cargo pocket of my BDUs (Battle Dress Uniform), with just his head peeking out. At night he's my pillow in the foxhole.

I am very proud of my fighting position. It is really deep. Combat Teddy has a great view. He will see the whole war. Also, he keeps me company. He's about the only one I can talk to and not get mad.

War is not nice! Every day and night we see B-52 bombers and fighters flying overhead — but tell Sis not to worry because I'm taking good care of Combat Teddy and myself.

Mom, can you get the enclosed rolls of film developed? Tell Sis there should be some pictures of Combat Teddy on them. She can get an idea of what he's doing over here.

And then…

Dear Mom & Dad. This will be the last of my letter writing for a long time. The moon and sun will only rise two more times before we move out for combat. So just remember I love you with all my heart.

The letters stopped when Desert Shield escalated into Desert Storm, and the actual fighting began. We didn't hear from Darren until the troops were back at Fort Bragg in North Carolina.

We learned later that Combat Teddy traveled in Darren's cargo pocket as the 82nd moved across the border into Iraq, playing a major role in achieving superiority over the enemy in the first days of the ground war. After five days (or 100 hours) fighting alongside our French Allies, Darren's company of 135 troops — 136 counting Combat Teddy — were airlifted back to Saudi Arabia. A little extra treat for Combat Teddy, according to Darren, was that the pilot let them take over the controls for a bit.

When Darren arrived at Portland International Airport, he walked off the plane to be greeted by lots of friends and family waving signs welcoming him and Combat Teddy home.

Darren strode straight over to Jacqui and me and handed us Combat Teddy in sentimental fashion. "I promised you we'd both come home!"

As we all hugged, there wasn't a dry eye among us.

I know that Combat Teddy may not have won the war and liberated Kuwait singlehandedly, but I'm pretty sure he helped to lift the spirits of many of those who risked their lives to do so. He's most certainly entitled to his place of honor on the shelf in our living room where he has been sitting for twenty-five years dressed in his camo T-shirt and proudly wearing his dog tags around his fuzzy neck.

~Connie Kaseweter Pullen

85

Traditions and Time Zones

*Christmas is a day of meaning and traditions, a special
day spent in the warm circle of family and friends.*
~Margaret Thatcher

Although I still had much to do before everything was ready for our annual Christmas Eve meal that we would have before heading to church, I plopped down next to my husband on the couch in our den. It was just noon in Sandston, Virginia, but at Camp Arifjan in Kuwait it was almost 8:00 p.m. and time for their Christmas Eve service to begin. We were going to worship with our son via a live broadcast of the service on the Internet, compliments of the U.S. Army.

Worshipping together on Christmas Eve was one of the annual highlights of our holiday, a tradition both Bobby and I had brought into our marriage and continued with our own family of five. It was a staple for me, much like putting up a real tree, making Chex mix, decorating the porch railing with tiny white lights and garland, and hosting our annual open house on the Friday before Christmas. It ranked right up there with one of my favorite traditions — watching our kids pick just one gift to open on Christmas Eve.

This year, for the first time, two of our three children were not home for Christmas. We wouldn't be sitting in the same pew on Christmas Eve. We would be worshipping together from three different time zones.

Our twenty-six-year-old daughter, Katie, had married a Navy doctor and moved to San Diego in May. Her husband, Michael, had just begun his medical internship and had no leave. Matthew, our twenty-eight-year-old son, had been deployed to Kuwait just weeks ago.

I missed them a lot. I'd been going through the motions of a festive holiday. I'd purchased and wrapped gifts for Sarah, our twenty-three-year-old daughter, who'd driven the two-and-a-half-hour trip from Winchester to come home. The bright packages with pretty fabric bows were under the tree, becoming littered now with dried pine needles. I'd shopped for gifts for Matthew, Katie, and Michael that had fit inside large priority mail, flat rate boxes. I'd wrapped the items in colorful paper, and then bubble wrap, before wedging them into the cardboard boxes that weren't quite big enough.

Since Thanksgiving, I had preoccupied myself with the tasks associated with carrying out our traditions — shopping, wrapping, mailing, baking, and decorating. Staying busy had helped me keep my emotions intact. Now as I sat still on the couch with my husband and our younger daughter listening to the words of the Army chaplain, I was struggling with the incredible emptiness I felt.

As the service came to an end, the video stream continued, giving every soldier the opportunity to extend a live greeting to loved ones back home. We waited patiently for a glimpse of our son and were finally delighted to see his smiling face fill the screen on our TV.

"Hi, everyone," he said, in a blanket greeting to me, his dad and Sarah as we watched together in Sandston and to Katie who was viewing the service from the West Coast. "Merry Christmas! I'll give you a call in a few minutes."

Minutes later, thanks to the technology of smartphones, iPads and free apps that enable real-time video chats, the five of us were all talking at once. We were in front of our tree, Katie was in front of hers, and Matthew was in a building with Wi-Fi service somewhere in Camp Arifjan. Even with the slight delay from Kuwait, it was happy chaos!

"We saw you!" "How are you?" "Did the mess hall make a special dinner?" "Did you get our Christmas packages?"

Through the barrage of questions, Matthew said, "Katie, Sarah, grab a present!" as he produced one of the small packages we shipped to him.

"It's Christmas Eve, and we each get to open one gift!"

~Carol Burge Mawyer

Chapter 10

Military Families

★ Saying Goodbye ★

86

Angel by My Side

Make yourself familiar with the angels, and behold
them frequently in spirit; for, without being
seen, they are present with you.
~St. Francis of Sales

My husband and I had been married forty-seven years when I got "the call" from the hospital. "I'm sorry," someone said in a steady, even voice. "He didn't make it."

I sat at the other end of the line, feeling my heart begin to break. "He didn't make it," a voice inside me kept repeating. It was Sunday, November 1, 2015. All Saints' Day.

The next morning, I set about making plans for the funeral. My husband had mentioned more than once that he wanted to be buried at the veterans' cemetery among those men and women who had served their country. "I will honor your wishes," I had assured him.

On the morning before Veterans Day, my children and I and a few friends gathered at the cemetery, waiting for the Navy to tell us where to go for the burial. I had never been to a military funeral before. We followed the procession to a sunny spot surrounded by manicured lawns and tall trees. In this hallowed space, military honors would be bestowed on a dedicated Navy Chief who, decades earlier, was a young sailor ready and willing to serve his country. The bright morning sun illuminated the colors of the flag draping the casket, making the red, white, and blue more vibrant, alive, and meaningful. My heart overflowed with pride.

At the opening of the ceremony, two Seamen reverently lifted the flag from its place on the casket and, from one to the other, meticulously folded the length of the flag into a perfect triangle. They handed the flag to the Chief who, in turn, knelt at my feet and placed the flag into my hands.

"Thank you. It's beautiful," I whispered, looking into the face of this young man who was honoring his fallen older brother. I clutched the flag to my chest, embracing its beauty and spirit until it was time to go.

I have taken great solace in the flag that was presented to me on that solemn day one-and-a-half years ago. This priceless keepsake is displayed in a United States Navy flag case and sits on my hearth next to a statue of a Bereavement Angel that my cousin sent me shortly after Bernard's passing. The angel's arms are outstretched toward heaven, and she is holding a lone star in her hands. The message written in the folds of her skirt reads: "Perhaps they are not stars but rather openings where our loved ones shine down to let us know they are happy."

Last fall, I was shopping for Christmas gifts and I found the website that offered the Bereavement Angel, along with a variety of other angels. I had just placed my order for a Hope Angel for my niece and a Comfort Angel for a friend when a Military Angel appeared out of the blue on my computer screen — one of those pop-up ads. She was dressed simply in blue and white, clutching the American flag to her chest, the flag folded in a perfect triangle. A price was listed, as well as a brief description. I immediately dialed the toll-free number noted at the top of the screen, as the site I was browsing did not offer this angel.

"I have to have that Military Angel!" I said to the representative who answered the call. I'm sure she detected the urgency in my voice.

"We only have a few left in stock," she said. "I'll see what I can do. It will probably take two to three weeks before you receive it."

A couple of days later, on November 1, 2016, the first anniversary of my husband's passing, this Military Angel appeared on my screen again when I opened my laptop. Just a picture of her. Spanning the screen. No words. No price. Just her. In a field of blue. I hadn't even signed in yet.

A couple of days later, the angel appeared on the screen again even before I logged in. She didn't stay long. Just long enough to have said, "Hi! I'm here," and leave. What was she trying to tell me?

The next evening, my daughter stopped by. I had told her about "my angel."

"Want to see a picture of her?"

I opened my laptop, and a message appeared on the screen that I had never seen before: *This page is having trouble loading.* I clicked on the red X in the upper right-hand corner several times, but I couldn't delete the message. I was just about to give up when the message suddenly disappeared. In its place, the angel appeared.

"It's her!" I cried. "She's here again!"

"Mom, this is a sign! I think Dad is trying to tell you something."

On the morning of November 8, 2016, the package containing the Military Angel appeared on my doorstep. I carefully unwrapped the package and placed the angel on the hearth next to the American flag and the Bereavement Angel.

On Veterans Day, November 11th, we would be commemorating and honoring all those men and women who served their country in the name of peace and freedom. And I would be honoring and remembering a young, zealous sailor who came into my life fifty years ago.

Suddenly, a voice inside my heart said: "Everything is going to be all right."

And I knew it would be.

~Lola Di Giulio De Maci

A Final Peace

Every parting is a form of death, as
every reunion is a type of heaven.
~Tryon Edwards

My brother, Captain Wilbur Dale Latimer, was a helicopter pilot in the Vietnam War. He was twenty-six when he died in 1971 during his second tour of duty. Although devastated by his death, we learned to live without him and found special comfort through the years when men who had served with Will contacted us to talk about him.

However, in 2011, the fortieth anniversary of Will's death, I was blindsided by a new wave of grief. My friends worried about me, and I even worried about myself. It seemed Will was with me every day, but just out of reach.

One Saturday night in July of that year, a friend who is a Vietnam veteran called from a helicopter pilots' reunion. Robert said when he went to his table at the banquet that night, someone was sitting in his place. Instead of making an issue of it, he found an empty seat at another table where he didn't know anyone.

In the course of the dinner, as the men told their war stories, he kept hearing the name Latimer. Robert didn't know Will, but he knew his story, so he asked if they were talking about Will Latimer. What a surprise to learn they were.

When he said he knew me, a man sitting beside Robert told him he and Will had been best friends during flight training. They had served their first tours in Vietnam together in the 71st Assault Helicopter Company (AHC). Pilots of Huey gunships were known as Firebirds while those who flew regular Hueys were called Rattlers. Will and Buddy were Firebirds.

During their second tours of duty, Buddy served in another location and didn't hear of Will's death for quite some time. He had never met or talked with anyone in our family, so he wasn't sure how I would feel about receiving a phone call after so long. Buddy asked Robert to find out if I would be willing to talk to him.

That night, after the banquet was over, Robert called to tell me about meeting Will's Firebird friends. It felt like a divine appointment to both of us.

I jumped at the opportunity to speak with Buddy. When he called, he encouraged me to attend a small reunion of Firebird and Rattler pilots to be held in June 2012 in New Orleans. He said I'd connect with men who had flown with Will. I already knew about the reunions from newsletters I'd received over the years and had actually daydreamed about going.

Although I was nervous, I felt compelled to attend. And so it was on June 21, 2012, that my husband and I walked into a New Orleans ballroom to meet a group of aging Vietnam veterans. We were welcomed with open arms.

Around the room, they had set up displays of war memorabilia and photographs of themselves — and Will — in their prime of youth. Two helicopters were on site. I sat in one like Will's.

I met Buddy in person, bonded with Ray, Will's door gunner, who dealt with PTSD long before it was acknowledged as a war disability. I met Carson who narrowly escaped capture after being shot down and another not-so-fortunate man who spent five years as a POW. I still hear from a woman whose brother was MIA until seven years ago when he and his crew's remains were returned for burial at Arlington Cemetery. Many men took the time to talk with me and express their admiration for Will.

We hugged. We laughed, and we cried. I saw that some of the men had lived full lives, while others hadn't been able to leave the nightmare of war behind. I also witnessed a special brotherhood among the organizers of the reunions and their struggling comrades. They are brothers in the truest sense.

At some point during those two days, like the final piece of a puzzle, a new acceptance slipped into place inside me. As I left that reunion, I was finally able to let my beloved brother rest in peace again.

~Dorothy Latimer Johnson

88

Lest We Forget

*And they who for their country die shall fill an
honored grave, for glory lights the soldier's
tomb, and beauty weeps the brave.*
~Joseph Rodman Drake

Between the two Dutch towns of Margraten and Maastricht in southeast Netherlands is an American cemetery. This beautiful, green open space with its acres of white crosses and Stars of David is the final resting place of 8,301 U.S. World War II soldiers, and the walls within the cemetery hold the names of 1,722 missing servicemen and servicewomen. These are the Americans who liberated Holland in 1944 and 1945 and never came home. One of the soldiers buried in the Netherlands American Cemetery and Memorial is my uncle, U.S. Army Pvt. Alfred Alexander Wang, Jr.

Uncle Alfred served with the 115th Infantry Regiment as it pushed into Germany prior to the Battle of the Bulge. The fighting was rugged as they struggled to push the German soldiers out of the small towns and countryside. The troops lived in trenches and foxholes, and they had to advance through cold, ankle deep water and mud. Historical reports tell us that on December 7, 1944, in a pre-dawn attack, the 115th advanced on the Jülich Sportplatz, fighting hand-to-hand in the dark. When the battle ended, the Americans had gained the ground, and the 115th continued their advance toward the Roer River the next day. But the war was over for my uncle. He was Killed in Action on

December 8. He was twenty-eight years old.

I grew up post-World War II knowing nothing about my uncle's service and not much more about him. Perhaps it was the pain of war; perhaps it was a tradition of not acknowledging sadness that kept the family from talking about him. Alfred's mother and two sisters never openly shared their deep sense of loss.

I did have some vague knowledge that I had an uncle buried in Holland, and that there was a man named John Silvius who took care of his grave. I knew this little bit because when I was a child in the 1950s, we regularly received postcards from the John Silvius family in Vaals. They were colorful postcards illustrated with spring flowers, chickens pulling carts filled with Easter eggs, a bucolic countryside, and ice skaters on a Dutch canal. One postcard had a handwritten birthday congratulations to a one-year-old me.

These postcards were tucked away in a keepsake book. I found them again while researching my family genealogy. As I dug into the Internet for more information about my uncle, I discovered a remarkable organization, the Foundation for Adopting Graves at the American Cemetery Margraten. This nonprofit organization began in 1945 when the American cemetery was first established. It continues today as an association of thousands of Dutch citizens who place flags, flowers, and photos on the graves of the fallen and next to the names of the missing.

Every grave and name at Margraten is adopted by a Dutch citizen. And, remarkably, five hundred people are on a waiting list to volunteer. The annual Memorial Day service in May is attended by thousands of people each year, and it's been that way since 1945.

The tradition of honoring the U.S. soldiers who gave their lives for Dutch freedom is so strong and so important to the community that the adoption of a grave passes from generation to generation within a Dutch family. This is how Uncle Alfred's current caretaker, Mr. Reijnen, became a gravesite volunteer. He sent me this e-mail:

My grandmother cared about the resting place [of Pvt. Alfred Wang] in Margraten for a long time… My grandmother passed away. After a few years I was called by people of the

American-Cemetery-Margraten with the question if I'll take over the adoption care what was earlier by my grandmother. And so I keep it in our family to care and honor the fallen soldiers.

When I started this journey back into my family history, I was saddened to think that my uncle was buried so far away, forgotten and erased from our family history through silence. But what I discovered is that, all this time, the mission of the Foundation for Adopting Graves at the American Cemetery Margraten was "Lest we forget — *opdat we niet vergeten.*" They were doing our remembering for us.

Since 1944, the Dutch people have been honoring and remembering their "Margraten Boys," their liberators, and keeping them in their hearts. Our soldiers, our family members, and my Uncle Alfred, who never came home from Europe, rest in peace forever among those with whom they fell in battle. And they are cared for with love by their grateful Dutch friends in the American cemetery between two small towns.

~Patricia Walsh

89

Pursuing His Passion

Grief is the price we pay for love.
~Queen Elizabeth II

Rewind years ago to my five-year-old son Ryan (third child, only boy) who wants to play with guns. I, his mom, am against violent toys. He is very persistent, to the point that he begins to bite his sandwiches into gun shapes to have a gun to play with.

I give in. But only water pistols!

Fast-forward a few years to Ryan at nine. His father convinces me that a Daisy Red Ryder BB Gun is an appropriate Christmas gift for a nine-year-old boy. Ryan is thrilled with his gun and the teeniest, tiniest BBs that it shoots.

Ryan grew up hearing all the magnificent stories from his military family members about how great they felt being able to serve our country—a country built on *freedom*. We were all very proud of this fact. Through the years, Ryan became quite a history buff. He was especially drawn to books about past U.S. wars. He joined a re-enacting Boy Scout troop as a teen. They re-enacted the Revolutionary War of 1776. Even though his troop re-enacted the British Loyalists, he would chuckle and say, "Well, someone has to do it!"

As time went on, we knew he wanted to follow in the family footsteps and join the military. At first, he wanted to join the Army. Ryan was a wrestler in high school and sustained a torn meniscus, which required surgery to remove part of it. The Army was hesitant to enlist him because of this, but that did not deter him. He checked into the other military branches and decided on the Navy. He wanted to become a sailor. His aptitude sent him on the path to become an Electronics Technician (ET). He followed that path to become an ET for a Navy Seal team. He was a hard worker, putting it "all in." He moved to San Diego, California, from Illinois to fulfill the next step in his journey. The Navy was the perfect fit for him. Now, he awaited his first deployment.

The day came. I received a call from my very excited son. He was going to an undisclosed location in the Middle East. My son was over the moon excited. Me, not so much! No mom wants to see her child going anywhere that close to war. I choked back the fear and tears and felt pride.

We had a wonderful time when he was in for his pre-deployment leave. Two really quick, memorable weeks! He was so excited. He insisted on spending as much time with his dad, sisters, and me rather than with his friends. Then he left to go back to base and get ready for his adventure.

The next thing I knew, he was texting me that he was on his way and "All is good!" The next couple of months flew by with periodic calls, texts, and even an occasional package (me to him, him to me). The last thing he mailed home was a very heavy box. It was filled with cartridges for his rifle. He found a sale online and wanted to stock up for when he got home and went to the range. It was that gun thing again!

It was a Thursday night. My husband and I had just finished dinner and settled down to watch *Wheel of Fortune*.

We saw a black SUV pull in our driveway.

Two people got out.

They stopped and put on their military hats.

They walked slowly to our door.

The whole time, my brain was questioning what was going on, but my heart was breaking. Time was going in slow motion...

"Are you Mr. and Mrs...? We are sorry to inform you of your son's death..."

Time stopped. They were talking, but I couldn't hear a word. The fog was rolling in around my brain.

In the days following his death, our Casualty Assistance Calls Officer (CACO) was very caring and helpful in making all the arrangements we never thought we would have to make for our twenty-three-year-old son. His commanding officers from San Diego arrived the next day and stayed with us throughout the duration of his wake and funeral. We went to Dover Air Force Base to be there as his body returned to the United States; he was autopsied by the Navy doctors before being sent home to us in Illinois. He was formally escorted by two of his friends from the Navy who were also from the same deployment. We were amazed by the overwhelming love and support shown to us, not only by the Navy, but by our community.

During the following days, we looked for an appropriate place to donate the money we received from Ryan's wake. We heard about a community project to rebuild and relocate our veterans' memorial to a more visible and accessible location. What a perfect place to donate the monetary gifts we received in his honor. We contacted the local park district that was involved in the plans. They told us the donation would be greatly welcomed, but what they actually needed was a steering committee to head the whole fundraising effort.

This became our passion. I called it our grief project. We gathered other couples that had a child in the military and began our quest with a self-imposed, aggressive timeline of fourteen months. Throughout this project, we learned that our community had a multitude of veterans and their families. They were very receptive to the plan, and on Veterans Day 2016 we dedicated our community's new, vastly improved Military Veterans Memorial.

In the days, weeks, months and year since I received the visitors that fateful Thursday night, I am learning to live without my son's physical presence. I miss his smile, face, voice, love, touch, hugs, conversations, and laugh.

I have learned to live each day as if it is the last, live life without regrets. My husband and I put our thoughts, sorrow, and grief into something positive. There is no way to bring back our son, but he will live on in our thoughts, words, and actions. He was passionate about the military and we honor that passion with our work on the memorial.

As I was cleaning out a closet today, I smiled! I continue to find the occasional teeniest, tiniest BB from oh so many years ago. He was here.

~Karen B.

Warriors' Pact

Praising what is lost makes the remembrance dear.
~William Shakespeare

It was shaping up to be a routine weekday afternoon for me as a volunteer at the USO of Raleigh-Durham International Airport Center. A few troops had come and gone, stopping in for a snack or drink before boarding their flights. Several retirees had also been in and out.

Then a young man in civilian clothes and carrying a backpack walked in. He promptly presented his ID that showed him to be active-duty Navy. We welcomed him and then ventured a logical guess that he was based with the Marines at Camp Lejeune since there are no Navy bases in the state. He affirmed this and also our query as to whether he was a Navy medic or Corpsman, which was also likely since Navy Corpsmen imbed with Marine units in combat and have earned the highest respect from Marines. We casually asked about his destination and suggested he could set his backpack in our bag storage area if he liked. He demurred on that, saying he would prefer to keep it with him; he would be flying to Christchurch, New Zealand. That destination aroused our interest, and so we asked what was taking him halfway around the world.

"Meeting up with a few guys," he answered vaguely. After one or two more probing questions, we sensed he was not up to chatting, and so we were about to respect his reticence for conversation by easing up on our small talk. Then, for whatever reason, he became very verbal.

We had no need to ask any further questions — except one.

He told us five men would be joining up in New Zealand — him, three Marines and a Corpsman who had served together in Afghanistan in 2011. It had been a tough deployment, he said; they saw a lot of combat and had taken casualties. He and the other four had become very close and had made a pact. If and when they had this all behind them, the five would reunite annually. They would make it special. None of the usual tourist locations would be on the itinerary; they would journey to meaningful, iconic places on every one of the world's continents, no matter the remoteness.

Our visitor expected to rendezvous with a Camp Pendleton-based Marine at LAX airport. From there, the two would board a New Zealand–bound flight. Two others had been discharged from the Marines and were living abroad in Japan and the Netherlands. They would meet up with them in Christchurch. This prompted a question that needed an answer. "That's four, but didn't you say five are in this pact?"

"He's in my backpack… the other Corpsman… killed in action," he replied. "His parents knew of our pact and asked that we take some of their son's ashes wherever we go to be spread to the winds. The first year, we went to Mount Everest. We climbed pretty high, never intending to reach the summit, and when we knew it was time, we scattered his ashes to the wind on the mountain."

"The next year, we went to Iwo Jima," he continued. "His ashes were scattered in the black volcanic ash where more than six thousand Marines fell taking the island from twenty thousand Japanese troops. This year, it's New Zealand. We'll hike and whitewater raft and release some more ashes to the wind and water. Machu Picchu in South America or someplace in Africa, maybe Mount Kilimanjaro, are on the list for the coming years. We'll talk about it on this trip."

These five Marines and sailors truly exemplify the meaning of the Marine Corps motto, Semper Fidelis, a dedication and loyalty to one another, to Corps and country.

~Bill Kretzschmar

The Bracelet

Strangers are just family you have
yet to come to know.
~Mitch Albom

I was more nervous standing in the middle of a race expo at a convention center than I had been two days earlier during a rocket attack in Kandahar, Afghanistan. It was the day before the Soldier Marathon, and I was going to meet the family of the soldier — the reason I would be running that day.

1LT Daren M. Hidalgo was killed by an improvised explosive device (IED) in Afghanistan on February 20, 2011. Four months earlier, on Halloween night, I met, talked to, laughed at, and fell in love with that same soldier. We were only on the same base for a few weeks, but that was enough to know he was spectacular.

When faced with his death, I felt trapped. I was still working in Afghanistan. I couldn't make it to his funeral, nor did I feel it was my place to. I wondered if his family knew that we had been close, or even that I existed.

In May, I visited West Point where he was buried. Overcome with emotion, I wanted to leave some memento that I was there. So I took a bracelet off my wrist and placed it next to his temporary wooden grave marker.

During one of his visits, Daren had requested that I make him a parachute cord bracelet. He picked the navy blue and camo colors, and I measured his wrist. Then I crafted the bracelet. On the night he was killed, I attended the ramp ceremony where a fallen hero is loaded on to a plane to begin the journey home. As USO staff, we send at least one person to attend every single ceremony to represent the American people and honor the fallen hero every step of the way home. We know we are the first people to say their final goodbyes and their first prayers for the fallen. I didn't know I was attending a ceremony for Daren until they called his name.

In the hours that followed, I had a secret to keep that I couldn't imagine in my worst dreams. I knew it would take time to notify his friends and family back in the States. So to calm my idle hands, I made myself a bracelet in the same colors and using the same cord that I used to make Daren's bracelet mere months before. I put it on my wrist and didn't take it off until I placed it on his grave three months later. It gave me comfort every time I looked down and saw a reminder of him. It lasted through countless miles of sweat, heat, and tears while I ran to train for the marathon in his honor. It helped me through the months of having no connection to him other than his sweet fellow soldiers.

In November, I returned to the States to run the Soldier Marathon with a group of Daren's family and friends to honor him. With hands shaking, I entered the race expo. No sooner had I walked in the room than a man with the same huge dimples as Daren came barreling toward me. "SARAH!" he yelled. Daren's father wrapped me in a big bear hug, and began introducing me to Daren's brothers and sisters.

He brought me over to a table and introduced me to Daren's mother. I greeted her nervously, and then I saw it on her wrist: my bracelet. It was the one I had crafted during the darkest hour of my life to remember the man I loved and had left on his grave. I told myself it was a coincidence, and she must have received it from somewhere else. Yet I could hear my heart pounding in my ears and my voice trembling when I asked her where she got the bracelet.

She told me that after Daren died, she had a Killed in Action (KIA) bracelet, but it created too much attention. It made her uncomfortable that everyone from a dentist to a stranger asked about her son who was killed. She wanted a way to remember him, but not have it displayed for all. Then she visited his grave. She saw the bracelet lying there and knew it was the answer to her prayers. It was a way to honor him, but not have everyone ask her about its meaning. She had worn it since that day. It gave her comfort.

With tears welling in my eyes, I whispered, "I made that bracelet. I wore it every minute of every day from the moment I found out he was killed."

Continents and oceans apart, we both found comfort from the same bracelet to honor the same man.

I wasn't sure Daren's family would even know who I was, and suddenly I was sobbing and hugging his mother. I felt the thick cord of the bracelet wrapped around my back as her hands pressed into me, and her heart unloaded the love she had.

Four years later, when I was turning thirty, I received a package in the mail. It contained a lovely card and a picture in a magnet frame from Daren's mother. It was a picture of her holding Daren's baby niece, and her arm was cradling the sweet baby's face with that same bracelet.

Daren couldn't be there to wish me a happy birthday, but I'm still receiving the gift of his love.

~Sarah Kemp

92

Chicken Soup for the Soul

Always a Mother

There is an instinct in a woman to love most her
own child — and an instinct to make any child
who needs her love, her own.
~Robert Brault

We quickly gathered up some clothes and threw them in a small suitcase. A dark van was waiting in our driveway to take my husband and me to the airport. Uniformed military personnel escorted us past staring eyes as we boarded our flight. Upon arrival, USO volunteers comforted us and guided us from the aircraft to another waiting van. They knew why we were there as they had done this duty hundreds of times before.

Hours later, as we waited in a beautifully appointed room of the Fisher House, we heard the roar of jet engines as the plane landed on a runway not far away. Our son was finally coming home from his tour of duty in Afghanistan. It was not the homecoming that we, his parents, were hoping for. It was his flag-covered casket that we came to receive. Following what seemed to be a well choreographed solemn ballet of sorts on the tarmac that concluded with a mortuary van taking our son's remains away, we returned to the airport on our way home. Once again, USO volunteers greeted us and offered us coffee, donuts, and comfort items to take with us on the long flight. The kindness of those USO volunteers greatly impacted my life. I had never met nor known what USO volunteers did. My limited understanding was that they hosted Bob Hope and Raquel Welch for the troops in faraway lands long ago.

A few months passed, and an article in the local paper announced the opening of a USO center at the airport near me. For the past five years, I have volunteered each and every Friday night at my USO for the closing shift. Another mother of a fallen soldier often volunteers with me. We do not let those we serve know who we are, for we are there to lift their spirits. Little do our special guests know that when I greet them, I see a bit of my son in each of them. I see their dedication to serve, their commitment to and love of country. I appreciate their service and their sacrifice more than they will ever know. And when I thank them for their service, I do it with all my heart.

When I enter the doors of my USO welcome center to fulfill my volunteer duties, it is like coming home. I find comfort, joy, and healing through serving our troops, and in doing so, my soul and spirit are lifted, and the memory of my only son lives on.

~Toni Gross

93

No Matter What, It Will Be Okay

What we have once enjoyed deeply we can never lose.
All that we love deeply becomes a part of us.
~Helen Keller

The 7:00 a.m. phone call contained the words that no wife ever wants to hear. "Ms. Seif, your husband was on the helicopter that went down and is confirmed missing at this time."

Just four days earlier, on March 6, 2015, my husband had received the Silver Star, the Marines' third highest award for valor, for his actions on a 2012 deployment that had taken the life of one of his dear friends. In 2013, I was by his side in Washington, D.C. as he received the USO "Marine of the Year" for those same heroic actions in Afghanistan — again surrounded by loved ones and family.

My husband was honored and humbled to receive the Silver Star that day, and to make things even better, it was also the day we announced to our friends and family that I was pregnant with our first child. Life was more than just good; it was phenomenal.

After that March 10th phone call, the next few months were a complete blur of paperwork, phone calls, and travel. There were seven funerals and memorials within a two-week period throughout the country.

In the beginning, the phone calls and text messages flooded in from friends and family. As time wore on they became far and few between, as is expected. Everyone returns to their normal daily life, except for the widows and children. These men were seen as heroes and Marines to most, but to us women they were our husbands, best friends, and the fathers of our children. No longer would they come home for dinner or give us a phone call to let us know they wouldn't be home that night because of work. We did not just lose our best friends that day in March; we lost our entire world, our everyday life.

I had thrown myself into the paperwork and phone calls. I wanted to get everything possible squared away before my son was born.

Our son was born in August. He was perfect and wonderful. I now had to navigate through a whole new life for the second time that year. Andrew and I had so many plans and dreams that we had wanted to fulfill together. Now, I would be doing them on my own, with his legacy.

These events have taught me that no matter what, I need to keep pushing forward and show my son how wonderful life can be. My husband and I had always wanted to do more traveling, so for the last two years that is what my son and I have done. We travel, and we see the beauty in life.

Our son is thriving in the only normal he has ever known. We have lost and gained so many family members, both blood and not. He knows nothing but love and the amazing stories of his daddy and uncles and what amazing people they were. I cannot help but see my husband in him in so many ways. His crooked little smile, the way he raises his eyebrows at me, and his constant need to know exactly how every single thing works in the world around him. All I have to do is look at the amazing legacy my husband left behind to know that no matter what life throws my way, everything will be okay.

~Dawn Seif

Military Families

Through the Generations

The Bronze Star

*You are not here merely to make a living. You are
here in order to enable the world to live more
amply, with greater vision, with a finer
spirit of hope and achievement.*
~Woodrow Wilson

"**M**r. Murphy is doing it again, Mom. Every morning he puts up the flag, and every evening he pulls it down," Peter said, as he watched our neighbor through the kitchen window.

"He's patriotic," I said to my ten-year-old son.

"We're patriotic, but we don't have a thirty-foot flagpole in our yard," Peter said. "Who do you think he is?"

"You'll find out tonight," I said. "I've invited our new neighbor to come to dinner and get acquainted."

When he arrived, I saw that Mr. Murphy had dressed in a suit and tie. His hair was still damp from his shower, and his cheeks were shiny from a fresh shave. It was obvious that getting invited to dinner was a big social event for him, and I was glad I'd used our good china.

Peter was never one to be shy. "Why do you put up that flag every day?"

"Lots of reasons, I guess," responded Mr. Murphy. He cleared his throat. "I'm glad to be an American. I think it's pretty to see the flag climbing up the flagpole to greet the morning. And it just makes me feel good."

"I thought maybe you used to be a general or something," Peter said.

Mr. Murphy laughed.

"No, I was just a seventeen-year-old private in the Army who got shot in both legs when our unit landed on Omaha Beach on D-Day in World War II," he said.

"Omaha Beach," I said quietly. "Not many survived that."

"No," he whispered, "not many."

"Did you get any medals?" Peter asked.

"Yes, I got a couple. I got a Purple Heart and a Bronze Star. I could show you the Purple Heart," he offered.

"Can I see the Bronze Star, too?" Peter asked.

"No, I never got it. Lots of soldiers earned medals, but never got them. Besides, we weren't trying to win medals; we were trying to win a war," Mr. Murphy said.

"You did," Peter said. "Thanks."

Mr. Murphy smiled. "You're welcome."

"No, I meant it," Peter said firmly. "Thanks."

"Couldn't you write to the President and get your medal?" I asked as I passed the potatoes.

"I don't want to bother the President," he laughed. "Besides, cutting through the red tape could take years."

I knew he didn't have many years.

That evening flew by. Before we knew it, Mr. Murphy was thanking us for a lovely dinner and heading home.

The next morning, Peter and I stood at the kitchen window and watched our neighbor raise his flag.

"I made something for him last night." Peter held out his hand. "It's a copy of the Bronze Star."

A gold foil star with slightly crooked points hung from a striped cloth. I recognized the material; it had been cut from the tail of Peter's favorite shirt.

"I know it isn't the real thing, but he'll never get the real medal, will he, Mom?"

"No," I answered simply. "Why don't you give that to him right now?"

"I feel embarrassed to go alone. Will you go with me?"

I phoned Mr. Murphy and asked him to meet us beside his flagpole.

"I know this is about fifty years late, but I brought you your Bronze Star," Peter said. He pinned the paper medal to the pocket of the old man's shirt.

Mr. Murphy snapped to attention and saluted, giving the ceremony unexpected dignity. Tears rolled down his wrinkled cheeks.

"I couldn't be any prouder if the President himself had given this to me," he said, wiping his eyes on his sleeve.

A few days later, I took a casserole to Mr. Murphy and saw a frame hanging over the mantel. It contained a faded Purple Heart… and a Bronze Star made from gold foil and a piece of a boy's favorite shirt. Both were precious to the old soldier.

The next morning, Peter looked out the kitchen window to watch Mr. Murphy put up the flag.

"Mom! Look!" Peter shouted and ran to the door.

Fearing the worst had happened to our neighbor, I ran after him.

A newly installed flagstaff was attached to the corner post of our back porch. A bright, new American flag was carefully folded across the rail. It was a special gift to a young boy from a grateful old soldier.

Peter quickly unfolded the flag and attached it to the staff. It gave a gentle flutter and settled into a rolling wave.

We turned and saw Mr. Murphy standing in his yard, watching us.

Peter saluted, and the old man smiled and saluted back.

~April Knight

Putting Things in Perspective

Gratitude turns what we have into enough, and more... It makes sense of our past, brings peace for today, and creates a vision for tomorrow.
~Melody Beattie

While our national policies are often debated, there is no misjudging the character and essential goodness of the service men and women sent in harm's way to carry them out. At times, it may appear that their good deeds, past and present, are submerged—washed over by the passage of years or the din of this morning's sound bites. Too often, much of what our soldiers, sailors, Marines, and airmen have done may seem to have been forgotten, ignored by an unappreciative world for which they sacrificed so much. When that happens, it is useful to recall the people and events that best illustrate the service and sacrifice of our heroes, and to pass those memories on to the generations yet to come.

Three very special episodes in three parts of Europe come to mind for me.

The first was documented on a PBS special, "D-Day Revisited," which focused on six WWII veterans of Omaha Beach returning to Normandy. They were greeted by French schoolchildren who still study the events of that day as an important part of their schools' curricula.

Many of these children had drawn pictures with the French flag along one side of the paper and the Stars and Stripes on the other. Dozens of children came to meet the veterans and hear their stories. Almost all asked for the veterans' autographs—many had them sign the crayon flags they had drawn—and waited in long lines to be photographed with them.

The second occurred in Bastogne, Belgium. A few years ago, a friend of mine, Reed Johnson, brought his father, a Bastogne veteran, to Europe to celebrate an anniversary of the battle. When Reed's father arrived at the ceremony, he was met by a tiny Belgian schoolgirl. She shook his hand, led him to his seat in the front row, and then, with a gesture that Reed said touched his father beyond measure, stood beside him as our national anthem was played... and sang it with him in English.

My own recollection of Bastogne occurred not long after when I took my family there on a visit. As we drove down the main street of the city—a Sherman tank still sits at the corner of a major intersection—my kids noticed the American flags that hung from almost every building. When we stopped to fill up with gasoline, I asked the station attendant what special occasion was marked by all those American flags. "Nothing special," he said. "They're there all the time." Like the French schoolchildren at Normandy, the people of Bastogne have not forgotten. Nor, I think, will they ever forget.

The third episode I want to tell you about occurred on a winding road, high on a mountaintop in Bosnia, where my small unit was one of the first to arrive in Sarajevo after the signing of the Dayton Agreement. A day or two after our arrival, I began making the rounds, visiting other units in and around the city.

One of the American communications outfits had set up in an old Ottoman fort high on a mountaintop overlooking the city. The road to the fort was along a mountain path, barely passable in our Humvee. At one point, the road squeezed between a sheer vertical drop on the left and a small village on the right. Pressed against the road, the tiny community was wedged into a miniscule space between the path and the wall of the mountain.

I was riding in the front side passenger seat of the Humvee with my arm out the window. In the arcane reasoning of the military, because we were a part of an international force, the national flag emblem was affixed on the right shoulder of our uniforms (not on the left as was customarily the case). Thus, the American flag was showing on the sleeve that was nearest the open window.

There were mixed emotions about the mission to Bosnia. But, whatever the headlines, it became clear to the troops who were there that the people who appreciated us most were the very old and the very young. Our presence allowed the old people to live their lives in dignity and the young to play in the sunshine, and both groups were grateful.

As our vehicle moved slowly through the village, two elderly Muslim gentlemen were drinking tea at a small table right next to the road. We were so close, that as we inched by, one of them reached toward the flag on my arm and said something to me in very passable English.

I nodded to him and wondered at his words for the rest of the drive. When I returned to my quarters, I asked about the significance of the expression the old gentleman had spoken. It turned out that he had used an ancient phrase — words with meaning so deep they were reserved for use in his culture only to express the most profound appreciation.

What the old man said when he pointed toward the flag on my shoulder was "We will love you for a thousand years."

Sometimes, when the headlines are bleak, I find myself thinking about all the people who appreciated the work of our American heroes, in Normandy, Bastogne, and Bosnia. That helps me keep things in perspective.

~Thomas D. Phillips

96

Lesson Learned

*As experience widens, one begins to see how
much upon a level all human beings are.*
~Joseph Farrell

A s a small child I earned a privilege from my grandparents that only a select few of their twelve grandchildren was allowed. I was entrusted to dust their home, an honor that involved moving, cleaning and replacing every photo frame, souvenir, and precious keepsake, including fine china, porcelain bells, and intricate glass figurines.

On one occasion, carrying out my delicate duty, I became curious as to why a particular object was considered valuable enough to be displayed with the others. It was a simple, tarnished, metal object resembling a small fireplace ash bucket. A bit dingy, it appeared crudely made and was entirely useless for the job it appeared to merit — unless it was an ashtray — but no one in my family smoked. It was poorly etched with the notation: "September 1945, Heilbronn, Germany." On the opposite side was scratched my grandfather's name: "Dell I. Powell."

When I asked my grandmother why this metal object was kept with all her fine things, she explained: "Your grandpa wasn't always a gardener and florist. A long time ago, many countries were involved in a terrible war called World War II. Your grandpa volunteered to represent his country as a soldier in the United States Army. Like he does at the flower shop now, he worked very hard and took great pride in what he did, and soon he became a Military Police officer."

She told me to hang on for a moment while she went to get something. I sat stunned. *My* grandpa? A soldier — with a gun? Shortly, she brought back photos revealing a skinny young man in uniform wearing a stoic, hard expression that I didn't recognize on my spunky, silly grandpa's face.

I was shocked. "He looks so… different," I murmured.

"So young or so serious?" she asked with a smile.

Crestfallen, I answered, "So… so… sad!" She looked closely at the face in the picture.

"Well, it was a very sad time then," she said softly. "People are very ugly with one another during war. Grandpa was far from home and missed his family. He saw things he never wanted to see and sometimes had to do things he wasn't proud of."

Grandma picked up the lackluster memento in question and admired it as she continued, "This, however, was something he *was* proud of. One of his duties was to capture and contain prisoners from the other country's armed forces. Prisoners of war weren't treated very well. It's not like prisoners in jails here. They didn't have beds to sleep in, clean clothes to change into or three square meals to eat each day. Many of the enemy's prisoners were simply killed. Grandpa's orders as an MP were to guard the prisoners to keep them from escaping. He was expected to be stern, firm, and uncaring."

My "Gramps" mean? I'd seen him angry — but I couldn't imagine him grumpy and marching prisoners along. The guy who called me "Little Red" and squeezed my nose and gave the best hugs in the world? The man who winked at my grandma when he called her his "Brown Eyes," and who whistled while he tended to his delicate flowers — rough, tough and ready to shoot?

"Grandpa's job was important, and he took it seriously," Grandma continued. "He always did his duty, accepted his responsibility, and never broke the rules."

"But," she said, her eyes twinkling with pride, "he also never forgot that his captives were also *men* — human beings just like him. They had families; they bled like him; they loved like him; they got hungry like him. They were doing what they were expected to do — just like him. So, while he wasn't friendly with them, he kept reminding himself to see the prisoners as men and treat them with mercy. Because of his kind heart, the prisoners were grateful. In secret, the German prisoners gathered bits of empty ammunition shells. They melted the brass to shape it and then hammered it into an ashtray to give him as a gift to show their gratitude and respect."

With that, she left me with the little ashtray that appeared a little shinier somehow — a gift from the heart that he treasured regardless of the fact he hadn't a use for it.

Later, when he came home, my grandpa — larger, older and more bent than the young Dell I. Powell in the picture — lifted me off the floor for a big embrace. I choked back a lump in my throat. My heart almost bursting, I felt for him at that moment more love and pride than I had had in all the years I'd known him. Though my grandma gave me the story, it was the man I'd never known in my grandpa who taught me a lesson I'd never forget.

We are all human beings; we love and are loved; we laugh, and we cry; we struggle and prevail. We will disagree and may even battle — but we are *all* worthy of compassion, because all lives matter.

~Angel Renee Perkins

97

Gratitude at the Gas Pump

The deepest craving of human nature
is the need to be appreciated.
~William James

My husband, Ted, is a proud Vietnam veteran. I can see his pride when he looks at the November 10, 1972 issue of *Life* magazine that featured his hometown of Massillon, Ohio. Massillon sent the largest number of young men per capita to Vietnam, and the article includes a large picture of Ted and his buddies standing shoulder to shoulder downtown. One of Ted's lifelong friends who was a fellow Vietnam veteran had the photo enlarged so I could frame it for Ted.

Ted doesn't talk much about the war, but occasionally something reminds him of a story and he will share it with me. One night, he and I went to a Billy Joel concert in Cleveland. One of the songs, "Goodnight Saigon," started with the sound of helicopters getting increasingly louder. In the large venue of the concert, they became deafening, and I could see and feel Ted tensing up. The song ended with the helicopters fading away, and Ted relaxed. Some days later, Ted told me about a horrific helicopter crash in Vietnam. Being a medic, he had to assist the wounded and see those who had been killed.

He's also told me stories of hilarious escapades while on leave, what it was like sleeping in the jungle, and how beautiful Vietnam is. He also tells me how scared he was at times. One time, on a recon mission, Ted had to jump out of a helicopter while it hovered above the ground. The helicopter couldn't stay long as it was a target, so the gunner was hurrying them along. When it was Ted's turn the gunner pushed him right out the side and he landed ten feet below, rolling on the ground.

Sadly, Ted's fears included coming home. The transition to civilian life was not easy. Ted had been used to intense structure and was afraid he wouldn't be able to adapt.

Vietnam veterans were not met with parades or crowds of thankful citizens at the airport. There was no fanfare, and even worse, they were met with protests and even spat on. This bothers Ted, and rightfully so.

Recently, Ted went to the gas station at our local club store. There was a young attendant watching over the pumps, and he approached Ted. The young man saw Ted's Vietnam veteran license plate and asked, "Are you the veteran?" Ted responded affirmatively. The young man reached out his right hand and said, "Thank you." Finally, Ted received the thank-you from a stranger that he didn't get when he returned home decades ago.

The young attendant said, "My uncle was in Vietnam. He never made it back. Well, physically, he made it back, but not really," as he pointed to his head. He asked Ted what he did in the Army, and Ted told him that he was a medic. The young man told Ted that his uncle was a tunnel rat. Ted knew what that was. Tunnel rats ran underground search-and-destroy missions. Often, the enemy put venomous snakes in the tunnels. Ted didn't disclose all of this to the young attendant, but did tell him that it was a very dangerous job, and that his uncle must be a courageous man.

Ted and his new gas station attendant friend stood and chatted for several minutes. As Ted told me, he kept thinking that he had to get home to mow the lawn, but the young man kept talking. Evidently, the young man enjoyed the conversation and asked more questions, so Ted didn't feel like he could just cut him off and leave. I wasn't buying that. Ted recounted to me almost verbatim the entire conversation. As Ted told me the story, I saw that pride again and got tears in my eyes. He told me that as the conversation was ending, the young man extended his right hand again and said, "Thank you, sir." I think Ted enjoyed the conversation, respect and well deserved recognition that he was shown after all these years.

~Lil Blosfield

Tragedy Turned to Treasure

The guardian angels of life sometimes fly so high
as to be beyond our sight, but they are
always looking down upon us.
~Johann Paul Friedrich Richter

On November 8, 1983, my mother awoke in the middle of the night with fearful thoughts that left her struggling to breathe. The next morning, those fears became a reality when an officer stood at her doorstep. My mother's husband of seven months, LTJG Cole "Bam-Bam" Patrick O'Neil, went beyond the call of duty and sacrificed his life for our country.

Knowing my mother's story, I was scared of the military life and falling in love with a military man. I feared I would experience the same heartache, but I had it all wrong. If my mother had had this same selfish mindset, her beloved Navy pilot would never have had the opportunity to experience love before he was called home.

Just over four years ago, I met my military man, and I fell hard and fast. After only one month, I knew I was in love with him, but I was scared. He had signed his contract with the U.S. Navy merely two weeks prior to meeting me.

Within four months of commissioning into the U.S. Navy, my husband had orders for deployment. I prayed that my mother's beloved late husband would be my husband's guardian angel during deployment.

I can say without a doubt that my prayers were answered. Shortly after my husband arrived at the ship, something miraculous happened. A recreational flyby was presented for entertainment by some of the U.S. Navy pilots over my husband's ship. As my husband stood on the deck gazing up at the jets, he heard one of the pilots flying over him being announced by the call sign "Bam-Bam" — the same call sign LTJG Cole Patrick O'Neil used during his duty as a U.S. Navy pilot. My husband called to share that experience with me, and I knew that my prayers had been answered. My husband did, in fact, have a guardian angel watching over him on that ship. This brought me comfort for the remainder of the time my husband spent away from home.

Before my husband commissioned, my mother came across some of her late husband's belongings that she thought she had mailed to his parents. Among the contents in the box were the Ensign and Lieutenant Junior Grade officer ranks of her late husband. Thinking of no better way to honor his memory, my mother approached my husband and gave him the shiny gold and silver bars. Upon receiving the gift, my husband confessed that before we were married, he had a dream about wearing LTJG O'Neil's ranks even though none of us knew at the time they were in my mother's possession. I had the honor of pinning LTJG O'Neil's final ranks onto my husband's collar and he wears them proudly. Those glistening bars serve as a subtle reminder of those who have fallen in the line of duty and those who are watching over us.

My husband commissioned into the military for a purpose — to be a part of something bigger than himself — and it has truly humbled him. I could not be prouder to be his support system on the home front and the one he comes home to at the pier. I thank the Lord for having brought my precious sailor to me. Without him, I might never have changed my perspective on military life. I would have missed out on friends who will forever be family and this truly beautiful life we cherish together. I used to never imagine a life with the military, but now I cannot imagine a life without it.

My advice to any current or soon-to-be military member or spouse is to not let fear stop you from something that could end up blessing you with some of your most treasured memories. Everyone has a story. Every story has both tragedies and treasures. But these are the elements that make each story beautiful.

~Lauren Nicole Adams

Giving Back at the USO

Life is a gift, and it offers us the privilege,
opportunity, and responsibility to give
something back by becoming more.
~Tony Robbins

There I was, a seventeen-year-old, chunky, baby-faced kid who didn't really have a clue what to do with himself after high school. Luckily, our school had a career fair during my senior year, and I ended up liking what a Navy recruiter had to say. A couple of months later, and while still in high school, I raised my hand and recited the pledge. My parents had to sign a document, since I was only seventeen, to give their approval. I was the third generation in our family to serve... a fact I am still proud of.

Fast-forward several months past boot camp, "A" school, and several other service schools... to a slightly more confident, less chunky, baby-faced kid... and my first encounter with the USO.

While flying home for leave before traveling to my first "real" duty station, I saw the signs at the airport. Stopping in, I found friendly people. (It wasn't always "friendly" in public for those of us in uniform back then — it was 1973.) There was food, soda, coffee, cards, books, TV... and it was all FREE and served with a smile. Over the next few years, as an E-2, E-3, and E-4 (PO3 for us Navy types), shuttling between schools, home, and my duty station, I would utilize — and actually seek out — the USO wherever my travels would lead me. And always, a smile, a kind word, and someplace to rest… FOR FREE… did I say it was FREE? To a junior enlisted, at the low end of the pay scale, anything FREE was a good thing.

As time went on, things got busier. Between advanced schools, survival training, flying overseas (I was enlisted flight crew now), and, oh yeah, getting married, my life got a bit more "complex," and I drifted away from the USO.

Our family moved several times during my career — not as much as many, but enough to make life challenging. We were always blessed to make friends along the way with whom we still keep in contact. In the military, the people we serve with become our family. We serve a common purpose, and the experiences we share forge a bond that few outside the military will know. While away from home, I knew my wife would continue to manage the household, raise our son, and solve life's problems — without me. I was confident that, should anything occur that was beyond her, friends would step in. That's what the military is about. As I advanced in my career, she too, "advanced" — working with Navy Relief and volunteering as an "Ombudsman" at one of the units we were with. The Ombudsman is a link between enlisted families and the command. If problems occur, especially while an enlisted member is deployed, family members call the Ombudsman, who contacts the command directly and finds a solution.

People (usually civilian friends) ask if I had a favorite experience while I was away. On one detachment overseas, we were flying round-the-clock ops, and our crew just happened to be stuck in a cycle that flew at night — all night. We were the "Bat Crew." After the cycle ended, and we were trying to readjust to a normal schedule, I remember walking out of the barracks one night and looking up. I was tired, lonely, and thinking about home (seven time zones away). *What were my wife and son doing? Was everything okay?* It was a clear evening, and as I looked at the sky, I saw a familiar constellation — I can't remember which one — but it was one of the "easy" ones — the Big Dipper or Orion. It was something I would see just about every night, and it brought me comfort. I knew that in several hours my wife or son might be looking up at that same constellation. A connection. Sounds hokey, I know, but it helped.

I retired in 1995 as a Chief, with twenty-two years in, the same girl at my side (the "Admiral"), and a son I am very proud of. (Did I tell you he made Eagle Scout?) When asked if I would do it again, I say yes. I miss the flying, the friends, the excitement, and the homecomings. It was a privilege to serve and I was honored to make so many friends along the way.

After retirement, there came a time when I decided to do something with my spare time. Around Christmastime, a buddy of mine (also a veteran) sent me an e-mail. It contained a link to a video of Bob Hope doing one of his USO shows in Vietnam. After watching several of his videos, laughing and crying, my solution of "what to do" was obvious—and my connection to the USO was re-established.

I am now privileged to "give back" during those times when a young, baby-faced kid needs a place to hang out. I get to talk with active-duty types, families, retirees, and guys and girls on their way to boot camp. And I usually tell a few "sea stories" along the way.

~Chuck Goebel

Ask Him If He Ever Saw Bob Hope

Out of pain and problems have come the sweetest
songs and the most gripping stories.
~Billy Graham

Early in 2001, I discovered an old, dusty basket full of love letters in the attic of our family home. They were written by my parents. My dad, Lt. Charles O. Hardman, and my mother Mary, pregnant with their first son upon his departure, endured a twenty-month separation during World War II. They wrote each other almost every day. Growing up in a small country town in Spencer, West Virginia, Dad talked about his combat experiences all my life; he spoke at Veterans Day ceremonies, Rotary Club, and schools. In his letters, he never wrote of the danger that he faced every day as an infantryman, but of life experiences sprinkled with meaningful and unusual happenings.

In one letter dated May 8, 1944, he wrote:

I had the most interesting evening. In fact, I enjoyed myself more than any other time since I left you. We had a traveling USO show play for our battalion this evening, and it was wonderful. I was in charge of the arrangements and had to mother the troop during their brief stay. It was composed of four girls and five men. Four of them Americans and five British. It was vaudeville but very refreshing and enjoyable. The actors really put everything they had into it, and the boys ate it up. I really had a lot of good laughs out of it.

I was so moved by the letter mentioning the USO show and the positive impact it had on Dad and his "boys" that I soon became a volunteer for the USO of NC in Jacksonville, North Carolina. I assumed that others who served also shared their war stories with family, friends, and their community. I took this for granted, but I realized I was wrong.

Recently, a journalist for a local neighborhood magazine, *Landfall Neighbors*, interviewed me about my parents' love letters. Bridget arrived at our home with pen and paper, eager to learn more about their letters. After showing her the letters, including my dad's war memorabilia of a Nazi flag, his helmet, and a silk map, she told me that her father served in the Marine Corps during Vietnam, but he would never talk about it. She said her teenage daughter is particularly interested in his experiences, but he won't even discuss the topic. She said her father is now in his eighties, and in her parents' garage is a box full of "war things." I encouraged her to search for the box and ask him about it. However, out of respect for him, she wouldn't dare investigate the contents and didn't want to ask.

It occurred to me that he must have seen a USO show "over there," and maybe he would talk about that. After all, Bob Hope entertained the troops during the Vietnam War. Surely, he saw one of his shows, and maybe he would remember this and share his memory. She mentioned this to her family as they gathered for New Year's Eve dinner the following evening.

On the morning of New Year's Day, an e-mail from Bridget was waiting for me:

We all went to New Year's Eve Dinner tonight, and I asked him if he ever saw Bob Hope with the USO. That simple question started a conversation about seeing Marilyn Monroe and several other famous people of his time. He did share that most of those shows were in Korea prior to Vietnam. However, he did recount a story about a Bengal tiger and his experience in the DMZ. My daughter asked him a few questions, and I couldn't believe how much he shared. My brother and I talked after dinner, and he couldn't recall Dad ever talking that much about the war in his lifetime.

Bridget thanked me for encouraging her to ask her Dad "one more time" about the war, using Bob Hope as her "way in."

I have met many active-duty service members and veterans during my experiences in volunteering for the USO of NC. Many refuse to talk about what happened "over there." I am one of the few whose dad shared an abundant amount of his combat experiences throughout my life. Only now do I understand that this was very unusual. The loved ones of these warriors want to learn more about their experiences, but their questions often conjure up memories that are perhaps too painful to reveal.

But maybe, just maybe, they will talk about the day when the USO came to their base to entertain them, and who knows where that discussion will lead?

~Sarah Hardman Giachino

Service for Eight

All good men and women must take responsibility to
create legacies that will take the next generation
to a level we could only imagine.
~Jim Rohn

We stand with our iPhones, ready to capture the very significant event we have traveled in heavy rain for over an hour and a half to witness. It seems like just yesterday we attended the graduation ceremony from basic training of our nineteen-year-old son. How is it possible that we are in the flag-filled induction room at the Military Entrance Processing Station in San Antonio, Texas, to record *our* son, now a thirty-eight-year-old Army captain, administering the oath of enlistment to *his* son, our eldest grandson? He will be nineteen when he graduates basic training.

Surely, it was just days ago when this grandson, four years old at the time, sat anxiously awaiting a video teleconference with his grandfather, Chief of Staff Colonel Patterson, from his post in the Balkans where he was serving on an important peacekeeping mission. As soon as his grandfather's face flashed onscreen, my grandson said, "Hi, Pawpaw! Mommy said we were going to see you on the screen just like the movies. Where is the popcorn?"

I smile at that memory. Then I pay attention. My grandson is taking his oath. A very important life decision has now become a spoken oath and a signed commitment. Three generations of military service are represented in that room — my husband, our son, and our grandson.

Shortly before attending our grandson's induction, my husband, who has a strong research gene, finished exploring generational information on Ancestry.com. It yielded quite a history of military service. Eight generations of Patterson ancestors have served as warriors in numerous world conflicts that include the Revolutionary War, the War of 1812, the Civil War, World Wars I and II, the Vietnam War, the Balkan Peacekeeping Mission, Iraq, and Afghanistan.

My husband's love for military detail in his research is matched equally by my history-teacher penchant for the stories behind our military history. The links were exciting to explore, but when a document of service or retirement appeared, written details became outlines of flesh-and-blood relatives to me. I could piece together the stories. They were not unlike ours. Wives and mothers sent their husbands and sons into harm's way. The men and their families did many of the same activities, felt many of the same emotions that my family has experienced. They wrote letters, filled in diaries and sent care packages. My generation has added e-mails, phone videos, texts, tweets, and Instagram, but they convey the same emotions and news.

In one of our closets, I have rolled up signs that are left over from five different deployments and five joyous homecomings — handmade by four grandsons and one granddaughter. We keep them as mementos with hopes that we will not have to experience another dreaded goodbye because of an additional deployment. We say the same prayers for peace, bind the war wounds our family has suffered, tell heroic stories, and show decorations of valor that include a Legion of Merit, a Purple Heart and a Bronze Star earned in conflict and peacekeeping. We also remain vigilant and ready. That is the paradox of a military family… praying for peace while remaining prepared for war.

Yes, we can count service for eight generations so far… eight generations of courageous warriors and their families, who have honored their nation with pledges of loyalty, honor, and sacrifice. Two sons and now one grandson are currently in the Army. There are three more grandsons and one granddaughter. If history repeats itself, who knows what future generations will see when they research our names and records. What a legacy they will find!

~Sharon L. Patterson

Meet Our Contributors

Hannah A. is currently a high school student. Her favorite hobbies include reading and writing.

Kristi Adams proudly served eight years in the United States Air Force as a weapons officer. She now lives in Germany with her husband, who is serving on active duty, and the world's neediest rescue cat. Kristi is also a travel writer for Europe's *Stars and Stripes*. This is her second story published in the *Chicken Soup for the Soul* series.

Lauren Nicole Adams received her Bachelor of Environmental Design in Architecture, with honors, from Texas A&M University. She is founder of The Navy Home and married to a United States Naval Officer. Lauren loves all things design and hopes to make a difference in the lives of military families through her donations and future charity work.

Helen Aitken is a science educator, writer and the "Safety First" columnist for *Lakeland Boating*. Married thirty years to retired USMC Col. Scott Aitken, they settled down in eastern North Carolina after their thirteenth move in nineteen years. Will, twenty-six, ignores the razor and sports a well-trimmed beard. Learn more at helenaitken.com.

Karen B. is a Gold Star Mom. She has worked as a secretary for forty years, currently employed at a junior high school. She has raised three amazing children and has been blessed with two grandchildren. Karen enjoys volunteering in her community. She plans on continuing to honor her son in the future.

Kristine Benevento will never be a comedienne but she has been around humorous situations. Kris wanted to prove to the naysayers, "If I think really hard and write it down I can make people smile!" Born on Cape Cod and one of nine siblings, she brings her thoughts to life so her children can cringe when they read her stories.

Lil Blosfield lives in Ohio with her husband Ted. Lil has written stories and poems for as long as she can remember. She has accumulated a large collection over the years, with each day being the opportunity for another story! E-mail her at LBlosfield40@msn.com.

Veronica Boblett is a Navy wife and full-time stay-at-home mom to their son and three daughters. She enjoys taking care of her family, being active in their church and children's schools, and traveling. Veronica and her husband Rex look forward to moving back home to Kentucky when he retires.

Tamara Bostrom-Lemmon has contributed to several magazines, but this is her first inclusion in a book. Tamara graduated as speaking Valedictorian from Dixie State University in 2015 with a BS in English. She lives in St. George, UT with her husband, their children, and one spoiled Golden Retriever. They love to ski and hike.

Laquita Brooks received her Bachelor of Science in Mass Communication at the University of North Carolina at Pembroke in May of 2008. Laquita enjoys volunteering at the USO and other community events. Her hobbies include writing poems, collecting vinyl records and DJing. She is also a die-hard Duke basketball fan.

Carolyn Brown began this story when her young grandson, age seven, proudly stated he wanted to grow up to be "just like Grampa." Proudly Carolyn dedicates this story to him, his grandfather, and our military families who, with love and resilience, live with the unseen wounds of war. This is our story.

B.E. Burda served over twenty-nine years in the United States Air Force and enjoyed sharing all the resulting adventures with his three children and lovely wife. He is with the USO and enjoys time with his family, golfing, reading, and traveling.

Cassandra Burns is an Air Force veteran. Her husband is currently on active duty. She is a full-time student and stay-at-home mom to three sons. Cassandra enjoys writing, traveling, photography, snowboarding, and spending time with family.

Jonathan Cervantes was born and raised in Wake Forest, NC. After high school he joined the United States Army and is still enlisted. He is married and has a beautiful newborn daughter. He plans to finish his contract in the military and work in the Information Technology field.

Jesse Childers is just a guy who is trying to make his place in this world, sharing life stories while he goes.

Jacqueline Chovan is a wife, mother, and amateur author. She has been happily married to her husband Matthew for fourteen years and has been immensely blessed with three beautiful sons. Currently living in Germany, Jacqueline enjoys traveling, writing, and photography. She is actively working on a novel and short stories.

Lola Di Giulio De Maci is an essayist and children's author. Her stories appear in numerous *Chicken Soup for the Soul* books, the *Los Angeles Times*, *Reminisce* and *Sasee* magazines. Lola is a retired teacher with a Master of Arts in education and English. She writes overlooking the San Bernardino Mountains.

Katie Denisar hails from Galesburg, IL where she taught first grade for eight years before marrying her husband Bradley and joining the Army family. They have one daughter Laura, and since they married they have lived in the D.C. area, Anchorage, Alaska and currently reside in Honolulu, HI.

Lisa Dolby is a Navy wife and a mom to two pretty fantastic Navy kids. She has been married for fifteen years and has found her own way to shine through multiple deployments, PCS moves, and new homes. Life was moving at a lazy, predictable pace until that one handsome pilot walked into the bar and the real story began.

Jo Eager has been writing for decades, starting off as a copywriter at a radio station. This is her fourth story published in the *Chicken Soup for the Soul* series. Jo also works as a voice actor, a reporter in a television news helicopter in San Diego, and a fitness instructor. She was in the military during the 1980s in Berlin, Germany.

Anthony Farthing served twenty-three years in the United States Air Force. He served with distinction while deployed all over the world. He couldn't have done it without the love and support of his beautiful wife Mari.

Cassy Fiano-Chesser is the wife of a Marine Corps veteran and Purple Heart recipient. She works from home as a blogger and freelance writer. She and her husband live in Jacksonville, FL. They have five children. Cassy is a devout Catholic and a proud Down syndrome mom and loves spending time with her family.

Karen Foster is a freelance writer, blogger, and speaker. Her devotions and true first-person stories have appeared in multiple magazines, ezines, and anthologies. Karen has also served as a jail chaplain for women inmates. In addition to being a military spouse, Karen served as an Air Force Public Affairs Officer for ten years.

Amy Fraher is a mom of two and wife of a USAF MSgt-Ret. Amy has also published a children's book, with a second one currently a work in progress. Being military herself and then continuing as a spouse, her story is one of a basic life for all military families to recognize.

BJ Gallagher is a popular speaker and author of over thirty books. She writes business books that educate and empower, women's books that enlighten and entertain, and gift books that inspire and inform. BJ's timeless business fable, *A Peacock in the Land of Penguins*, is an international bestseller, published in twenty-three languages.

Karina Garrison is an award-winning author and speaker. Her stories appear nationally in books and other publications. Karina enjoys volunteer work, traveling, and making new friends through the release of her inspirational novel, *Tempting Faith*. Learn more at karinagarrison.com.

Carol L. Gee served over twenty-one years in the Air Force and Air Force reserves. She also worked for over twenty-eight years in higher education. She is the author of four books, her most recent *Random Notes: About Life, "Stuff" and Finally Learning to Exhale* and *Gilded Pearls*. Her work has also appeared in numerous magazines.

Sarah Hardman Giachino lives in Wilmington, NC, and serves on the USO-NC Board of Directors and the Jacksonville Advisory Committee. She is writing a book called *Dearest Darling, Dearest Sweetheart*, a twenty-month collection of her parents' love letters including memories of when they returned to the battlefields in Europe.

Heather Gillis is a United States Air Force wife, mother, and nurse. She is founder of Bowen's Hope, a ministry that helps kidney disease kids and their families. She is a blogger for Alaska Christian Women's Ministry and her own personal blog. To learn more about Heather or read her blog visit heathergillis.com.

Chuck Goebel was born in 1955 in Elmhurst, IL, and at seventeen joined the Navy to see the world (and get out of Elmhurst). After twenty-two years, he retired as a Chief, manages rental properties with his family, and enjoys life with friends and family. He is grateful to his wife Tammy and son Jason for their love and support, and to the many others he calls family.

Dianna Beamis Good is married with two grown children and four grandchildren. She is a member of the Northern Arizona Word Weavers. Her stories have appeared in *Christmas Story Collection*, *A Time to Blossom*, *Spoken Moments*, *Stupid Moments*, and coming in the spring *Loving Moments*. Dianna is currently working on a devotional.

Antonia Gross, "Toni," is the daughter of United States Navy Lt. Frank R. Hankey, who served for twenty-nine years. Toni and husband Craig have been married for forty-one years and reside in Oldsmar, FL. Their daughter Natalie lives in Ft. Lauderdale. Toni co-owns Frankie's Patriot BBQ. Her motto is "We honor through service."

Nicole Hackler is a Civil Engineer in North Carolina who has lived all over the country as a military wife. She loves to travel, take pictures of all the places she's been, and document her adventures by writing short stories and scrapbooking.

Jamie Handling received her Bachelor of Arts in English from California State University, Hayward and her Master's in Education from Walden University. Jamie and her husband Mike are both high school teachers and live with their two children in Northern California. In her free time she writes YA novels.

Teresa Anne Hayden is a writer living in Cayce, KY. Her treasures in life are her three children, six grandchildren and dog, Boomer. Her work has appeared in several publications including *Chicken Soup for the Soul: A Book of Miracles* and *Chicken Soup for the Soul: Food and Love*. Learn more at teresahaydenwriter.com.

Cherilyn Hearn lives and writes in southeast Kansas with her husband and three children. She received her Bachelor's degree from Wichita State University and has written fourteen books ranging from a cookbook to women's fiction. Cherilyn enjoys researching her work, home décor, and traveling.

Kathryn M. Hearst is a southern girl with a love of the dark and strange. Besides writing, she has a passion for shoes, vintage clothing, antique British cars, and all things musical. Kate lives in Orlando, FL, with her chocolate Lab Jolene and rescue pups, Jagger and Roxanne. She is a self-proclaimed nerd, raising a nerdling.

Miriam Hill is a frequent contributor to the *Chicken Soup for the Soul* series and has been published in *Writer's Digest*, *The Christian Science Monitor*, *Grit*, *St. Petersburg Times*, *The Sacramento Bee*, and Poynter online. Miriam's submission received Honorable Mention for Inspirational Writing in a Writer's Digest Writing Competition.

Andrea Holt worked passionately for USO Okinawa for nearly five years. In her time there, she encountered many touching moments, from just a smile, to a thank-you, to stories from volunteers and customers about how the organization made an impact. Andrea enjoys traveling, music, roller derby, and plans to work in marketing.

Dolores Incremona earned her BA as a non-commissioned officer in the U.S. Air Force. She then became a commissioned officer in the Air Force and earned her MS in International Relations. Now a retired veteran, she volunteers for the USO weekly and is on the Board of Directors for the Tampa Chapter of MOAA.

Taylor Jackson developed a passion and earned recognition for writing early in life. She has one son, and works as an admissions advisor in Northern California. Taylor enjoys make-up artistry, painting, and science. She plans to write science fiction, horror, science-based children's books, and to earn an MA degree in astrophysics.

Daphne Jasinski was a Navy brat. She lived in nine states and Spain, moving thirteen times by age fourteen. She now lives permanently in western Washington State with her husband. They have three children and two grandchildren. Daphne enjoys genealogy, sewing, reading, and writing. She is working on stories about her ancestors' lives.

Home-front mom **Linda Jewell** supports our troops, veterans, and their families. She's involved in Cookie Deployments and writes about patriotism, parenting, and prayer. Linda provides practical tips, inspiration, and encouragement to strengthen moms of the military during tough times. E-mail her at Linda.Jewell@icloud.com.

Dorothy Johnson is a retiree, who shares her thoughts about life and faith on her blog, *Reflections from Dorothy*. She also contributes devotionals to FaithHappening.com. She has just completed her first novel.

Lisa Hyman Johnson, a writer and retired teacher, received her MA in English from Auburn University. She has an actress/singer daughter, an Air Force officer son, a wonderful daughter-in-law, and enjoys living with her husband and rescued cats and dog in coastal Alabama where she is active in their church and community.

Sarah Kemp has worked for the USO for seven years in Kandahar, Afghanistan; Washington, D.C.; and now Stuttgart, Germany. She has a degree in journalism from Marshall University. She loves her home state of West Virginia, supporting the troops, and international travel (just one continent left!).

Lois Kiely received her BA and MS degrees from Monmouth University. As the 1988 New Jersey Teacher of the Year, she was presented with an Honorary Doctorate. She is an award-winning teacher, artist, and writer. Lois has one son and a granddaughter. She lives in New Jersey and winters in Arizona.

A "military brat," **Michael Kincade** knows firsthand the importance of the military spouse. He holds a BA in Business, has been married for forty years to his wife Nancy, has two adult sons and a new grandson. His work, *Positively America*, will be available this summer. They reside on the Central Coast of California.

April Knight is a freelance writer. Her latest romance novel is titled *Stars in the Desert*. When she's not writing she can usually be found riding a horse. She collects letters written in the 1800s and antique inkwells.

Bill Kretzschmar has been a USO of North Carolina volunteer for thirteen years. In addition to his weekly shift, he is a member of the Honors Support Team and edits the quarterly newsletter. A Marine veteran, he served two tours in Vietnam. He resides in Cary, NC, with his wife of fifty-two years, Jan.

Mitchell Kyd writes frequently about the joys and poignant moments of small town living. As a self-proclaimed tale weaver, she reminds others that we are no longer a culture of oral storytellers and that our stories are lost in two generations unless we preserve them through writing.

Erica Kyle has always had a passion for the arts. She recently started a blog at ejablonski959.wordpress.com to share her writing in hope that her story will inspire and encourage others. Outside of work and her family Erica enjoys painting, drawing, and doing DIY projects around her home.

Ranishley Larsen is an energetic native of Sydney, Australia. Currently residing in San Antonio, TX, Mrs. Larsen attended the University of Sydney and graduated with a BA in 2004. Leaving behind her corporate career, she is currently a freelance marketing executive and graphic designer. E-mail her at ranishley@gmail.com.

Mary Elizabeth Laufer was a Navy wife for twenty years. She attended five colleges across the country and finally earned a degree in English

Education from SUNY. Her jobs included substitute teacher, library assistant, and private tutor. Over the years she kept extensive diaries and now draws from them to write her stories.

John J. Lesjack and Carol Lee are retired schoolteachers who live in Northern California. Responses to "Up Close and Personal" can be e-mailed to jlesjack@gmail.com.

Gary C. Lilly has been in the Pastoral ministry for forty-seven years. Gary enjoys writing personal devotionals for people going through difficult times and uses poetry to encourage and inspire others. He and his wife Pamela are both avid readers and love to play with their dog Seemee.

Donna Lorrig is the Media Relations Specialist for the Colorado Ballet Society and a homeschooling mother of seven children. She attended MTSU and Pikes Peak Community College, where she studied art, animal science, and politics. She thrives on the creative process and is a previous contributor to the *Chicken Soup for the Soul* series.

Kevin Matthew is a Chicago-based ghostwriter specializing in both nonfiction and fiction stories, as well as working on full-length books for his clients. When not locked away in his office typing, Kevin enjoys spending time with his wife. He received his BA in Communication.

The daughter of a retired sailor, **Carol Mawyer** grew up in a military family. She earned her BA from Virginia Tech in 1983 before marrying her college sweetheart two years later. Carol works as a public relations practitioner and enjoys reading, exploring Virginia wines, and texting her adult children in her spare time.

A native of Sandston, VA, **Matthew W. Mawyer** is a 2010 graduate of the Virginia Military Institute where he earned a Bachelor of Science degree in Civil and Environmental Engineering and an Army commission. He enjoys music, backpacking, and traveling, and resides in Richmond, VA, where he is active in his church.

Bob McDonnell is a husband, father, and grandfather living in Loveland, CO. He spent four years (1963-1967) in the United States Air Force, including one year in Thailand. He labels himself as "semi-retired." He is in his tenth year as a freelance writer for a weekly newspaper in Colorado.

Beau McNeff received his Bachelor of Arts in Economics, Political Science, and Public Policy from Southern Methodist University in 2002. He also received his MBA from Marylhurst University in 2010. Beau and his wife, Cecilia, have four amazing children. Beau served in the U.S. Army Reserve in Afghanistan during OEF 13-14.

A twenty-three-year Navy wife and mother of three, **Lisa Smith Molinari** writes the award-winning blog and syndicated weekly column, "*The Meat and Potatoes of Life*" which appears in military and civilian newspapers including *Stars and Stripes*, the newspaper for the U.S. Armed Forces. Learn more at themeatandpotatoesoflife.com.

Craig Morgan served in the United States Army before coming home to Tennessee and launching a recording career. He has charted seventeen times on the Billboard country charts and had seven singles make that chart's Top Ten, including "International Harvester" and "Almost Home."

A visual artist by training, **Susan Mulder** left a career teaching and speaking in her field to pursue new directions. A chronic maker of handcrafted goods, book nerd and doting Mim (as her "grands" call her), she also loves to cook and writes a little here and there. Susan resides in Michigan with her husband and an ornery cat named Bo.

Linda Newton is a counselor and the author of *12 Ways to Turn Your Pain Into Praise*. She frequently speaks at retreats, conferences, and seminars both in the U.S. and abroad. You can contact her online at LindaNewtonSpeaks.com and check her out on Facebook with her husband at facebook.com/answersfrommomanddad.

Anne Oliver, a native of Bluefield, WV, holds Bachelor's and Master's degrees from the University of Georgia. She and her husband George reared three Army brats during his thirty-one years with the Army. (HOOAH!) She enjoys volunteering, reading, and looking forward to more great adventures. E-mail her at armygrl74@aol.com.

Shannon Patterson is a devoted military spouse who loves traveling, finance, and writing. She is currently a stay-at-home mom in Southern Georgia.

Sharon L. Patterson is a retired educator and military wife. She has published spiritual encouragement for thirty-five years, including *A Soldier's Strength from the Psalms*, *Healing for the Holes in Our Souls*, *Where Is Happy?* and a calendar "Wisdom from the Rearview Mirror." Sharon is a past contributor to the *Chicken Soup for the Soul* series.

Angel Perkins is a former newspaper editor. She is a mother of three adult children and recently welcomed her first grandchild. Angel currently manages a manufactured home community for seniors, and she and her husband manage a campground in Michigan. She enjoys reading, singing, writing, and quality time with family and friends.

Perry Perkins is a frequent contributor to the *Chicken Soup for the Soul* series. Perry has written for hundreds of magazines, and has published several novels, short story collections, and cookbooks. His work can be found at perryperkinsbooks.com.

Tom Phillips (Col, USAF-Ret) led a detachment through a Red Brigades terrorist episode, served as Director of the Air Force Personnel Readiness Center during Operation Desert Storm, and commanded troops in

Italy, Bosnia, and Germany. He and his wife Nita live in Lincoln, NE, where he writes about history and baseball.

Elisa Preston has been a military wife for over ten years. She and her husband have an active toddler, a nervous dog, and a sassy cat they share with the grandparents. Elisa writes for Operation Blessing and is a school counselor on Fort Bragg. She loves reading, running, dancing, and is working on her second novel.

Connie Kaseweter Pullen lives in rural Sandy, OR, near her five children and several grandchildren. She received her Bachelor of Arts, with honors, from the University of Portland in 2006 with a double major in Psychology and Sociology. Connie enjoys writing, photography, and exploring nature.

Trevor Romain is a best-selling author and illustrator as well as a sought-after motivational speaker. Trevor's books have sold more than a million copies worldwide and have been published in 20 different languages. For more than twenty years, Trevor has traveled to schools, hospitals, summer camps, and military bases worldwide, delivering stand-up comedy.

Misty Sanico is a writer, editor, and afternoon tea enthusiast from Honolulu, HI. Her work has appeared in the *Bamboo Ridge, Journal of Hawaii Literature and Arts* as well as various magazines and newspapers. She is most passionate about reading and sharing Pacific Island literature.

Retiring about the same time her twin daughters left home and looking for something to do, **Tanya Schleiden** entered a Harlequin writing contest. Writing as T.R. McClure, she publishes her third heartwarming book this year. After leaving the military, Rocky and his family have settled in Tennessee. They visit often.

Dawn Seif is a mom and the widow of Staff Sergeant Andrew Seif, a decorated Marine having received USO's 2013 Marine of the Year Award and the Silver Star. March 10, 2015, Staff Sergeant Seif, along with ten other service members was killed during a training mission. On August 22, 2015, James Andrew Seif, Andy's legacy was born.

Sarah Smiley's weekly newspaper column is syndicated to newspapers and magazines across the country. She is the author of three books, including *Dinner with the Smileys*. In 2014, Sarah was awarded the American Legion Auxiliary Public Spirit Award for her efforts bringing attention to military family issues.

C. Solomon grew up in the military culture, the daughter of a United States Army soldier and spent the majority of her life overseas on military bases in Germany.

Mati Stark is a self-employed mother of five. She enjoys reading and writing, studying family history, and spending time with her kids. She and her husband of nineteen years make their home in Illinois. When the nest is empty they hope to visit a few street rod shows across the country and retreat to their cabin on the family farm.

Lauren B. Stevens is a freelance writer and proud Air Force brat. She is currently writing a book about her experiences as a "third culture kid," growing up in Europe during the Cold War. Lauren lives outside of Baltimore with her husband and son.

Candy Storey lives in Neptune, NJ, with her husband Jesse and their very large family. She is the pastor of a local church and is very involved with young people in her community. She loves to write and has a million stories.

Gloria Orioles Talbot is living the dream in Central Florida. Her three children: Katherine, Matthew, and Carolyn continue to amaze and inspire her. Gloria has worked with faith-based communities, youth serving nonprofits and addiction resource organizations for the past thirty years. In her spare time she enjoys travel.

Kathryn Taliaferro has a BA in Religious Studies and a Master's in Religious Education. She is married to an Air Force pilot and they have four children who they homeschool. She enjoys blogging at DailyGraces. net, as well as reading, crocheting and crafting, and hopes to write a book about God's presence in our daily lives.

Kamia Taylor took her experiences of constantly moving in the military and used them to manage businesses, real estate and deal with a wide diversity of cultures throughout her legal career. She has retired to a small organic farm in Southwest Missouri where she enjoys the diversity of wildlife instead. E-mail her at bigblackdogrescue@gmail.com.

Kasinda Thomas received her BA in English from Huston-Tillotson University and is currently pursuing her MS in Professional Counseling. She likes to travel and spend quality time with her family and friends. She loves to give back to her military community and hopes to help them build stronger relationships in the future.

Mary Varga is a Certified Personal Trainer and Senior Fitness Instructor. She is also the survivor of a Traumatic Brain Injury in 1997 that left her with very poor balance. The classes she teaches are like physical therapy for her. Mary is a devout Christian and member of Louisville Christian Writers. Writing and working out are her passions.

Patricia Walsh is an alumna of Northwestern University and has written several nonfiction children's books. Now living in Arizona, this former Midwesterner enjoys hiking, editing her high school newsletter, and genealogy, which led to her discovery of the Dutch volunteers who honor the graves of WWII American soldiers.

Jennifer Mears Weaver is the wife of a former Sergeant in the United States Marine Corps and the mom of four very active children.

Beth Wiggins is the wife and high school sweetheart of LTC (ret) Scott Wiggins and the mother of three sons: Walker, Andrew, and Benjamin. She taught in the American DOD schools in West Germany, worked for EDS in Dallas, TX, and home-educated her sons for twenty-three years. She currently teaches Senior English in El Dorado, AR.

Arthur Wiknik, Jr. served in Vietnam with the 101st Airborne Division and was featured on the History Channel and the Military Channel for his participation in the battle of Hamburger Hill. Arthur frequently shares his military experiences at schools and civic organizations. Learn more at namsense.com.

David M. Williamson is a grateful husband, father of four, and Air Force aircrew veteran living on Okinawa, Japan. He writes songs, plays piano, and drinks unhealthy amounts of coffee. When not at work or playing online games, he writes fantasy novels, short stories, and the occasional haiku.

Kristi Woods is a writer and speaker who shares her words of encouragement at KristiWoods.net. She is published in *Chicken Soup for the Soul: Dreams and Premonitions*, *Proverbs 31 Encouragement for Today*, and ibelieve.com. Kristi, her retired-from-the-military husband, and their three children live in Oklahoma.

Andrew Yacovone was born in Hollister, CA and attended University of California Davis. He joined the Army in 2013 as a 2nd Lieutenant and has won multiple awards in songwriting competitions. His band, Interstate 10, can be found on iTunes and Spotify and all social media with the handle @i10music.

Angela Young attended Sam Houston State University with a major in English. She married her Marine Corps husband in 2010 and moved to North Carolina. She and her husband now live in Florida. In her free time Angela enjoys reading, journaling, hula hooping, hiking, camping, lip-syncing, and volunteering at her church and library.

Meet Amy Newmark

Amy Newmark is the bestselling author, editor-in-chief, and publisher of the *Chicken Soup for the Soul* book series. Since 2008, she has published 140 new books, most of them national bestsellers in the U.S. and Canada, more than doubling the number of Chicken Soup for the Soul titles in print today. She is also the author of *Simply Happy*, a crash course in Chicken Soup for the Soul advice and wisdom that is filled with easy-to-implement, practical tips for having a better life.

Amy is credited with revitalizing the Chicken Soup for the Soul brand, which has been a publishing industry phenomenon since the first book came out in 1993. By compiling inspirational and aspirational true stories curated from ordinary people who have had extraordinary experiences, Amy has kept the twenty-four-year-old Chicken Soup for the Soul brand fresh and relevant.

Amy graduated *magna cum laude* from Harvard University where she majored in Portuguese and minored in French. She then embarked on a three-decade career as a Wall Street analyst, a hedge fund manager, and a corporate executive in the technology field. She is a Chartered Financial Analyst.

Her return to literary pursuits was inevitable, as her honors thesis in college involved traveling throughout Brazil's impoverished northeast region, collecting stories from regular people. She is delighted to have come full circle in her writing career — from collecting stories "from the people" in Brazil as a twenty-year-old to, three decades later, collecting stories "from the people" for Chicken Soup for the Soul.

When Amy and her husband Bill, the CEO of Chicken Soup for the Soul, are not working, they are visiting their four grown children.

Follow Amy on Twitter @amynewmark. Listen to her free daily podcast, The Chicken Soup for the Soul Podcast, at www.chickensoup. podbean.com, or find it on iTunes, the Podcasts app on iPhone, or on your favorite podcast app on other devices.

About Miranda Hope

Miranda Hope, granddaughter of comedian Bob Hope, serves as Vice President of the Bob & Dolores Hope Foundation, which "supports organizations that bring HOPE to those in need, and those who served to protect our nation." In that role, she spearheaded partnerships with FoodCorps, SuperFood Drive, and the Monarch School for homeless children. She is an active participant in partnerships to help active military and veterans with Easter Seals' "Bob Hope Veterans Support Program," the WWII Museum in New Orleans, the USO, and Operation Homefront.

Miranda worked for a decade as a teacher and counselor in the public school system in Virginia. She founded and directed "Next Step," a nonprofit that helps low-income, first generation teens figure out what they want to do with their lives and how to pay for it. She is a musician, a singer-songwriter (www.mirandahopemusic.com), and a certified yoga teacher, trained to offer trauma-sensitive yoga and meditation to a military population. For more than four years, she offered a weekly class in the locked-down psychiatric ward of the VA Hospital in San Diego, CA.

Miranda holds a BA from Stanford University and an MFA from Columbia University and currently resides with her husband, child, and dog in the Blue Ridge Mountains of Virginia.

About the USO

For more than seventy-six years, the USO, a private, non-profit organization, has served the men and women of the U.S. military and their families throughout their service — from the moment they join until they transition back to their communities.

Today's service members need the care, comfort, connection and support that can only be provided by an organization that is with them at every point of their military journey, wherever they serve. The USO continuously adapts to the needs of our men and women in uniform and their families, so they can focus on their very important mission. The organization is a family of volunteers who are united in their commitment to support America's service members by keeping them connected to the very things they've sworn to defend — family, home, and country. The USO's work is America's most powerful expression of gratitude to the men and women who secure our nation's freedoms.

We often hear from people who say they want to give back to our nation's service members, but they don't know how to get involved. The USO provides a variety of ways to show support and appreciation for our military heroes and helps make a difference in their lives. Individuals, corporations or organizations can find creative ways to give at www.USOWishbook.org, choosing from the virtual gift catalog. Americans can also visit www.uso.org/force to learn how they can join Force Behind the Forces by making an online donation, sending a message of support to our service men and women or by finding a local USO to learn more.

Thank You

We are grateful to all our story contributors and fans, who shared thousands of stories about military life and heroism. We are also very grateful to the USO family, in particular Gayle Fishel, and her incredible team: Kristin Barry, Kayla Greenwalt, Leah Kartun, Joe Lee, Ashley McClellan, Sandra Moynihan, Rachal Pichette, Erica Schultz, Chad Stewart, Mari Villalobos, and Ann Weller for the incredible work they did soliciting and reading stories for the book. This was a true collaboration.

On the Chicken Soup for the Soul side, Elaine Kimbler read the thousands of stories that were submitted and helped us narrow them down to a few hundred finalists. Susan Heim did a masterful job editing the first manuscript and finding those excellent quotes we put at the beginning of each story.

Associate Publisher D'ette Corona continued to be Amy's right-hand woman in creating the final manuscript and working with all our wonderful writers. Barbara LoMonaco and Kristiana Pastir, along with Elaine Kimbler, jumped in at the end to proof, proof, proof. And yes, there will always be typos anyway, so feel free to let us know about them at webmaster@chickensoupforthesoul.com and we will correct them in future printings.

The whole publishing team deserves a hand, including Maureen Peltier, Victor Cataldo, Mary Fisher, and Daniel Zaccari, who turned our manuscript into this beautiful book.

We are especially grateful to Miranda Hope, Bob Hope's grand-daughter for her thoughtful foreword for the book. There is no one better to introduce this book, given that royalties from it are going to the USO to support all their good work across the globe.

Sharing Happiness, Inspiration, and Hope

Real people sharing real stories, every day, all over the world. In 2007, *USA Today* named *Chicken Soup for the Soul* one of the five most memorable books in the last quarter-century. With over 100 million books sold to date in the U.S. and Canada alone, more than 200 titles in print, and translations into more than forty languages, "chicken soup for the soul" is one of the world's best-known phrases.

Today, twenty-four years after we first began sharing happiness, inspiration and hope through our books, we continue to delight our readers with new titles, but have also evolved beyond the bookstore with super premium pet food, television shows, podcasts, positive journalism from aplus.com, and licensed products, all revolving around true stories, as we continue "changing the world one story at a time®." Thanks for reading!

Share with Us

We all have had Chicken Soup for the Soul moments in our lives. If you would like to share your story or poem with millions of people around the world, go to chickensoup.com and click on "Submit Your Story." You may be able to help another reader and become a published author at the same time. Some of our past contributors have launched writing and speaking careers from the publication of their stories in our books!

We only accept story submissions via our website. They are no longer accepted via mail or fax.

To contact us regarding other matters, please send us an e-mail through webmaster@chickensoupforthesoul.com, or fax or write us at:

Chicken Soup for the Soul
P.O. Box 700
Cos Cob, CT 06807-0700
Fax: 203-861-7194

One more note from your friends at Chicken Soup for the Soul: Occasionally, we receive an unsolicited book manuscript from one of our readers, and we would like to respectfully inform you that we do not accept unsolicited manuscripts and we must discard the ones that appear.

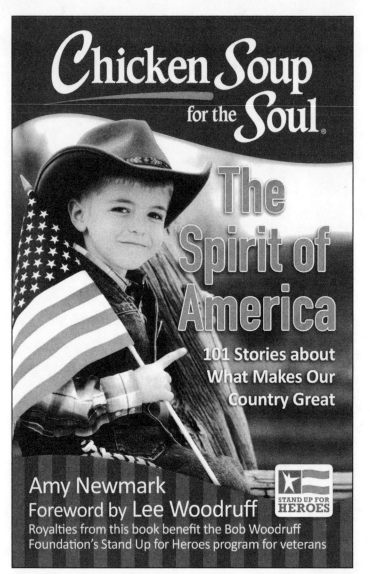

Paperback: 978-1-61159-960-2

eBook: 978-1-61159-259-7

American Spirit

Random Acts of Kindness

101 Stories of Compassion and Paying It Forward

Amy Newmark

Paperback: 978-1-61159-961-9
eBook: 978-1-61159-260-3

& Kindness at Its Best

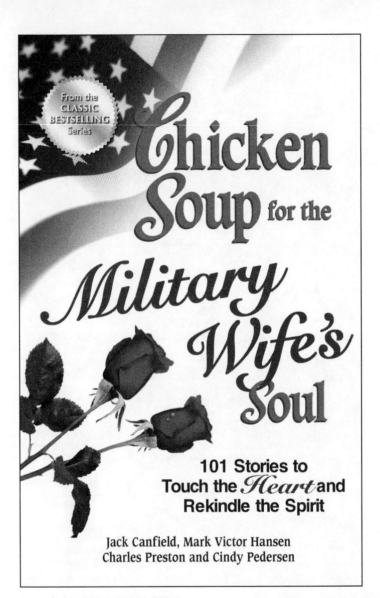

Chicken Soup for the Military Wife's Soul

101 Stories to Touch the *Heart* and Rekindle the Spirit

Jack Canfield, Mark Victor Hansen
Charles Preston and Cindy Pedersen

Paperback: 978-1-62361-028-9

eBook: 978-1-45327-642-6

More Heartwarming

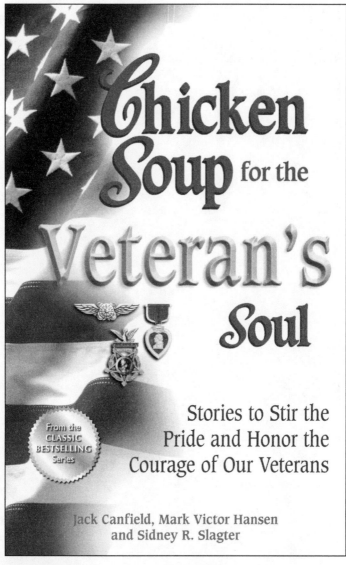

Chicken Soup for the Veteran's Soul

Stories to Stir the
Pride and Honor the
Courage of Our Veterans

From the
CLASSIC
BESTSELLING
Series

Jack Canfield, Mark Victor Hansen
and Sidney R. Slagter

Paperback: 978-1-62361-103-3
eBook: 978-1-45328-054-6

Military Stories for You

Changing the world one story at a time®
www.chickensoup.com